History of Limington, Maine

Robert L. Taylor

Published as a Project for the Limington Historical Society

HERITAGE BOOKS
2008

HERITAGE BOOKS
AN IMPRINT OF HERITAGE BOOKS, INC.

Books, CDs, and more—Worldwide

For our listing of thousands of titles see our website
at
www.HeritageBooks.com

Published 2008 by
HERITAGE BOOKS, INC.
Publishing Division
100 Railroad Ave. #104
Westminster, Maryland 21157

Copyright © 1991 Robert L. Taylor

Other books by the author:

Early Families of Limington, Maine
Early Families of Raymond, Maine

David C. Young and Robert L. Taylor:
Death Notices from Freewill Baptist Publications, 1811-1851

New material by Edward S. Lord

Cover illustration by Art Hahn, courtsey of Mrs. Author Hahn

All rights reserved. No part of this book may be reproduced or transmitted in any form or by any means, electronic or mechanical, including photocopying, recording or by any information storage and retrieval system without written permission from the author, except for the inclusion of brief quotations in a review.

International Standard Book Numbers
Paperbound: 978-1-55613-377-0
Clothbound: 978-0-7884-7055-4

TABLE OF CONTENTS

Preface   v

Chapter I Geography   1
   Location, Mountains, Emery's Corner, Ponds, Streams and Rivers, Bridges at East Limington.

Chapter II Land Titles   12
   Frances Small and the Indian Deed, Claiming the Ossipee Tract, Incorporation.

Chapter III Indians   21
   The Pequawkets and their Trail, Indian Stories.

Chapter IV Early Settlers   27
   Surveying the Land, Squatters and Early Settlers.

Chapter V Early Days   38
   Moving to a Wilderness, Early Traditions, Stagecoaches and Mail Service.

Chapter VI Religious Societies   51
   Congregational Church, Free-Will Baptist Churches, Bullockites, Baptist Churches, Friends Church.

Chapter VII Education   76
   District Schools, Limington Academy, South Limington Seminary.

Chapter VIII Industries   88
   Mills on Little Ossipee and Saco Rivers, Stabstreet, Ruin Corner, Bean Neighborhood, Barbel Creek, Limington Corner.

Chapter IX Prominent Citizens   114
   Leaders in Town Affairs, Doctors, Aged Persons, Death Statistics.

Chapter X Military   130
   Revolutionary Soldiers, Militia and Early Musters, Old Byington, Civil War.

Bibliography	136
Limington: Then and Now	147
Limington in Profile	149
Index	159

Preface

The town of Limington has never had a written history. Hon. Arthur McArthur, a life long resident and son of the third settler, took an interest in collecting material relating to the town shortly before his death but committed little to paper. The early documents that he did manage to gather were given by his son to the Davis Library. In the 1880's William G. Lord, acting as local correspondent, wrote articles on Limington people and events for the *Maine Sentinel*, a newspaper published at Biddeford. During the 1940's Miss Elizabeth Ring, a teacher of history at Deering High School, was hired by Walter Davis of Portland to write a history of the town, but she was unable to finish it.

My interest in local history grew out of an assignment given by Miss Esther Wood while I was a student in her Maine History class at Gorham. In 1965 I purchased Francis Meeds' day books containing a year by year record of the deaths in town from 1816 to 1845. As a result I became interested in gathering more information about these people, and while teaching at South Berwick, I had the opportunity of using the newspaper files at the Dover, New Hampshire, Library. A number of volumes of *The Morning Star*, a newspaper first published at Limerick and later at Dover were found which contained much relating to vital records. It was also from this source that information was obtained on Limington's Free-Will Baptist Churches. York county newspapers located in the York Institute at Saco and the McArthur Library at Biddeford were also studied, and required many weeks of research.

During the summer of 1966 I canvassed the town and managed to find and copy the inscriptions from over one hundred cemeteries. In the winter of 1968 I had permission to go through the numerous town books and papers that were stored in the town hall. From these sources I was able to learn and gather much pertaining to early town affairs and to genealogical data. I sought to expand the study in scope in order to present as complete a history as possible of the town and her families. Interviews were granted and private records copied, enabling me to complete a genealogy of the families in town up to the 1890's. This family data proved an invaluable source while writing the chapter on the early settlers and their times.

I am grateful to many townspeople who have aided me in my research. Mrs. Ada Manson loaned the original records of the First Free-Will Baptist Church of Limington. Mrs. Laurence Graves loaned the militia book and diary of Rev. Wescott Bullock and Mrs. Edith Peters gave scrapbooks and old photographs. Photographs were also loaned by Mrs. Maude Chick, Ruth Meserve, Annis Holmes and Louise Haley. I am especially indebted to Edith McCauley of Gorham for proofreading my manuscript.

Chapter I — Geography

Location:
"The town of Limington comprises the eastern portion of the lands lying between the Saco and Little Ossipee Rivers located in the very northeastern part of York County. It is slightly over nine miles long, with an average width of five miles. It is bounded on the north by Baldwin, on the east by Standish, on the south by Hollis and Waterboro, and on the west by Limerick and Cornish. The Saco River forms the boundary line on the north and east sides while the Little Ossipee separates it from Waterboro on the south."[1]

Land:
The land is fertile and productive and was originally covered in places with rocks that were later removed and used in the construction of stone walls. The surface of the town is much broken with steep hills and narrow valleys. On the declivity of the hills at some distance from the bottom the best land for cultivation is found. In the part of town known as Emery's Corner that was annexed from Limerick there are several lofty eminences where a limited amount of granite was quarried.

Plains lands bordering the Saco and Little Ossipee Rivers vary in width from one to three miles, constituting about one-third the area of the town. With the exception of a few small pieces of intervale land this sandy soil is too poor for cultivation. The plains once covered with pine timber on the bank of the Saco River in Steep Falls and Hardscrabble section have been cut and now, especially in Hardscrabble, scrub oak and pitch pine are found.

Mountains:
The surface of the land is varied and undulating, the highest points being Sawyer and Libby Mountains in the west, Mulloy Mountain in the south and Moody Mountain in the north. The mountains in all cover 1,200 acres of the town.

The highest point of land in town and in York county as well, is Sawyer Mountain, which rises 1,100 feet above sea level. In 1884 the U.S. Geological Survey placed a stone tower fifteen feet high upon its most prominent point. Later the tower was struck by lightning and now only scattered stones remain of this landmark built by Autien Sawyer, great grandson of William Sawyer for whom the mountain is now named.

Sawyer Mountain Monument, erected in 1884.

The first white man to occupy the mountain was Samuel Morrison, a native of Wells, who came to Limerick early and is said to have trapped in the area.[2] In 1810 Morrison moved to New Limerick in Aroostook County after selling his land on the mountain to George Meserve, who had settled on its eastern side.[3] The mountain was named for the Meserve family before it received its present name.

Rising four hundred and eight feet in the southern part of the town is Mulloy Mountain, named for Dennis Mulloy who in 1777 settled on its north side. This mountain once had a huge pine tree which stood on its summit and was said to be seen on clear days thirty miles out to sea, serving as a guide to sailors entering Portland Harbor. "But at last, the old tree which stood the storm for so many years was broken off before the fury of a November gale in 1885."[4]

Moody Mountain, the smallest of Limington's hills, located in the northern part of town was named not for an early settler, but for Leander Moody who returned to his native town in the late 1840's and settled on its southwestern side.

Libby Mountain rising eight hundred and seventy-six feet in the northeastern part of town is made up of numerous rocks, with ledges on its southern end. The mountain was owned early by Abner Libby and inherited by his son John Billy. These Libbys for whom the mountain was named lived at at Limington Corner.

A little to the west and adjacent to Libby Mountain is a mountain named for John Douglass, the first settler in the immediate area. He built his log cabin south of the steep incline of Libby Mountain near the old road going into the Edward Littlefield place. Leonard Douglass, a grandson, had formerly occupied the house within the ravine between the two mountains.

DOUGLASS MOUNTAIN

"Old Douglass Mountain stands among its fir-trees
Like a proud beauty in a gown of green,
And, looking down upon our little village,
It seems to say: 'Peace be upon this scene.'

How many times I've climbed its rugged summit.
Well paid by all the view spread out below,
With the 'White Mountains' gleaming in the sunlight
And lovely Saco River winding slow.

Sebago Lake lay like a jeweled bracelet
Among the green expanse of hill and plain,
And seen among the fir trees and the hemlock
The rising smoke of a far distant train.

Down at the foot of the old apple-orchard
Limington Village seemed a thing to love,
With tall elm trees along its hilly main street
And the Academy that gleamed so white above.

Old Douglass Mountain, I shall not forget you
Where'er I roam, whatever lands I see.
And when I sleep my last below the village
I'll know that you are looking down on me."[5]

Emery's Corner Section

West Limington made up a tract almost two and one-half miles long by one and one-half miles wide, comprising about fifteen hundred acres of land. In March 1870, by an act of Legislature it was annexed to Limerick and now is known as Emery's Corner. It was accessible by the old proprietor's road leading from Limington Village and up Paul Lombard's hill. The hill obtained its name when Paul Lombard, an early settler, won a bet from another man by backing a team of oxen with an ox cart up the hill.

The early settlers of this western section of town came from Gorham. Andrew Cobb the first settler came in 1786. He was followed several years later by Nathan Cobb, John Greenlaw, and Paul Lombard. James Emery, for which the area is named, came in 1798 and settled near the present corner.

"'In the winter of 1869, the people residing in what was then known as the 'Burnt District' of Limington petitioned the legislature to be set off to Limerick. Every resident real estate owner of property in this district together with owners of property in said district but resident at Limerick signed the petition. The division line between the two towns was changed as follows to wit — commencing on said division line at the north-west corner of land of Daniel Weston and thence run due north on the range line for a distance of about three miles and a half to the north-west corner of land of Thomas Smith, and thence run due west on a check line to the Cornish and Limington town line."[6]

The reasons assigned for the set off can be briefly stated as follows: the petitioners said that living in the remote section of the town many town meetings were held of which they had no notice; that Limerick Post Office was nearer their residences than the one at Limington; that their place of worship and of business was in Limerick; that their residence was nearer Limerick than Limington village; that between the center of their section, Emery's Corner, and Limington Village there was a very high hill difficult to ascend.

There were hard feelings on the part of those living in Limington because the town had lost one-twelfth of its valuation and for several years a division war was waged between the two towns. Inhabitants of Limington said that the people who lived in the Emery Corner section when teaming from Portland, were still obliged to pass over the hill about which they had complained and that by the set off they had no better accommodations than before the change. They also felt that Limerick offered no superior advantages and that by actual survey the distance from Emery's Corner to Limington was less than to Limerick Village, although the elevation is slightly greater. With one exception every person residing in that district who attended worship anyway worshipped at a church in his own territory. The Limington residents said that the men who signed the petition for a set off stated they owned houses and lands there, but in fact they did not live there and only owned land.

Ponds:

There are seven ponds which cover 1,635 acres of the town. Four of these, are in South Limington. The remaining three, Horn, Ward and Webster Ponds are all in North Limington.

Boyd Pond named for David Boyd, Esquire, who settled at its west end in 1803, covers an area of .06 square miles and is 0.4 of a mile north to south[7]. Although the pond has a depth of twenty feet at its deepest point, it is shallow in parts and has an average depth of fifteen feet. The pond which empties into Little Ossipee River is fed by springs and yields several kinds of fish including pickerel, yellow perch, hornpout and sunfish.

Dole Pond is one-quarter mile in length and has no more than twelve feet of water at its' deepest point. It is fed by a brook running from the outlet of Foss Pond which pours in from its northeastern side. This boggy marsh was originally named for Richard Edgerly, an early settler of Gove Ridge, who purchased the land on which the pond is located. Loren Dole purchased the Edgerly property and since 1893, the pond has been known by its present name.

Foss Pond is a three-quarter-mile-long marshy area. While the northwestern and southeastern ends have open water, the rest is shallow and mostly covered by heath bushes. "If one would jump up he could shake an acre," was one native's description of the bog.[8] The older natives remember a large boulder some distance from the marsh stream where different parties fished.[9] The area is now covered by large trees.

Sand Pond, so named because of the sandy area surrounding it, is spring fed and is 0.2 miles in length. It is at times stocked with fish and several cottages are located around its edge.

The principal lake in town is Pequawket Lake, but the natives call the pond by its original name, Horn Pond. The pond is shaped like an ox head with horns on its east end, hence the name. It covers an area of 0.26 square miles and is 1.2 miles long with a depth of fifty feet at the deepest point.[10] The lake is comprised of clear water fed by Stone and Hanscom Brooks as well as by numerous springs. Many cottages are found on the lake.

Ward Pond, is fed from Rhoda Brook, named for Mrs. Morrill (Rhoda) Sanborn. The pond coveres sixty-five acres and is thirty-five feet at its deepest point. The pond was named for Elijah Ward of Falmouth to whom the Proprietors granted the land on which it is situated, for his assistance given them on lotting out land in 1774.[11] The name it bears, with the exception of the word "Ossipee", is the most ancient given to any landmark in town. Its waters empty into Hamblen Brook. In April 1969, a trailer park was established on the pond's northern shore.

Webster Mill Pond is fed by water pouring out of Horn Pond. It was made when a dam at its present outlet was constructed for a gristmill in the 1790's.[12] The pond was known as the Small Mill Pond up to the turn of the century because the descendants of Captain James Small had owned and run the mills there.

Streams and Brooks:

Hanscom Brook is a tributary to Horn Pond and was named for Daniel Hanscom who settled at the "north corner" near the brook in 1789.

Hamblen Brook was named for Gershom Hamblen who settled at Wheelwright Corner on its northern bank in 1798.[13] The source of the brook is formed by waters running out of Ward and Webster Mill Ponds. In the course of its one-mile length the brook falls forty feet before it empties into the Little Ossipee River.

The Merrifield Brook originates from a spring in Cornish near the Limington line. It is located in the northwestern part of town and was named for Levi Merrifield. Its length is three miles and it falls four hundred feet before it empties into Pease Brook, which helps form the boundary between Cornish and Limington before running east into the Saco River. Pease Brook, formerly known as Salmon or Tannery Brook, falls 660 feet.

Davis Brook rises in the western highland of the town, flowing easterly for a way before turning due north. It runs into the Saco River near a place which was called Whaleback because of the ridge along its eastern bank. The brook was named for Ezra Davis who in the early part of the last century had a sawmill in the area where Route 25 now crosses the brook.

Barbel Creek is a small stream running through the community at South Limington, nicknamed "The Creek." It is fed by water running from a small dam, mostly coming from the "Johnny Brook." Older residents remember when barbels were speared and caught as they ran upstream. It flows in an easterly direction and is a tributary of the Little Ossipee River.

Pine Hill Brook is formed by water flowing out of Sweat's Meadow below Limington Corner. The brook flows easterly for about two miles and runs into the Little Ossipee River.

Springs:

The town is well watered by springs and streams. Cold Boiling located at the foot of Dyer's Hill and the Mineral Spring nearby can be found within the sandy soil of the Steep Falls section. In the early 1880's efforts were made to have the mineral spring water from these two springs used for commercial purposes. It was then felt that the water was equal, if not superior, to any water yet brought to public notice for the cure of liver and kidney complaints and humors of all kinds.[14] Charles A. Anderson served as local agent, suppling it by the gallon or barrel.[15] Negotiations were made with a party in Boston to introduce it in that city and bring it before the public.[16]

Octagon House on the Little Ossipee River built by Captain Josiah E. Chase, 1861.

Little Ossipee River:
In the beginning the land which now includes the town of Limington was described in early deeds as the land between the rivers of the Great and Little Ossipee. The name Ossipee, borne for more than three centuries by the largest tributary of the Saco River, had much to do with the town's early plantation name, "Little Ossipee." In Indian dialect Ossipee means "River of Pines," particularly appropriate as are most Indian names, since the region at that time was noted for its remarkable growth of pine.[17]

The Little Ossipee River unites with the Saco River at East Limington and flows from a southerly direction. At Nason's Mills where there were early saw and grist mills, it turns westward, skirting the south of the town for about two miles.

Starting from the river's mouth which empties into the Saco, the southern side to the Waterboro line is one stretch of pitch pine plains, while on the northern bank the soil is hard and productive. The river has seven or eight branches, each one having in the past driven one or two mills.[18]

Saco River:
The Saco River is a beautiful stream, taking its rise in the White Mountains of New Hampshire, with in a few yards of the Ammanoosuck River, which runs in an opposite direction. The river empties itself after a meandering course of some one hundred fifty miles into the ocean between Saco and Biddeford. Much of the way it has rocky banks along which flows clear water. In parts where the descent is great, the current, of course, is rapid. It has numerous falls presenting scenery of great sublimity and beauty.[19]

Pulp Mill and Falls, looking toward Steep Falls.

The natural descent of "Great Falls" at Hiram before the present dam was built was seventy-two feet. This was within sight of the acclaimed "Sundy Hills", one of the disputed boundaries of the Ossipee tract.[20] At Steep Falls, once a busy manufacturing place, the river falls twenty feet. At Salmon Falls, a place where the Indians often camped when coming down from Fryeburg in the spring to spear salmon, the descent is thirty feet.[21] At Saco Falls, a part of Indian Island, where Squando, the chief of the Sokokis lived, the descent is forty-two feet.[22] These are not all, but are among those of the greatest magnitude.

The Saco River is subject to freshets in the spring, but being mainly supplied from springs and rivulets from the mountainsides, it is not so subject to severe droughts in mid-summer as the Kennebec and Penobscot, which draw their resources from large but shallow lakes and ponds.[23] In ordinary freshets the river rises 10 to 15 feet in the spring, so frequently bridges were carried away along its course.[24]

Several times the Saco River has overflowed its banks and threatened to do much damage. The first record of any great freshet in the Saco River was in October, 1785.[25] References are also made in various newspapers and town records of a freshet in 1814. In the spring of 1843, following a winter of unusual severity and a heavy fall of snow, the river again raged. On the third of March 1896, after several days of continual rain and snow, the water rose within eighteen inches of the mark of the year before, bringing extensive damage all along the valley of the Saco.[26]

In the days when Maine was a part of the Colony of Massachusetts and a little explored wilderness, the original growth of pumpkin pine covered the land from the mountains to the sea. "The river had more good 'privileges' on it, as they are called, than any river in Maine — has rich and fertile bank — abounds in valuable fish — presenting from its source to its mouth, the most beautiful and picturesque scenery."[27]

Bridges over the Saco at East Limington:

This town's first bridge over the Saco was built at East Limington about 1786 at the cost of three hundred pounds. In 1792 when the town was incorporated three other bridges had been built over the Little Ossipee River for nearly the same sum. The expense of these early bridges was divided among the settlers of a then infant plantation consisting of no more than about a hundred families, the greater part of which were miserably poor.

The old bridge was disposed of and a new bridge known as "the Hemlock Bridge" was secured over the Saco below Parker's Rips in 1832. In April 1833, a freshet occurred and carried away about half of the new bridge. The bridge had to be rebuilt but in 1843 it was washed out again by a spring freshet.

Next the Parkers and Bragdons built a bridge by subscription a little above the location of the first one. They had a plan to build a road from the stage or Steep Falls road across the upper end of Ward's Pond through the property now belonging to the Winfield Weeman heirs and there connect with the Baldwin road. This road, however, was never built.[28]

Meanwhile, Colonel Henry Small, who had moved to East Limington from Gray, became county commissioner and by his political influence had a bridge built nearer his tavern than the Parker bridge. This one was not covered, but was on the site of the covered bridge. It was a log structure with no center piers. The huge logs were reinforced top and bottom where they joined, and stretched three hundred and fifty feet from bank to bank.

As time went on, this bridge, too, became unsafe. The time-stained timbers were removed and a covered bridge was built by "Jake" and Horace Berry of Conway, New Hampshire. The spruce to build the bridge was shipped by freight from Bartlett, New Hampshire. The bridge was framed in Baker's field and then moved on the stone piers in one piece.[29] The piers were built by the Bradburys of Hollis Center from stone quarried on the island above the bridge. It was finished in January 1885 at a cost of about six thousand dollars.

The bridge was boarded only half way up from the bottom at first, as the builders thought that the snow would blow in and keep the bridge "snowed" for winter travel. This did not work out as expected and the bridge was completely boarded about 1894. There were doors above the two center piers and the planking left a space at the sides so one could look down and see the rocks and water underneath. During the 1896 freshet one of the piers was undermined and reinforcement had to be bolted to the frame.

Covered Bridge at East Limington built in 1884.

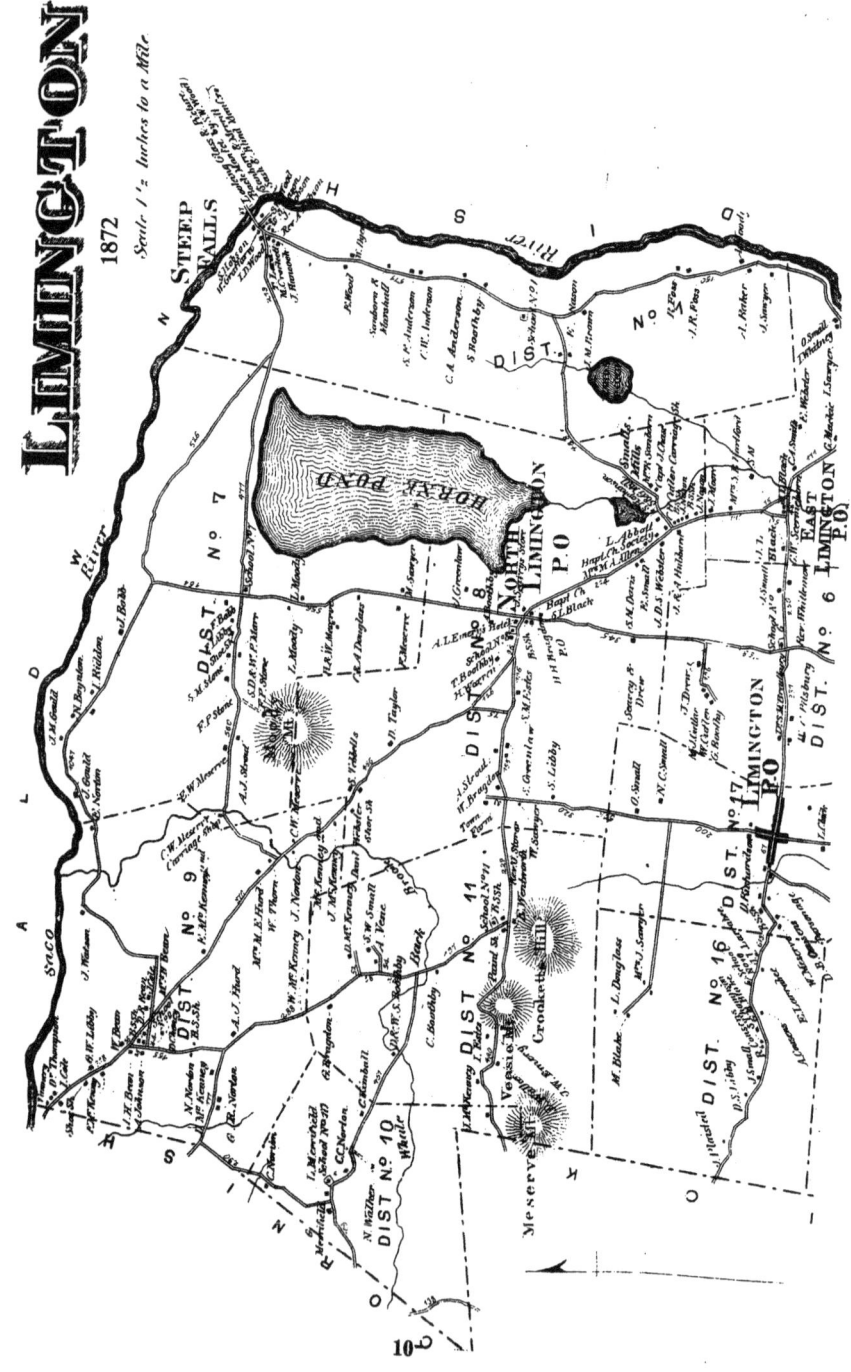

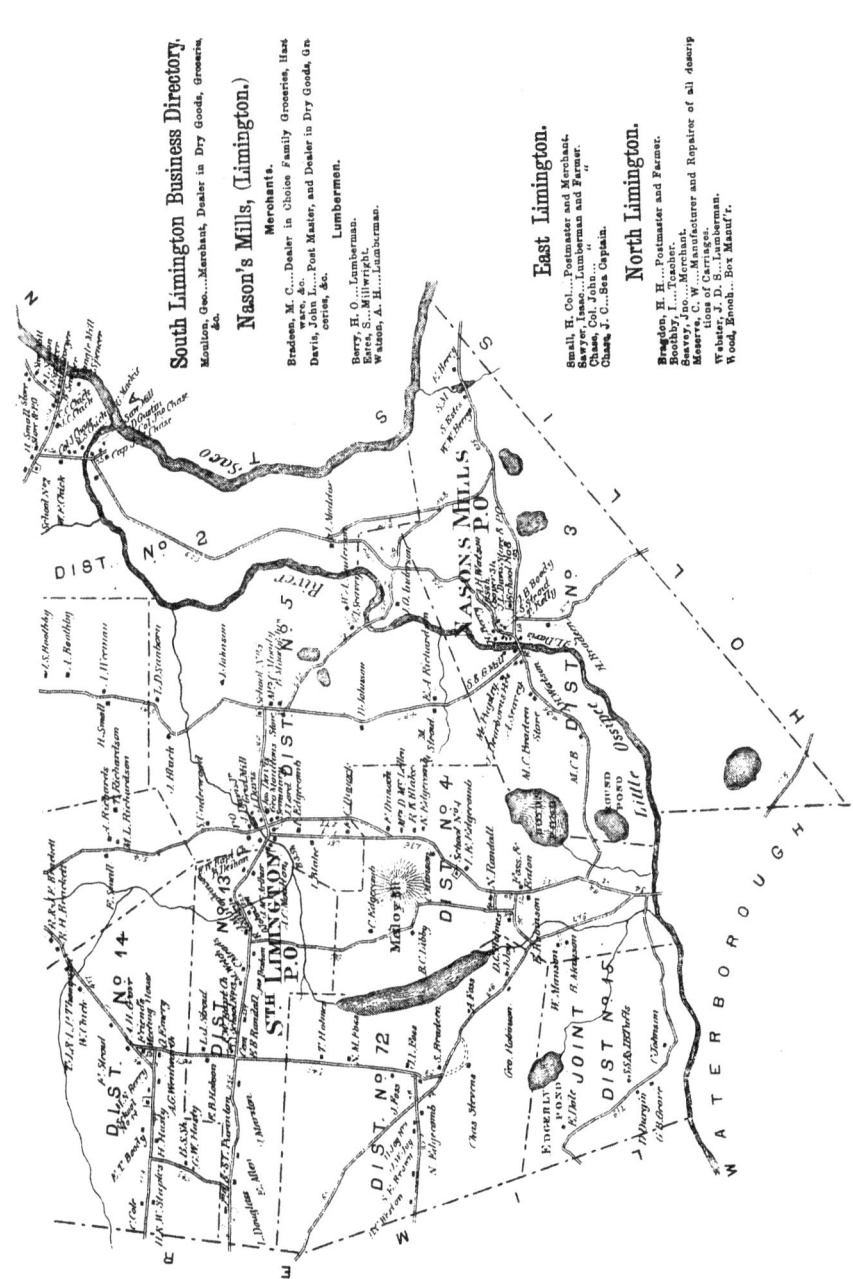

South Limington Business Directory.

Moulton, Geo....Merchant, Dealer in Dry Goods, Groceries, &c.

Nason's Mills, (Limington.)

Merchants.

Bradeen, M. C....Dealer in Choice Family Groceries, Hardware, &c.
Davis, John L....Post Master, and Dealer in Dry Goods, Groceries, &c.

Lumbermen.

Berry, H. O....Lumberman.
Estes, S...Millwright.
Watson, A. H...Lumberman.

East Limington.

Small, H. Col....Postmaster and Merchant.
Sawyer, Isaac..Lumberman and Farmer.
Chase, Col. John... "
Chase, J. C...Sea Captain.

North Limington.

Bragdon, H. H....Postmaster and Farmer.
Boothby, I.....Teacher.
Seavey, Jno....Merchant.
Meserve, C. W..Manufacturer and Repairer of all descriptions of Carriages.
Webster, J. D...Lumberman.
Wood, Enoch..Box Manuf'r.

Chapter II — Land Titles

In the year 1622 the council of Plymouth made its first grant of land in Maine to Sir Ferdinando Gorges, and in 1629 another more definite grant was made by the council, called the Plough Patent, forming the province of Lygonia. This patent included all the Ossipee lands, but as possession was never taken by the proprietors, the Indian tribes remained in undisturbed occupation, and titles given by their sagamores were, and always have been, held to be valid in law. In 1668 Captain Sandy, an Indian Sagamore, sold a large tract of land embracing the territory between the Great and Little Ossipee Rivers to Francis Small.

Francis Small, regarded perhaps as the father of the leading American families by that name, came with his father to Kittery about 1634.[1] In 1662 when he assigned George Mountjoy all his debts due from Indians, he mentions "housing at Ossebey," proving that he had then established a trading post in that region.[2] He had tramped all the way through the wilderness and built a trading house at the junction of the Ossipee and and Saco Rivers where the village of Cornish now stands. The present site of George F. Clifford's house is declared to be the spot upon which Small's house stood. A little later Small established himself at Kittery continuing his trade in peltries with the Indians.

"In the summer of 1668 Francis Small sold goods to the Newichewannock tribe of Indians on credit, for which they were to pay in furs during the autumn; but when the time of payment drew near, the red men deemed it easier to kill Small than to pay him, and they decide to fire his house and shoot him when he came to escape the flames. Captain Sandy, the chief of the tribe, was friendly to Small and told him what the Indians were planning to do; and, as he could not control them in the matter, he advised Small to flee for his life. Small thought the tale a cunningly devised fable to frighten him away in order to avoid payment; but when night came on, thinking it wise to be on the side of safety, he secreted himself in some pines on a hill near by and watched through the long November night. With the coming of the dawn, a flame of fire shot up from the burning house, whereupon Small took to his heels with all possible speed, probably seeking the nearest settlement."[3]

The chief, "Nick Sumbe," or "Wesumbe," by the English called "Captain Sandy," followed Small and made good the loss caused by debt and fire, conveying to him the entire Ossipee tract of nearly twenty miles square between the Ossipees, the Saco and the Newichawannock Rivers, signing the document with his mark of the turtle, the ancestral totem of his tribe.[4] Date of the instrument was November 28, 1668, but it was not recorded until over one hundred years afterward, on August 28, 1773; and thereby hangs a tale, for probably no conveyance of property in this state ever was the cause of so many heart-burnings, law-suits and almost endless litigations for three generations afterward.

Its particular value consists in the fact that six towns hold title under it: Shapleigh, Newfield, Parsonsfield, Limerick and Cornish, and all of Limington except that part annexed from Hollis in 1798. Following are the considerations of the Indian deed!

"To All People to whom this Present wrighting shall Come I Captain Sandy of ossobe in New England Sagamore send greeting.

Kno ye that I the said Captain Sandy for and in consideration of two large Indian Blankets two gallons of Rum two Pound of Powder four Pounds of muscet (musket) Balls and twenty Strings of Indian Beads with several other articles by me Received of Frances Small of Kittery in the County of york Indian Trader have given granted Bargained allianed Enfeofed confirmed and delivered and by these Presents do fully freely Clearly and absolutely give grant Bargain sell alline Enfeof convey confirm and Deliver unto him the sain Francis Small his heirs and assigns forever all that my great Tract of Land at ossobe (Ossipee) containing Twenty miles Square Lying and Being Between the two Rivers of great ossobe and Little ossobe so called and Being the Same Land where the said Frances Smalls trading house now Stands and from the River nechewannock near Humphrey Chadborns Loging Camp and to hold unto him the said Francis Smalle his heirs and assigns forever with all the Priviledges of hunting Fishing Trading together with all water and water courses mines minerals wood under wood Stones Swamps medows Ponds with all Emumts (Emoluments) Priviliges and Propritees Belonging to the afore said tract of Land unto him the said Francis Smalle his heirs and assigns forever to his and their own Proper vse benefit and behoofe forever and I the Said Cpt Sandy Do hereby Convenant Promise and Ingage for my self and my heirs unto him the Said Francis Smalle his heirs and assigns forever Peasibely to have hold use ocquyre and Possess the aforesaid Tract of Land without the Least hinderance or molistatn from me the said Capt Sandy have hereunto sett my hand and seal this Twenty Eight Day of November one thousand six hundred and sixty and Eight."[5]

The original deed which is over three hundred years old is now in the custody of the Maine Historical Society at Portland and may be seen there. Its various transferors and owners are as follows. The document passed from Francis Small of Kittery to his son Samuel Small of Kittery; from Samuel to his son Deacon Samuel Small of Scarboro, from Deacon Samuel to his son Joshua Small of Limington, from Joshua to his kinsman, Wingate Frost of Limington, who was clerk to the early proprietors; from him to his son Joshua Wingate Frost who later went to Virginia. In 1890 Lauriston Ward Small, a native of Cornish and then a broker in Chicago, was loaned the "Indian deed" as it was familiarly called and subsequently sold the same to Mrs. Ada (Small) Moore of New York City, whose father was the seventh generation from Francis Small, the trader.[6] She gave it to the Maine Historical Society.

At the time of the deed's transfer in 1668 Francis Small was gaining a great reputation as a planter, fisherman, and Indian trader. He doubtless spoke the Indian language and lived with them at various trading camps. Small was a resourceful man, venturesome, fearless, alert and somewhat given to speaking his own mind. He was fast becoming a large land owner and there is no doubt that he owned more acres than any other man who ever lived in southern Maine.

During the King Philip's War, Francis Small and his family lived at Major Shapleigh's garrison house at Sturgeon Creek, later living at the old family house at Kittery.[7] Finally tired of fighting Indians, troubled with conflicting claims in the hands of speculators, he deeded his property at Kittery together with the Ossipee lands to his son Samuel. He then went to live with another son, Daniel of Truro, Cape Cod, where in the year 1713, he died at the age of ninety-three years.[8] Many years later the heirs of Francis' two sons, Samuel and Daniel, each produced a deed to the same Ossipee tract acclaimed to be signed by the old Indian trader. The deed held by the heirs of Samuel Small was proven valid by the courts and was later upheld.

On January 28, 1669, a year after Small's purchase of the Ossipee tract, he deeded to his friend Major Nicholas Shapleigh an undivided half of the Ossipee lands. This deed was not recorded at the time,[9] and much trouble and various litigations followed the deal, for on April 30, 1711, Francis gave his son Samuel a deed to the entire Ossipee tract as originally given by Captain Sandy. This deed together with the original Sandy instrument came to light in 1771 after remaining lost so long.[10] Both were recorded at the same time, August 28, 1773.[11]

Samuel Small, the last sole owner of the Ossipee land, never made any attempt to prove his claim because of the many Indian disturbances of that time. It, however, remained for his children and his children's children finally to obtain claim and settle upon the tract after almost endless litigation.

On August 17, 1773, the heirs of Major Shapleigh and Samuel Small met at the inn of Samuel March of Scarboro to discuss and determine what revisions should be made of the Ossipee lands. It was then agreed by both parties that the Ossipee territory should have the following divisions: To the Shapleigh heirs, that part which afterward became Shapleigh, Parsonsfield and part of Limerick; to the Small heirs, that part which afterward became Newfield, Cornish, Limington and the rest of Limerick. During this meeting when a final division of the land was being made among themselves, each party agreed to give James Sullivan, "the one half of thirteen thousand acres of land where he was laid out, called by the name of Limerick town....provide said Sullivan oblige himself to defend our title against other claims."[12] The following listed names were determined as the rightful Small heirs: Samuel Small Jr., Joshua Small, Samuel March, James Small, Nathan Chick, Peter Cobb, Isaac Nason, Edmund Coffin, Edward Chapman, Benjamin Small, Christopher Hammond and Benjamin Meads Lord.[13]

Not until "August the 4th Day, 1777, did the Proprietors let it be known and explained by what right they had been taken possession. It was "voted that the following persons are proprietors in the shares and proportions following: viz. Heirs and assign of Samuel Small late of Scarboro, deceased, eldest son of said Samuel Small, under whom the proprietors hold, two-fifths. The heirs and assigns of Joseph Small, late of Falmouth, deceased, another son of Samuel Small, last named, one-fifth. The heirs and assigns of Elizabeth March, wife of Benjamin March, late of Kittery, deceased, a daughter of said Samuel Small, one-fifth. The heirs and assigns of Mary Davis, late of Gloucester, deceased, another daughter of said Samuel Small, last named, one-fifth."[14]

From this it appears that all the children of Samuel Small of Kittery were then dead, and that the claim was being pressed by his grandchildren and great-grandchildren, the latter being four generations removed from Francis Small.

When the long-lost deed of Ossipee lands was found and measures were taken as early as 1771 to claim the land and settle on it, the way was opened for Deacon Samuel Small to take an active interest in the tract. It is assumed that he had the old Indian deed recorded, for that same year, 1773, he conveyed to his sons Samuel and Joshua three-eigths each of his share; to his favorite grandson Benjamin and his two daughters, Anna and Elizabeth, one-twelfth each, therefore disposing of his entire share and interest.[15]

On May 17, 1774, Samuel Small signed the warrant and notification for the first meeting of the Ossipee Proprietors held at the inn of Colonel Samuel March in Scarboro. The signatures to the call of that meeting were: Samuel Small, Samuel Small Jr., Samuel March, Joshua Small, Benjamin Small, Nathaniel Milliken, John Wright, Nathan Chick, Joseph Small, James Small, and Benjamin Meads Lord.[16]

The first legal meeting of the settled proprietors was held on August 1, 1774, at the March Inn where the following special business was transacted:

"1. Samuel Small Jr., chosen moderator.
2. Samuel Small Jr., chosen proprietor's clerk.
3. That James Sullivan, Esq. Joshua Small, and James Frost to be the committee to manage the Prudential affairs of said Proprietors.
4. Voted the sum of forty pounds lawful money be raised and assessed on the several original shares of the immediate descendants of Samuel Small, late of Kittery, deceased, under whom the Proprietors claim, for making roads and bridges on their land. That Samuel Small Jr., Samuel March, Joshua Small be assessed that sum as aforesaid. That Samuel Small Jr., collectors to collect that sum, and that Samuel March be the Proprietors' Treasurer."[17]

A second meeting of the Proprietors of Ossipee was held on August 15, 1774, at the March Inn in Scarboro. It was:

"voted that Mr. Joshua Small be directed and is hereby impowered to proceed as soon as may be in taking a plan of a tract of land called Limington, being a part of the Proprietors' land, and lot the same into lots, that part thereof next to the Saco River into thirty acre lots and the residue into hundred-acre lots and return said plan to the Proprietors immediately."[18]

These, the first town lots, were laid out in an irregular, oblong figure formed by the Saco River on the north, by a sharp bend in the same river on the east, and by the Little Ossipee on the south.[19]

"On October 7, 1774, the Ossipee Proprietors met at the inn of Colonel Samuel March in Scarboro, where all their earlier meetings had been held, and voted that seventy-five lots of one hundred acres each should be drawn, according to the proprietors' shares or rights respectively."[20] Later all the agents for the heirs of Samuel Small drew lots. The number and range of each lot corresponding to a map drawn up by Joshua Small were placed on separate pieces of paper and drawn by chance, so one person would not get the best lots.[21]

In the Proprietors' Records of November 10, 1784, "mention was made that certain lands had been apportioned to the heirs of Mary Davis, Colonel Samuel March family, James Frost for the family of Joseph Small, Samuel Small, Joshua Small, Benjamin Small, James Harmon, and Nathaniel Milliken. On September 20, 1786, settlements had been made with 'the heirs of James Harmon, Benjamin Meads Lord family, Edward Kennard, Daniel Small, Nathan Chick, Peter Cobb, Daniel Small (of Gray) and Isaac Nason."[22]

The accredited agent of the Davis heirs, most of whom resided in Gloucester, Massachusetts, was David Plummer. In 1796 lots A to H were set off by the Ossipee Proprietors to these heirs. This constituted what was later termed the "Cape Ann Right," a tract of eight hundred and forty acres upon

Pine Plain in the north-easterly corner of the town at a bend in the Saco River below the junction of the Great Ossipee and the Saco. The town lots were laid out in squares; and the irregular or triangular lots along the banks of the Saco River in this "Right" mentioned as "certain jibs of land," were given to David Plummer "for his pains."[23] Two years later in 1798 the Proprietors agreed that he should have "300 acres of the best land in said claim."

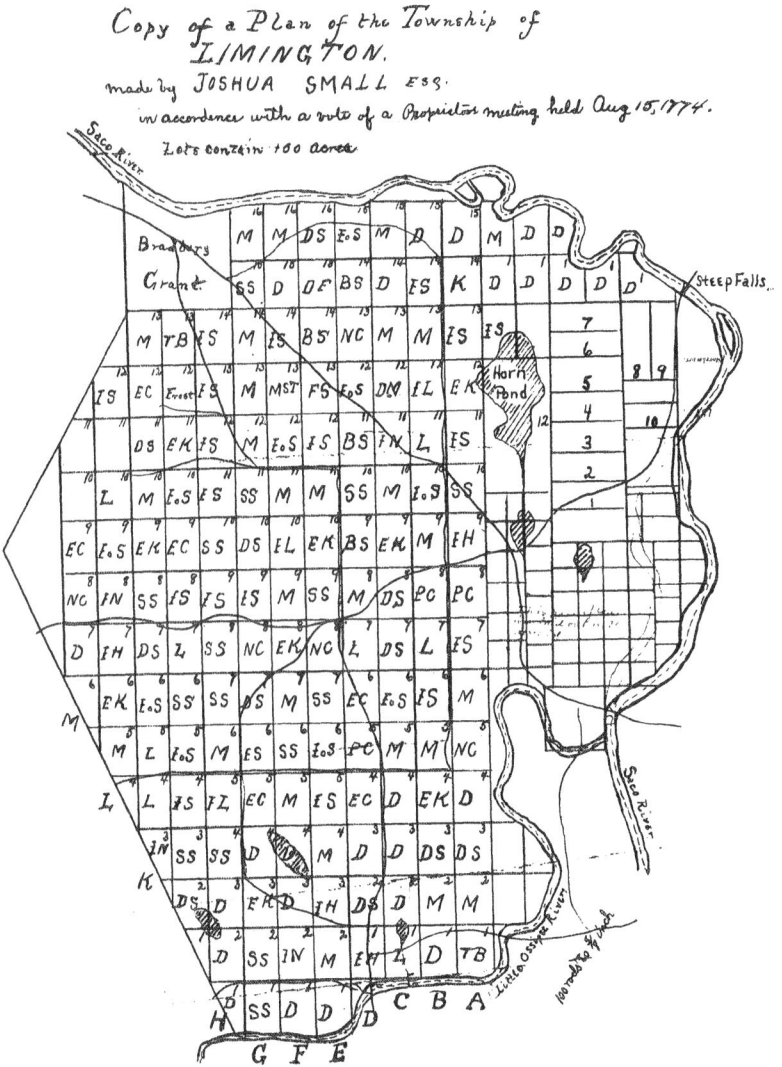

These abstracts, all taken from the Proprietors' Records of the town of Limington, starting with the first settlement extending from August 1, 1774, to June 28, 1803, have been preserved by a copy formerly owned by Leonard P. Thompson[24] and show the various measures pursued to gain a foothold on the rocky hills and valuable pine lands.

By the time the heirs of Samuel Small commenced an organized effort toward a settlement at Ossipee in 1774, as shown by the Proprietors' Records, there were already a few "squatters" upon their lands who were dealt with in different ways. Some merely paid a nominal sum for their few acres, while others were taken into court. Amos Chase, said to have been the first pioneer of that region, was granted two hundred acres "in consideration of his having built a mill within the proprietors' claim."[25] Theophilus Bradbury of Falmouth and later of Newburyport was granted five hundred acres by the Proprietors in the northwestern part of the town for legal counsel rendered.[26]

"Bewteen 1778 to 1784, the Ossipee Proprietors were obliged in self defense to bring suits against John Weeman, Dennis Mulloy, Eliakim Tarbox, Nicholas Edgecomb, Joseph Libby, Theodore Graffam, all of Limington, and many others."[27] The majority of these suits brought by the Ossipee Proprietors, were for "one acre of land...and the Dwelling wherein he now Dwells," though in the cases of Edgecomb and Tarbox, twenty acres are mentioned.[28] In some of these actions the lower court decided against the Ossipee Proprietors; but whenever a case reached the Superior Court, the Proprietors were always sustained. For instance, the Inferior Court of Common Pleas of January 1778, "found for John Weeman" the "cost of suit", while the Proprietors who appealed at the next session of the Superior Court of Judicature, held in June following, recovered "against the said John Weeman, the possession of the Premises sued for and the Cost of Court."[29] John Weeman paid his fines and, like many of the others, remained where he originally settled and later purchased his farm.

"November 1793, in the Court of Common Pleas, the Ossipee Proprietors, under Samuel Small late of Kittery deceased, brought suit against Joshua Sawyer, Daniel Sawyer, Nathan Sawyer, John Nason, Thomas Spencer, William Sawyer, Samuel Berry, Richard Berry, Thomas Morrill, and Benjamin Norton all of Limington, 'in a plea of a ejectment; with damages at five hundred pounds. The jury sustained the Proprietors in each case, except that of Samuel Berry. Having appealed in the Supreme Court at the session beginning June 8, 1796, the Proprietors recovered from Samuel Berry 'the premises and all the land except seventy-five acres...and costs $90.90.' The original plot contained two hundred and one acres."[30]

This suit of the Proprietors against Samuel Berry appears to have been the last to reach the Supreme Court.

Limington, was first surveyed in 1772 by James Warren in the interests of the Shapleighs and Smalls, and by Joshua Small in 1774 for the Ossipee

Proprietors. It was again surveyed by Nathan Winslow about 1775 or 1776 as ordered by Peter Woodbury of Cape Elizabeth, agent for the heirs of Daniel Small.

"The government survey by 'Heath and Wing' was submitted to the Secretary of the Commonwealth of Massachusetts with the 'Note: the above Plan is as Correct as the Roughness of the Township would admit of.' The boundary line is 'Thirty-two miles two hundred and thirty three Rods.' The 'seven ponds cover 1635 acres,' and 'the mountains cover 1200 acres.' The plan was 'taken and Actually Surveyed between the tenth of April and the tenth of May 1795,' and drawn on a 'Scale of three Miles, two hundred Rods to an Inch.' It was further attested by the autograph signatures of the three selectmen of that year, Joseph Libby, Benjamin Small, and Abner Libby."[31]

A likeness of Joshua Small's map drawn up in accordance with the Proprietor's meeting held on August 15, 1774, has been preserved and can be found at Alfred Court House. The Proprietors' initials are written on the lots drawn by them. The first division consisted of thirty-acre lots next to the Saco River, and the residue was divided into hundred-acre lots. The third and last division consisted of eight hundred and forty acres known as "the Cape Ann Right," located on the sandy plains in the northeast part of town.[32]

Incorporation

On January 27, 1791, a group of inhabitants of the Plantation called Ossipee petitioned the Senate and House of Representatives of Massachusetts for incorporation. The following is the petition:

"That your Petitioners have made a settlement in the County of York on a tract of land originally purchased by Francis Small of the native savages. Situated on Saco River, the boundaries of this tract, which is supposed to contain between twenty and thirty thousand acres, appears by the plan herewith exhibited; altho it is now more than one hundred and twenty years since this purchase was made by Francis Small, yet such has been the condition of his descendents and of this part of the country that not any attempt has ever been made to settle this estate left them by their progenitor, till within sixteen years past. The family is now become so numerous that by giving away a part, by selling and settleing themselves, they have grown to more than one hundred poor families on this plantation from the adjacent towns who had little if any other means of subsistence but to push themselves out into an uncultivated wilderness. But altho these settlers were poor, we presume to say they are an industrious people, and have made great exertion to clear and subdue this stubborn soil. They begin to wish and hope for some of those important priviledges enjoyed by people in the towns from whence they removed — That while they are labouring for a temporal, they may not forget an eternal inheritance, and their families sink into a state of savage ignorance and barbarity. The plantation is greatly embarrassed and their property retarded by the want of public roads. It is usual that townships granted by the Legislature are held by proprietors, non resident who are men of large property who are under obligations from the court on conditions of holding the grant and whose interest it is at the same time in order to raise the value of their land, to build a meeting house, settle a minister, and lay out and clear roads, the want of these advantages has been very sensibly experienced by the plantation. The inhabitants are sensible that it is a common opinion that to petition for incorporation is to invite publick taxes, but for this they are not "afraid" to confide in the justice and equity of the Legislature. They are convinced that it must be for the publick good that children as well as the dumb creatures should have "strength" of body before they are put to hard service. That plantations should have the means of instruction and of supporting themselves that they may be the better able to bear publick burdens and be more usefull to the common wealth, they therefore pray that the plantation may be incorporated, that they may be able to assess themselves, to build a meeting house for the worship of God, to settle a gospel minister, to institute schools for the instruction of their children, and they also pray that the taxes which have been charged on the said plantation may be applyed to clear their public roads, and your petitioners as in duty bound shall pray."[33]

The first page of the First Book of Records of the town of Limington embodies the Act of Legislature "to incorporate the Plantation called Ossipee, in the County of York, into a town by the name of Limington," with a full description of its' boundaries. The further passage of this bill is shown upon its pages by the autograph signatures of David Cobb, Speaker of the House, dated February 8, 1792; Samuel Phillips, President of the Senate, February 8, 1792; John Hancock, Governor of Massachusetts, February 9, 1792; attested by John Avery, Jr., Secretary of State.

The first town election was held at the schoolhouse, Monday, April 2, 1792, under a warrant issued by Amos Chase. Joshua Small was elected Moderator of the meeting; Asa Edmonds, Town Clerk; Captain Robert Boody, Captain Nicholas Edgecomb and Samuel Sawyer, Selectmen. The meeting was adjourned until April ninth, when John Boothby was elected Treasurer; Jesse Libby, Constable and Collector, with three percent for collecting.

Jonathan Boothby, Benjamin Small, and Amos Chase were elected a committee to call a minister to preach out the sum of fifteen pounds which the town voted for the support of the gospel; twelve pounds were voted for town charges, thirty pounds for schools, and three hundred pounds for highways.

Chapter III — Indians

The Saco River and its tributaries were the home of the Sokokis Indians. The tribe was located chiefly in two divisions, the Pequawkets had their principal village at Fryeburg, within the great bend of the river, and the other known as the Ossipees had their lodgment on the shore of Ossipee Lake at the head of the Great Ossipee.[1]

The Sokokis or the Pequawkets as they were sometimes called, were originally a very powerful people in the days before the whites came. Indications have been found of extensive settlements all through the Conways or around Ossipee Lake, and up and down the Saco valley. On the western shore of Ossipee Lake there is to this day a large burial mound ten feet high and fifty feet in diameter from which several Indian skeletons have been taken, all buried in a sitting position as was characteristic of Indian burials. In Fryeburg there are many of these mounds and other indications of their ancient encampments.

The principal residence of their chiefs or Sagamores was upon Indian Island just above the Lower Falls where now stands Saco village.[2] It was here where two noted chiefs, Fluellen and Captain Sandy had their headquarters and it was by their deeds to Francis Small and others that the whites hold title to the large tract of land that make up the Ossipee Towns.

The chief who succeeded to the command of the Sokokis at the death of Fluellen and Sandy was Squando, one of the most peculiar and marked among the Sagamores of the different tribes. He also had his wigwam on Indian Island, at the Falls.[3]

He possessed great strength of mind. His manners were grave, his address impressive. In the superstitions devotion of the Indians he was a leader and an enthusiast. He made them believe that he had intercourse with the spirits of the visible world who imparted to him revelations of human events. Cotton Mather said, "He is a strange enthusiastical Sagamore, who some years before pretended that God appeared to him in the form of a tall man in black clothes, declaring to him that he was God, and commanded him to leave his drinking and strong liquors, to pray, to attend the preaching of the gospel, and had made known to him the entire extinction of the English by the Indians in a few years.'"[4] These commands he is said to have observed strictly for a long time.

But in 1675 as he said, the fulfillment of the latter part of his vision came. The specific act that caused the first uprising of the Indians on the Saco and wrought up the earnest chief to revengeful eloquence, was an inhuman act of some drunken sailors near the mouth of the Saco River. Josselyn had reported that young Indian children could 'swim naturally, striking their paws under their throat like a dog, and not spreading their arms as we do; some sailors, to prove the truth of the assertion, had overset the canoe in which were Squando's wife and child. The child sank rapidly, and was only saved by the mother, who by diving brought it up alive.[5] Not long after this the child died, and its death so aroused the great chief that he was said to have cursed the river, saying that every year Manitou who dwelt on the farthest heights of the Great White Rocks would take his toll of white men's children, and be the curse true or false, every year full toll is taken by the Saco's rushing waters.[6] This legend, called the curse of the Saco, is still told by the older residents who live on its bank.[7]

Factory Island, or Indian Island as it was called by the early English, located in Saco was a great rendezvous for the whole tribe, especially in the spring when the shad and salmon were abundant in the foaming waters of the falls.[8] The high picturesque cliff which rises above the site of Gray's brick yard below the falls was also a favorite dwelling place.

This race knew not the use of metals; their implements were made of bone, wood or stone. The bone and wood have long since molded into dust and only an occasional stone relic is found to tell by its construction the artistic character of their long buried makers. Some are rough and rude in shape showing that they were made in the beginning of the Stone Age, others are smooth and well finished indicating progress in art. Many Indian artifacts have been found in the past. In one such case, James A. Gray of Saco in 1891 found in his brick yard two stone gouges of unusually skillful workmanship which he gave to the York Institute.[9] Similar artifacts, including numerous arrow heads, have been found on a small island reserved for traveling Indians on the Saco near the mouth of the Little Ossipee at East Limington.[10] Small groups of Indians would at different times come up the river and camp here to fish. One of the last such visits of an Indian family was reported on the Little Ossipee River in October 1845.[11] This small area known as "the Indian Reservation" was flooded when the dam was built at Bonny Eagle.

The Pequawket Trail

The "Pequawket Trail" not used by the Pequawkets of Lovell's Pond for at least two hundred years has mostly been obliterated by time. It was originally the main thoroughfare between the coast and the ramparts of the White Mountains. It has been said that the Pequawkets made an annual trip from Fryeburg, the ancient home of the tribe, down to the coastal area for the summer months where clams, fish and the like were easily obtained.[12] Jasper and flint arrowheads found at Biddeford Pool and clam shells found in Scarboro were no doubt left by these Abnaki Indians. One of their routes came down from Fryeburg and went by way of Alfred to the Berwicks, a former home of the tribe. The redskins used to go along the shores of the Mousam River and through the village. The water from the Conant Mill Dam at Alfred covers the fording place directly below the old Came homestead.

The coastal terminus of the Pequawket Trail was at the mouth of the Saco River at Biddeford Pool and at Saco on Indian Island. From there it went northward through Biddeford, Dayton, Lyman and on into Waterboro.

The Pequawket Trail that in its prime so meandered through the Saco Valley is now almost forgotten. The trail, although bare and plainly marked, was a thing of the past when the settlers first arrived in town. An attempt will be made to discern its course, picking up this ancient footpath at Waterboro, as that town bounds Limington and had much to do with tracing the trail as it probably existed. The trail is said to have followed Deerings' Ridge, emptying into the Webber road east of Ossipee Lake.[13] Near here is an Indian cave, where Indians used to stay nights on their journeys. From this cave, now said to be somewhat caved in and shallow, have been found arrowheads and other artifacts.

Leaving the Indian cave, the trail went up the New Dam Road as it now goes, but somewhere before reaching the Limington town line it must have had a branch that went to the west. Indians taking this western route followed the southern bank of the Little Ossipee River, and walked on stepping stones in damp spots above the present site of Scratch Dam. These stones said to be in a straight line along the bank which marked the trail are now covered by back-up water from the dam. The path came between the present Day and Scribner fields joining an Indian trail leading from Berwick before crossing the river into Limerick just below the present bridge.[14] The trail then made its way northward, superimposed by the road-bed of Route Five.[15]

The other route of importance continued in a more or less northward direction from the present New Dam Road above Ossipee Lake, following the flow of the Little Ossipee's southern bank into Hardscrabble.

It was joined here on the plains by another well-worn trail that lead from the falls at West Buxton Village where the tribe came at stated seasons to spear salmon with which the Saco then abounded. The crossing farther down the river at the site of the old Davis Bridge and where Samuel Berry first settled in 1774, has been mentioned as "the Pequawket fording place."[16] Horseshoe Bend, just below the crossing place, is where Indian relics have been found at different times.[17]

The trail proceeded in a northerly direction along the bank of the Little Ossipee River until it reached the mouth of Pequawket Brook.[18] It then left the river, following the course of the brook which bears the old Indian name, then continued in a more easterly direction into Slabstreet, hitting the southwest end of lot number three on range G.[19] Crossing this section of North

Limington, it led to the east side of Horn Pond, a favorite Indian camping place. It then continued in a northerly direction across sandy plains land and either crossed the Saco River at the Goshen, below Half Moon Pond, or went west on the Whaleback Road which followed more or less closely the Saco. The Indians had a village at the mouth of the Great Ossipee below Cornish Village. In Hiram, just across the river on a high bluff the Indians had a fort.

Before King Philip's War, fearing an invasion by the Mohawks, the two branches of the Sokokis Indians employed English carpenters to go up from the coast and build two stockade forts fourteen feet in height, constructed of heavy, hewed, hardwood timber, set in a trench three feet deep, then tri-nailed together and reinforced with heavy horizontal bars.[20] One was located on the west shore of Ossipee Lake. The other fortification was built close to the confluence of the Great Ossipee and the Saco in Hiram. Some of the early settlers of Cornish who cleared the land where the stockade once stood must have discovered the ruins there.

It was at this settlement located on the mouth of the Great Ossipee that the trail of the Pequawkets formed a junction with that of the Ossipee.[21] The Pequawket Trail went up the Hiram Road skirting the western bank of the Saco heading toward their village at Fryeburg. The other trail crossed the Ossipee River only a few rods north of the present village of Cornish and entered the village precisely as the road now enters, separating at Thompson Park. The Ossipee Trail which formed the northern branch crossed Little River where the bridge now is and led on to Ossipee ponds. The southern branch or the main trail led up the High Road as the road now goes and continued as far as the south side of Trafton's Mountain, at which place the present road deviates from the trail.[22] This trail used by the Pequawkets continued southward through Limerick into Waterboro and on to Berwick.

When the earliest settlers came to town almost two hundred years ago and fixed their habitation upon the banks of the Saco and Little Ossipee Rivers, the territory even then was ceasing to be the hunting ground of the Sokokis or Pequawkets. There remains little evidence that this was to any extent an Indian hunting ground.

In the 1830's, some Indian remains were found on the Randall Foss farm near the river within reach of the East Limington Bridge. They were the bones of natives slain by white men, sometime near the period of the French War.

"It was said that three hunters from Buxton came upon an Indian camp, containing three men and one squaw. The Indian men had secured, by their trapping and gunning excursion, a large and valuable lot of Beaver, Otter, and other furs, which excited the cupidity of the white rangers. At that period, the slaying of an Indian was deemed a light matter, and more especially when pelf in the shape of pelts, could be gained by it. The hunters conspired, and brutally murdered the Indians in their sleep, thus repaying their hospitality with treacherous slaughter. The old Squaw was awakened by the blows inflicted upon the unconscious victims, and begged for her life in most piteous accents. But the hunters fearing that she would inform against them, and that others of the tribe would avenge the foul deed of blood, determined to put her also to death, in order to insure their own safety. They had, however, some compunctious visitings in the matter of murdering a weak defenseless Squaw; and, as no one would commit the deed alone, they all agreed to take aim at her person, shut their eyes and pull trigger, that they might not know whose gun discharged the fatal bullet. But the aim was too true, and the three bullets lodged in the body of the beseeching woman. They then, after burying the bodies, secured their booty, and turned their faces towards home, deeming the secret of the murder safe in their own bosoms.

For a long period of years the first settlers in the neighborhood of Limington Falls, were surprised and terrified by Indian whoops and yells, mingled with the imploring shrieks of a female voice, long after the last traces of Indian occupancy had been obliterated from this region. The wild war whoop was invariably heard as the precursor of every storm, and agonizing cries mingled with mists that rolled in from seaward direction.

The foul deed would have remained a secret if it had not been for the full confession of the last pale-faced hunter previous to his death in the neighborhood of the scene of the unprovoked murder. From that period, the war-whoop ceased, and the avenging cries of the murdered Indians has not since been heard. The other two of the hunters had previously died, and kept their secret with them unrevealed. But justice would not permit the deed to perish unconfessed, and it was reserved for the one dying last, to make the disclosure."[23]

Indians were no doubt a thing of the past when the first settlers migrated into town, but tradition tells us they did occasionally appear and were feared. An interesting incident occurred in the frontier life of Mrs. Dennis Mulloy of South Limington.

"On one of those occasions when it was necessary for the father to be away, mother and the children were keeping the home fires burning against his return when they were startled by a scratching sound on the roof. Believing it to be made by Indians attempting to enter the little cabin through the chimney, the young mother dragged the straw and cornhusk mattresses from the beds — rent them open and stuffed their contents onto the fire to create a smoke barrier and keep the Indians from descending the chimney. An anxious night was spent; when morning came, the family dared at last to go outside and check — to their amazement they saw 'their Indians' had been a tree branch stirred by the wind rubbing along the roof."[24]

John Foss, the nearest neighbor of Mulloy used to go up through the woods until he could see the smoke arising from their cabin, then feeling assured of their safety, would return home. One day Foss came into the cabin greatly excited having missed the column of smoke from the cabin for several days he feared that they had been murdered by the Indians. Once an Indian had approached the Foss cabin one night seeking help for his squaw who was having trouble giving birth to a baby. Mrs. Foss volunteered her services in assisting as midwife. The Indians were grateful and always remembered the Foss family for this kind deed.[25]

One other story of kindness concerned the family of Andrew Cobb, who settled early on the lower part of Sawyer's Mountain in West Limington; now called Emery's Corner. The story goes that an Indian squaw with her baby ran away from her husband and took shelter in what has been since called "Indian Rock" on the Cobb farm. There she stayed unnoticed for about eleven weeks, secretly milking the Cobb cow to get food for her child. Cobb, noting that the cow was coming home dry each night, decided to stake out a watch. At last the squaw with a baby strapped to her back was sighted coming from the cave with a birch bark pail. Cobb then came out of hiding and approached the woman. She feared he would kill her, but overcame her fears when consoled by food fetched from the house for her and her child. This act of good charity in the Indians behalf continued for about two weeks, at which time she left. Soon after, her husband appeared at the Cobb place, from Waterboro way searching for his wife and child, all the time threatening he would kill them if he did find them. The Cobbs, not wishing harm to the mother and her child, told the Indian that they hadn't seen anything of the party mentioned.[26]

In other instances some gave the Indian reason to fear them. John Sutton, an early settler of Ruin Corner did have an apparent dislike for Indians. One evening as dusk was approaching, John told his wife that he smelt an Indian. He took his gun and once outside sighted and shot dead a savage getting over the pasture fence, north of the house on the ridge. Later generations while plowing the field where the killing is said to have taken place, came across a part of a tomahawk which they claimed to be the Indian's.[27] The farm has since been owned by the Willard Boothby heirs.

Chapter IV — Early Settlers

By 1776 families were beginning to be found on that part of the large tract of land lying between the Great and Little Ossipee Rivers which was conveyed by Captain Sandy to Francis Small in 1668. Limerick and Cornish each had four settled families,[1] while Limington had at least a dozen settlers, more than half of which were Small's descendants.

The first settler of this large tract between the two Ossipees was Isaiah Foster, who settled under the Limerick Proprietors. He came with his family in October 1772, and settled on a southerly slope about a mile below the present village at Limerick. His track at the time was a crude logging road which followed up the west bank of the Saco to Buxton and thence westward, striking the Little Ossipee River where the logged road disappeared and only a line of spotted trees remained to guide him and his family to the wilderness home which they were seeking.[2] It was at the Foster place that Joshua Small, Philemon Libby and others slept on a March night in 1773 when they first got between the rivers to lot out their unexplored lands.[3]

Two months later in the same year Samuel Small and Joshua Small, the two principal proprietors, led a second surveying party to the Ossipee lands. This time they ran out lines about seven miles from the Saco River, westward between the rivers of the Great and Little Ossipees, where they cut down a number of trees and built several camps on their land. They further continued to "survey southerly as far as Limerick from thence easterly near Little Ossipee River and so to the said Saco River."[4] The surveyors on this trip noticed no improvement or settlement had been made on any of the land that was surveyed, excepting the tract occupied by Isaiah Foster who lived in Limerick.

The Small Proprietors conducted their third surveying trip to the Ossipee tract in October 1773. This time after crossing the Little Ossipee at the Indian ford, and turning a little north-westerly, they soon saw a man putting up the wall of a log house. This squatter was Ezra Davis who had come that summer up the Saco River from Saco. When Samuel Small asked him by what right he was there, Davis gave a short answer.[5] Further on and nearer the Saco they came upon Deacon Amos Chase and his son, Amos, putting up a sawmill. As in the previous case, the Chases were also warned off by the

Proprietors who told them that the land between the two Ossipee Rivers was being taken up and claimed.[6] However, both Davis and Chase persisted and continued to hold on to their claims, becoming the first settlers of Little Ossipee, later Limington. Many of the other early squatters were eventually hauled into court, however, the cases against Davis and Chase were settled in a more peaceful way. The Proprietors later, on August 22, 1788, conveyed to Davis the two hundred and thirty-two acres where he lived for two hundred pounds.[7] Whereas, in the latter case, old Amos went in August 1774, to the Proprietors' meeting and for a small fee was granted two hundred acres of land in consideration of him and his son having built a mill within the Proprietors' claim.[8] This first mill built on the southern side of the Little Ossipee River was on the site of the present mill ruins, having been run and owned by the Chase family for over one hundred and eighty years.

Chases' Falls on the Little Ossipee River where Amos Chase settled. It was the site of his sawmill and later a fulling mill.

Chase, one of two squatters to reside within the limits of town, apparently remained undiscovered by the Proprietors in the month of November or December 1772, on the mouth of the Little Ossipee River. He states that soon afterward they started to build a sawmill.[9]

Some questions have arisen as to which has the honor of being the towns first settler, Chase or Davis! While it is true that Chase, by his deposition, came earlier although he further states that he wasn't sure of the exact date, his was more of a commercial venture, and by most standards he was not a true settler. That title would then go to Ezra Davis, the man to strike the first blow to make a farm. It was Davis making a home, who first felled the heavy growth which was so abundant in those days.

Ezra Davis was soon followed by his small family from Saco. Ezra Davis, Jr., the eldest son, was about two years old at the time. When Ezra, Jr. died on April 2, 1836, he had been a resident of Limington for about sixty years, probably the only person then living who had lived in town that long.[10] The second of Davis' sons, and a brother to Ezra, was Robert, the first white male to be born in town on August 28, 1775.[11] Robert Davis died on or near the site of his birth at South Limington on November 14, 1826.

Ezra Davis, the first settler in town, became its leading citizen in his time, and was with consistency given the title of Esquire. In December 1793 he was chosen agent to take the town's petition to the General Court at Boston, asking for abatement of taxes in order that the public money might be spent in building roads, settling a minister, and building a meeting-house.[12] He was Justice of the Peace for many years, frequently moderator of town meetings, grand juryman, tithingman and holder of lesser offices.[13] In 1801 he was one of a committee of three appointed to draw up a petition favoring the removal of the York County Court from Wells to Alfred, and was also elected town treasurer from 1801 to 1804.[14] His gravestone in the Johnson graveyard in South Limington where he and his wife are buried reads: "Ezra Davis, Esq., the first settler of the town, died Oct. 15, 1826, aged 79 years, 7 months, 5 days."

John and Nicholas Davis, two younger brothers of Ezra Davis soon followed. John settled as early as 1775 on the eastern bank of the Little Ossipee River within a part of Little Falls Plantation that was annexed to Limington.[15] Nicholas and his new bride settled near his brother, Ezra, on the western bank of the Little Ossipee immediately after his discharge from the army in January 1777.[16]

Major Nicholas Davis House located on bank of the Little Ossipee River at Horseshoe Bend, Hardscrabble. The place was moved to Cape Elizabeth by Walter G. Davis.

Deacon Amos Chase who accompanied his son and helped build the early sawmill was one of the very early settlers of Buxton, coming originally from Newbury, Massachusetts. Soon after establishing his son, Amos, at East Limington he moved to Saco where he died on March 2, 1818, at the age of nearly one hundred years. Deacon Chase is said to have been a commanding figure, six feet in height, vigorous and erect in old age, eloquent in conversation and pre-eminent in prayer.[17]

Amos Chase, a son of Deacon Chase, was a young man when he and his father camped at the mouth of the Little Ossipee. A descendant who still lives on the old Chase grant and within sight of where Chase settled mentioned a family tale about Amos. One morning, as the story goes, soon after Amos' arrival a rooster was heard crowing, whereupon investigating the sound young Chase was led up river and was surprised to see another white settler.[18] This could well have been Ezra Davis.

Amos Chase, the first resident to be married in town, continued to occupy a prominent place there, exchanging tracts of land from his large farm, making up the heart of East Limington. Later he and his sons built a gristmill on the falls opposite his sawmill on the north bank of the Little Ossipee. The name of Amos Chase is found in the Limington Congregational Church records as one of its original charter members in 1789 and later one of its first deacons.[19] He died March 25, 1825, aged 72 years, and was buried in the little family cemetery in an unmarked grave located at the mouth of the Little Ossipee River where he first settled.

In June 1774, when Elijah Ward assisted Joshua, James and Samuel Small in running out tracts of land in the present town, lotting them into hundred acre lots, not one settler nor any sign of improvements were reported except those of Ezra Davis and Amos Chase.[20] This Proprietors' surveying party was employed as many as forty days during the summer, running the course from the mouth of the Little Ossipee to the mouth of the Great Ossipee. Corners of lots were marked by letters and figures cut on trees. For his services, Mr. Ward was granted the lots around Ward's Pond, which still bears his name.

Sometime in the summer of 1774, Jonathan Boothby came from Scarboro and felled trees on land bought from Samuel March in 1773. He moved back to his native town and didn't make a permanent settlement until at least January 1778 when he married Mary Small, also of Limington.[21] The farm that he settled was south of Pine Hill and later occupied by Alvah Weemen, a descendant of the old settler. His obituary in the local newspaper, reads "Sunday morning, (May 27, 1832) in Limington, Jonathan Boothby, age 79 year: He left a large circle of relatives and friends to mourn his loss; by his death, the church has lost a zealous and active member; the poor and helpless a ready and kind benefactor and society its brightest ornament."[22]

In the summer of 1774, Joshua Sawyer, having migrated from Cape Elizabeth, began to cut down trees on part of the land that Amos Chase then had in his possession near Limington Falls on the Saco River. Amos went to see Sawyer with the intent of forbidding his working on the land, but changed his mind on arrival. Shortly afterwards Amos Chase's father went to the Small Proprietors and purchased two hundred acres, giving up all the remainder of the land that they had run out.[23] Twenty years later, Chase was approached by Ezra Davis, agent for Sawyer, and urged to give a quit claim deed of the land on which Sawyer had settled, but Chase refused.[24] Sawyer was taken to court by the Proprietors and ordered to pay thirty dollars for the land on which he had years before squatted. The description of Sawyer's land as taken in 1795 by the Small Proprietors is as follows:

"Beginning at a bunch of maple trees by side of the Saco River, run north sixty-eight rods, thence west seventy-two rods, south twenty-four rods to Dea Amos Chase's land, thence continuing in a line that shall strike two rods south of said Sawyer's house to said river, thence by said river to first mentioned, thirty acres or there about."[,25]

Joshua Sawyer was followed in the next year or so by his brother, Nathaniel, who settled on land adjoining his northern line by the river. Nathaniel Sawyer lived on this place at East Limington until his death, June 4, 1821, and lies buried near the mouth of the Little Ossipee River. He had nine boys and three girls by his two marriages.[26]

Samuel Berry seems to have been the fourth permanent settler, in Little Ossipee Plantation, now Limington, about the same time as Joshua Sawyer.[27] His campsite was near the old Pequawket fording way, later the site of the Davis Bridge which crosses the Little Ossipee River at what is now called Horseshoe Bend.[28] Berry came from Biddeford and late in life married the widow of Thomas Boothby. A couple of years later in 1795 his claim was contested by a suit brought against him by the Small Proprietors. The description of his lands taken then by the Proprietors is as follows:

"Beginning thirty-five rods north of Samuel's house, thence run west until it strikes the eastern line of range A, then run south by said range line to Nicholas Davis' land, thence running easterly by Davis' to Little Ossipee River, thence northerly by river until a west line will strike first mentioned, seventy-five acres."

Berry lost his case and sold the part remaining, moving to his bride's residence at Ruin Corner at North Limington where he remained until his death, November 21, 1829, aged eighty-six years.[29] Samuel Berry lies buried in an unmarked grave on a knoll west of the Baptist Church near the site of C.Y. Boothby's shingle mill.

John McArthur came to Little Ossipee in January 1775, and settled his family on Barbel Creek at South Limington.[30] Mr. McArthur, came to this country in 1765, and three years later he married Mary Miller of Cape Elizabeth. Margaret McArthur, their fourth child, born November 5, 1775, was the first white female child born in town.[31] Soon after his arrival, McArthur built a house now occupied by Hollis Hogle where he died on August 30, 1816, aged seventy-one years. "He was a man possessing in full measure the traits peculiar to the Scotch character; was conservative, opinionated, argumentative, and logical; a man of sound mind who availed himself of every source of information".[32] His sons Arthur and James, were leading citizens in Limington and were extensively known in York County, being highly respected for their intelligence, probity, and public spirit.[33]

In February 1775, Joshua Small came with his mostly grown-up family from Scarboro and was the first of the Small Proprietors to take formal possession of the acres which Francis Small, his great-grandfather, had bought from the Indians one hundred and seven years before. He built his log cabin near the bank of the Little Ossipee River and cleared a farm at the foot of Pine Hill. Here he continued his occupation, that of a tanner. His tannery was on Black Brook, a branch of Barbel Creek, two miles west of the mouth of the Little Ossipee River.[34]

For many years, Joshua Small transacted the legal business of the early settlers; and to him, the principal Proprietor of the town of Limington, much of the early prosperity of the settlement was due.[35] He was instrumental in getting the town incorporated and was moderator at its first meeting held at the village schoolhouse. Joshua Small died in the early summer of 1803, aged seventy-eight years. He had thirteen children, all except one marrying members of early Limington families.

The Joshua Small House located in the Whittemore field on the Pine Hill Road before it was taken down about 1887. It was last occupied by his son, Dea. Nathaniel Small.

Family tradition claims that Samuel Small, Jr. came about the same time as his brother, Joshua. He is said to have settled where David Richardson once lived going up the Shaving Hill Road from the village. Samuel, unlike Joshua, went to Limington with intentions of returning to Scarboro, which he soon did, after giving his farm to his son, William Small. It is believed that one reason he returned home was to care for his father, Samuel, Sr., "both men being burdened by years".[36] Samuel and Joshua Small, leaders of the early surveying parties to the Ossipee lands, were each deeded a three-eighths share by their father. Joshua Small sold his share for about $10,000.00. Samuel Small was supposed to have received much more for his share because he peddled it out to the settlers in one hundred acre lots.[37] Samuel's oldest son, Benjamin, a favorite grandson of the older Samuel, later became one of the Proprietors and settled in town about 1776 one-half mile north of the village.

Colonel Nathan Small House owned by Rev. Howard Wells.

Still another early settler in town was David Young, Jr. of Saco. He and Thomas Young first came to Amos Chase when he was working on his mill, telling Chase that they were going to run out lines.[38] Thomas Young settled on land next to the Saco River in Hollis. David Young did lot a piece of land out in town, but was of Hollis when he sold it to Samuel Berry in 1793.[39]

David Young's oldest son, David, baptized at Saco in 1763, was an early settler in town; grandsons give the date as 1776.[40] Much later in 1792, David Young purchased one hundred acres on number four on range B.[41] He died on the farm on April 14, 1843. His father-in-law, Francis Small, who died in May 1792,[42] lived next to him near what is now the Charles Thomas place on the road going toward Hardscrabble. Francis Small was an early settler and one of the founders of the Limington Congregational Church.

In the fall of 1776 Joseph Libby came to South Limington and settled on what was later the George Manson, now Ralph Hasty farm where he died on

October 6, 1835, aged eighty-five years. Two years before he had gone to Samuel Berry who lived on the banks of the Little Ossipee River to be shown land, and finding none returned to Saco. Several years later in 1776, he again appeared at Berry's and was shown land. Libby went on to see Ezra Davis who he heard would show him land.[43] The area beside Mulloy Mountain where he settled was made into three farms when Thomas Rumery and Nicholas Edgecomb the next two settlers who very soon followed settled within the neighborhood. Libby, being the first discoverer, was offered his choice, but chose to decide it by lot. The center lot fell to Edgecomb, the south side to Rumery and Libby drew the east side.[44]

Nicholas Edgecomb and Thomas Rumery came from Saco, probably together, for Nicholas was a brother to Rumery's wife.[45] Rumery, after 1793, returned to Biddeford where he died. Nicholas Edgecomb remained, serving on the town's first board of selectmen and dying at his homestead in the fall of 1814, aged sixty-four years.

By the time that these three families that settled beside Mulloy Mountain had made a clearing, Dennis Mulloy of Cape Elizabeth and Eliakim Tarbox of Saco, with their new brides, moved into the area. Mulloy and wife, a sister of Mrs. John McArthur, settled on the north side of the mountain which bears his name.

Edward Mulloy House, South Limington.

In the month of November 1778, all of these South Limington squatters before named were warned off by the Small Proprietors. Joseph Libby was approached by Samuel and Joshua Small who told him that he was a trespasser on their land, and that they would sue.[46] These frontiermen remained on their clearings and between December 1778 and April 1784, they were taken before the courts and sued. Mulloy, Libby and Edgecomb purchased the land that they had cleared and thus remained. Tarbox, discouraged in the loss of his labor and improved lands, left town.

By the spring of 1776 two other families, Bartholomew Jackson[47] and Jesse Libby,[48] both having married Proprietor's daughters, came from Scarboro. Jackson settled on Quaker Lane and in 1793 moved to Wales, Maine, where he died September 27, 1837, aged eighty-nine years. Jesse Libby and family settled at East Limington near Wheelwright Corner. He later became the town's first tax collector. In 1797 Libby sold out to Gershom Hamblen and moved to Hampden, Maine.[49]

Jesse Libby was soon followed by two other brothers. Philemon Libby and wife settled on a one hundred acre lot, number 10 on range E, received from his wife's grandfather, Deacon Samuel Small. Philemon Libby, a licensed innholder for many years, lived in the McArthur house in the village. Aaron, an older brother was here before 1780, and is said to be the first man that ever kept shop inLimington. His farm was on lot number 9 on range B, lying on the old road between the ball field and Ruin Corner.

Up to this time only squatters and a handful of Samuel Small's heirs had settled within the bounds of Ossipee Plantation. Soon other claimants, beside Joshua and Nathaniel Sawyer, were to appear at Ossipee, believing themselves lawful owners to the tract purchased by Francis Small, the Indian trader. This group, known as the heirs of Daniel Small, assumed they owned the land under title of a deed Francis Small gave to Daniel, his youngest son, dated "ye last day of October, 1712."[50]

For the further development of their claim Nathan Winslow was sent to the Ossipee region to make a plan of it; and Peter Woodbury, a prominent citizen of Cape Elizabeth, was chosen:

"agent to the heirs of Daniel Small, late of Truro, deceased, by virtue of the vote of said heirs impowering me for the same, for and in consideration of the settlement brought forth by James Small of a certain place called Ossipee in the county of York . . . part of the tract belonging to the heirs above said joining Saco and Little Ossipee Rivers which tract was purchased of Capt. Sandy by Francis Small and conveyed by deed to his son Daniel."[51]

Accordingly, a number of the heirs of Daniel Small, of Truro, were allotted their portions of the Ossipee lands in March 1777, as marked on a plan taken by Nathan Winslow; they were, without exception, mentioned as being residents of Ossipee.[52] The first six of the following left by 1780:

1. Jeremiah Small, yeoman . . . Lot No. 67. (He was of Cape Elizabeth when he married Jerusha Woodbury, October 26, 1776.)
2. Jonathan Fairbanks, yeoman . . . Lot. No. 65. (He was of Cape Elizabeth when he married Sarah Foot, October 25, 1776.)
3. Peter Sawyer, yeoman . . . Lot No. 5.
4. Ithiel Smith, tailor . . . Lot No. 83.
5. Samuel Small, yeoman . . . Lot No. 85.
6. Mary Smith, seamster . . . Lot No. 46.
7. Daniel Small, mariner . . . Lot No. 66.
8. Timothy Small, mariner . . . Lot No. 66.
9. John Weeman, yeoman . . . Lot No. 88.
10. Joshua Sawyer, yeoman . . . Lot No. 2.
11. Nathaniel Sawyer, yeoman . . . Lot No. 3.
12. James Small, yeoman . . . Lot No. 67.

The heirs of Samuel Small, late of Kittery, claimed the same tract by virtue of a deed given Samuel by his father, the same Francis Small, bearing the date 1711. To test the validity of their title, Samuel March, acting for the "Ossipee Proprietors", (or the heirs of Samuel Small), brought suit in the Inferior Court of Common Pleas of York County against Pelatiah Fernald and Elisha Small, of Cape Elizabeth, for cutting down and carrying away trees on what was described in full as the Ossipee tract. The case was heard and tried at Inferior Court of Common Pleas held at York on the first Tuesday of January 1778.[53] The Ossipee Proprietors claims were sustained and the defendants fined for damages.

At the same session of court the Ossipee Proprietors brought an action against Timothy Small and John Weeman, two other heirs of Daniel Small, "in a plea of ejectment of one acre of land with the buildings thereon and appurtenances thereof . . . wherein they now dwell."[54] The Superior Court found in favor of the Small Proprietors.

The heirs of Daniel Small, late of Truro, were never heard from after their defeat in January, 1778. Most of those who were living on Ossipee land in March 1777 when they were deeded land soon left. Timothy Small, having no legal title to the land, returned after 1784 to Cape Elizabeth. John Weeman whose land adjoined Small's remained on his land, eventually purchasing it in 1799. Shortly after Weeman sold the farm on which he first settled and moved to a section of Standish near the bridge at East Limington. Two of Timothy Small's younger brothers, Jacob and Reuben, moved to Ossipee and were there before 1780.

In March 1777, when the agent to the heirs of Daniel Smith, acted to prosecute their claims, James Small was firmly established at Ossipee, now Limington. He probably took advantage of a period of good sledding in the winter following his discharge from the service in November 25, 1776, to move his family. Although Captain James Small appears to have been one of the earliest to take measures to prove his claim at Ossipee, neither he nor his sons became involved in the lawsuits which so disturbed the other settlers. Instead he — James Small of Limington ... mariner — "showed his acquiescence in the decisions of the courts against other descendants of Daniel Small, and others more or less connected with that family, by purchasing, on October 12, 1795, of Samuel March, Esquire, of Scarboro, "one of the Ossipee Proprietors, a hundred acres of land on the brook that runs out of Horn Pond."[55] Here, in the northeastern section of the town, he built in 1799 a sawmill on what is now known as Webster Mill Pond. His homestead was known as the Leslie Greenlaw place, located on the road going toward Camp Moy-Mo-Da-Yo.

In 1792 when the town was incorporated, it having "not been more than seven years since the town had increased to any considerable degree,"[56] the population of Limington was over seven hundred. One half of the families as of that date came from Scarboro and Cape Elizabeth. Scarboro not only contributed the majority of Small heirs but other families, making forty-five in all. As many more came from the other towns bordering Scarboro with Cape Elizabeth contributing twenty-two families, Gorham eighteen and about ten each from Saco and Falmouth. One third of that number found in Limington at that time had married into the family of or descended from Francis Small who purchased the Ossipee tract in 1668.

The reason why so many Scarboro settlers, came to Limington, other than being descendants of Francis Small, was perhaps the land and what could be grown on it. Accustomed to the crops of their former town, after some land was cleared and crops planted, the men from Scarboro, found that the early crops were enormous.[57]

Chapter V — Early Days

The Revolutionary War and fear of Indians did much to check the early immigration to this wilderness, but men came occasionally, built cabins and made clearings. Most of the earliest settlers were squatters and, proving no title to their land, were years later haled into court to be sued by the Small Proprietors. Many of the inhabitants who did purchase their lands under the Proprietors, "were in total and painful uncertainty as to the security of their lands," the title to the whole of it being then in litigation, pending decision in the Supreme Judicial Court.[1] From this uncertainty respecting the title to their lands the inhabitants had been discouraged from those improvements which they otherwise would have made. This caused the settlement and advancement of the Plantation to be slow in its early development.[2]

When the early settlers came here there were no existing roads to travel on. Those coming by way of Standish, the principal route of migration, had to follow a blazed trail through the wilderness guided by spotted trees. Not much in the way of worldly goods was first taken. It has been said that when Simeon Strout first came into town from Gorham in 1786, he brought only a cow and a sack of meal.[3] Strout was the first to clear land on what has been called the Alpheus Spiller farm south of Limington Corner. When Benjamin Meserve and Mark Marr, his brother-in-law, came with their brides in 1794 from Scarboro, they brought what little they had on tied poles dragged by a horse.[4] Most settlers came with cattle loaded down by packs.

The first settlers made bridge paths from their place of origin to their lots using spotted trees for a guide. The next settler would lay out a path from the last clearing to his lot and so on across the town.

For many years the mode of traveling was on foot or horseback. The main course, and no doubt the first road in town, started at the Saco River at East Limington about eighty rods up from the mouth of the Little Ossipee River, continued up Pine Hill, passing straight through the corner and by way of the Shaving Hill Road ran to Emery's Corner. Four miles south of Limington Corner another road commenced at right angles with the former, leading from Edgecomb's bridge to the Cornish line as it now goes. The way the early settlers laid out roads accounts in a measure for their leading over such steep hills. While some roads followed the line of least resistance when first cleared others followed the blaze marks of the range line or property lines of settlers hundred acre lots.

Snow Rollers made by Charles Chase, East Limington.

The roads first beginning as paths were widened after oxen were used.[5] It was on such a road that Reuben Gilkey, an early settler from the southern part of town, once traveled hauling logs by ox team to Portland. Crossing the Standish plains on the way back, his oxen were startled by a bear. Gilkey gave chase and finally caught up with them at the Saco River crossing, causing him much trouble and a loss of time.[6]

In 1818 there were five country roads leading through town on which many bridges had to be supported. The town had bridges over several large streams, being obliged to support one half of a bridge over the Saco River, and three and a half over the Little Ossipee River. These bridges were often swept away by freshets and other casualties thereby continually burdening the town's people with new and heavy taxes.[7]

As business and the number of settlers increased, they began to grade the roads. This was a hard, slow task. It was about this time that carriages started to be used. According to evaluation books, Lewis Whitney, the town doctor, had a carriage in 1835, but this was rare. The first ones had the seat set directly upon the axle tree.

Ezra Davis was the first settler to begin a farm in town. He first built a house which was probably made by cutting logs of uniform length, and by notching each at the ends and placing one above the other. The roof was covered with hemlock boughs or bark. A space about two feet square was left in one side to admit light. The chimney was made of stone rudely laid up in one corner, about eight feet high, then poles or pieces of bark were stood up to guide the smoke.[8]

After a house was rendered habitable, the next thing was to clear the heavy growth from the land. The way was made for cultivation by staging a "cut-down". It was the usual procedure to cut in June and burn the next May. First the settler would select a large tree with broad, spreading limbs for a driver, then go forward and partially cut all the other trees so as to leave them weak, until he had been over a territory as large as he wanted. When this was accomplished he would go back and cut the driver which fell against the first trees cut, those against others, and so on until all the trees were down. It would take about two hours for a large drive to fall. Then he would go over the fallen trees and cut off as many limbs from the lower side of the tree as he could so the trees would lie as near the ground as possible. He then cut the limbs from the upper side of the trees so they would lie close together.[9] When the fallen trees had become dry, they were burned. It was hard and tedious work clearing the land with two, five or ten acres annually cut on each farm.

Planting a piece of corn was next in order and as no plowing could be done as yet among the stumps and roots, a picked stick was used to raise the turf. It would take a man one day to plant an acre. When the ground was properly cleared, rye and grass seed was sown and "hacked in" with a hoe. The third year they had grass to cut, which was a slow and tedious job, as the hay grew very stout and lodged among the rocks and stumps.

Joshua McKenney House on Sawyer's Mountain last owned by Charles Estes.

When Henry Small came to carve out the first farm west of Shaving Hill in April 1787, he staged a "cut-down." After he had cleared the land and was able to raise corn, he moved his wife and three children to this vast wilderness and installed them in an old hunting camp upon his farm. Then he built the four walls of a log house, but before putting on a roof he was forced to go on a three days' journey back to Scarboro for corn meal. Upon his return, his wife and three babies were gone, and the camp was deserted. Henry made a dash to his house which as yet was but four walls without roof, to get his ax to defend himself from the wild animals which he thought had destroyed his family, and there he found his wife and babies safe. The wife had made a bed of hemlock boughs and a roof of peeled bark to keep the rain out.[10]

A list of poll and estates for 1792 shows that 7,400 acres were still owned by the Proprietors, three hundred seventy acres used for roads and 8,614 acres of unimproved land owned by settlers with five hundred forty acres of pasture and orcharding land being pastured, producing four hundred ninety-five tons of hay for the year. There were two hundred fifteen acres of tillage land, including orcharding tilled, yielding 1,020 bushels of Indian corn and one hundred and one bushels of wheat for the year.[11] The crops usually found in pioneers' gardens were corn, rye, clover, flax, beans and peas for porridge and a very few potatoes.[12]

Tillage was mostly on plowed land. It took from eight to twelve oxen to break the land the first time it was plowed. One old time witness reported having seen twelve oxen hitched to the plow, with three teamsters, one man holding the plow, one with an ax to cut roots, another with a hoe to clear the small parcels that gather on the colter. Sometimes the plow would be drawn into a place so snug and tight it would take four men with handspikes to get it out.[13] The first iron plow in town was owned by Frank Stone.

The produce was about fifty bushels of corn, thirty of wheat and rye and from one hundred to one thousand bushels of potatoes to the acre. The work was all done with coarse, rough tools until about 1835.[14] Then very few farmers used a cultivator. Grain was cut with a small tool called a sickle, used with one hand while the other grasped the grain. When cut, it was laid on the ground in small bundles, then gathered together and bound into larger ones with bands made of the grain. It was first stored in the barn until fall, next threshed with a flail, then carried out and turned from a basket upon the winnowing cloth, the wind blowing the chaff from the grain.

Marshall Lewis Richardson and wife at their home at South Limington, 1896.

Hurd House built 1815. Last owned by John F. McKenney.

Edward B. Randall House once located near the Emerson School.

Benjamin Manson Place on Holmes Road Burned in 1916.

Major Joseph Meserve House near Hanscom Corner. Pictured is John H. Moody and family who lived there.

Home improvements were slow in coming for in the spring of 1791, "only one finished house could be found in the whole plantation — but eighteen or twenty houses which had brick chimneys. The remainder were wholly log houses, many of which had no floors, and the whole affording but a miserable shelter from the severities of a cold climate."[15] Those who had a log cabin were fortunate as in November 1792, when the polls and estates had been taken only thirty-seven out of the one hundred twenty-one listed settlers had even a dwelling house with forty-five of them having only barns. It would appear more shelter was provided for their cattle than was provided for themselves. Barns were simply for protection of the animals while the feed was established outside. The number of livestock reported for that year was forty-nine horses, one hundred fifty-seven swine, one hundred forty-two oxen and two hundred thirty-one steers and cows.

Rude log shelters did not give way to frame houses until years later when sawmills were in operation. They were constructed by the more enterprising families soon after the incorporation of the town. These more permanent homes were hewed from the timber of white pine;

> "The sills and beams were at least eight inches square; the rafters were seven inches square at the ridgepole, seven by twelve at the beams, and the purlines were four inches at the small end. The houses were boarded and shingled. The walls were battened or feather-edged boards; windows were of seven by nine glass. The houses were divided into rooms by unplaned board partitions. They used cleat doors with wooden latch and string."[16]

Amos Chase House oldest house in East Limington. It was moved down from its original site across from the church years ago.

Several early houses are still standing in town, any one of five might be the oldest. The second frame house is said to have been built by Isaac Small who settled near Pine Hill.[17] The old James Frost place located on Pine Hill dates to before 1789, as does the Ben Evans house once occupied by Deacon Amos Chase.

The old Chase homestead originally stood nearly opposite the present East Limington Church, but was moved down the road to its present location near the Saco River about a century ago. It was described by a descendant at the turn of the century as being "never painted; the front having two rooms separated by a narrow entry-way with a precipitous stair case, with a huge inside."[18] The house was once occupied by Amos Chase's daughter-in-law, the widow of Abner Chase.

South Limington, the first settled area, may well contain the oldest dwelling in town. Ezra Davis, the first settler, may have built the same house occupied by his great-grandson, Joseph Davis, Jr. now owned by Harold Jenson. John McArthur, another early settler, came to Barbel Creek and built the house afterward occupied by his son, James. It has been said that this house had the first glass windows in town.[19] Further south down the road and east of Mulloy Mountain is the ancient Nicholas Edgecomb place, one of the town's first houses.

Some kinds of wild animals found early in the area were numerous. Hunters and trappers had traversed the woods even before the Indians left. Plenty of beaver dams were found but very few beavers.[20] They had been diligently hunted for their valuable fur. Deer were seldom seen, except by those who hunted them regularly. They sometimes mated with sheep, and in a few instances came near the barn with them. Wolves were numerous at first, and in winter ferocious. High pens were needed to protect the sheep at night but when daylight came the wolves would skulk away.

Levi Merrifield House, North Limington. The place is now gone.

Stories about wolves have often been told, but traditions do not mention a single loss by wolves or by any other wild animals in the Ossipee Valley.[21] Once Levi Merrifield an early settler near the Cornish line was obliged to carry burning pitch knots to keep the wolves away while working on his land.[22] Wingate Frost, the last clerk for the Proprietors told a tale of encountering a wolf in his youth. "Once, when Frost was sent to the mill with a bag of corn on the horse's back, a wolf came from the woods and faced him, looked the situation over then departed and he returned home safely with his meal."[23]

There were not as many bears as wolves, neither were they as easily driven away. Being very fond of green corn they often broke into the fields, eating freely, but trampling more than they ate.[24]

An early tradition involving a bear was told by an aged Brackett descendant. When Joshua and his brother Abraham Brackett first came to the wilds of Little Ossipee after the Revolutionary War a strange incident is said to have occurred just within sight of where they were to settle. When the parties were nearing the present curve west of the village, their pack horse became startled. Joshua Brackett realizing the danger of a nearby foe went farther into the forest with the trusted rifle that he had used in the late war and shot a bear.[25] The two brothers soon married and the family believed this incident to be some kind of an omen. The farm that they cleared is owned by Manley Brackett and has been occupied by that same family for over one hundred and ninety years.

It has been said that the first settlers endured many dangers and hardships. When the plantation was in its infancy; there were no gristmills and the settlers had to haul or lug their corn great distances to have it milled. One of the first gristmills in town was built by William Manson at his place on the brook which flows through the Benjamin and William Manson's farms on the present Homes Road. The mill was a great blessing to the struggling settlers.

Isaac Dyer and his family, living in the Steep Falls section of Limington, did their milling business at Scarboro. When Isaac's boys were old enough, they brought grists of grain either on their own backs or on that of a horse through the woods, thirty miles or more to their Uncle Watson's mill at Nonesuch for grinding. Since most of the day had gone when they arrived at the mill, they got their corn ground, slept overnight and returned the next day.[26]

Another story is told of John Foss, an early settler of South Limington, who took a trip to the mill when wolves were hunted and killed in the area between the Great and Little Ossipees. It being the time of year to have his corn gristed, Foss placed one or two bags of corn on his shoulders and carried them to Catarack Falls at Saco, it being the nearest mill at the time, finding his way by spotted trees. On the way back with his freshly ground meal just south of the Little Ossipee River near the present Edgecomb Bridge, Foss was chased by a pack of wolves. Once safely across the river he found a place to sit down to rest and watch. Shortly one of the wolves on the other side gave a howl, whereupon the pack fearing perhaps the cry would give nearby hunters their location, attacked that one wolf, tearing him to pieces and eating him.[27]

Since Foss may well be called a typical settler, a few circumstances in his life will be given. Mr. John Foss came from Saco. He moved to this town in 1780 and settled on the north side of the pond which still bears his name. His wife's maiden name was Susannah Milliken. They brought with them two children. Three of his sons, Joseph, John and Isaiah, settled on the south side of Foss Pond within a mile of each other. The sons individually lived to be over eighty years of age. Their descendants who lived on these farms were Allen W. Foss, on Joseph Foss' farm, Jeremiah L. Foss on Isaiah Foss' farm, and Charles Small on his grandfather's Foss' farm.

Mr. Foss was a man of great fortitude and of strict integrity. When not clearing his land he worked at Saco, a distance of twenty miles from his home, going by spotted trees through the woods and bringing heavy loads of provisions on foot for the support of his family. His wife was necessitated several times to take the same journey, carrying a child in her arms and leading another by the hand, returning in the same manner. They did not suffer as many of the settlers did from depredations by the Indians, but the hungry wolves often came around the lonely cabin, howling dismally. The brave mother would gather her children around her at such times, soothe them and commend them to the protection of the Almighty. She stated that at one time while her husband was absent they had eaten the last particle of provision that they possessed; her children were crying for food but she had nothing to give them. In her distress she thought of a piece of rye, which her husband had sown on the clearing. It was beginning to ripen, and as it waved in the bright sunshine, she took a pair of shears and went out, cutting a quantity of the precious grain. She carried it home, dried it by the fire, beat it out, pounded it in a mortar, then made bread which she baked by the fire and made a comfortable meal.

There were no fruit trees at that early date in Limington. Mr. Foss was sick and hearing that a settler in Limerick had an orchard of apple trees beginning to bear fruit, sent his eldest son to get him a few. The owner kindly gave the boy as many as he could carry in a large old fashioned handkerchief. But on the way home the boy being hungry was tempted to eat some. When he arrived home few apples remained.

Stagecoaches and Mail Service

Before the year 1820 there was no mail route through the little towns and settlements stretching from the White Mountains to Portland.[28] If anyone wrote a letter, the next man who went near its destination carried it in his hat. In 1820 Eben Irish of Fryeburg previously an early settler of Limington, carried the mail from Fryeburg to Portland once a week on horseback. A Mr. Tucker carried the mail weekly, in saddle-bags from Limington Corner to Cornish, thence to Limerick Corner and then back to Limington, a distance of about twenty-five miles.[29] The mail carrier was allowed to take mail matter in his pocket or cuff of his coat to those who lived far from the post office, and drop it at their doors. Those who lived off the road had a box to receive their mail nailed to the gate-post or a tree. In due time the carrier collected the postage and paid it to the office where it was due.

In 1830 Ben Gould of Conway drove his team twice a week from Fryeburg to Portland, and the people rejoiced in two mails a week.[30] Although this line, known as the White Mountain Line, did not pass through East Limington which was a thoroughfare for much of the travel from the upper country to Portland, it did pick up mail and passengers at Steep Falls.

A stage run by Andrew R. Bucknell commenced August 1832, and connected the White Mountain Line with the Boston and Augusta Line. It ran from Hiram to Waterboro, three days coming and two in going. Passengers were taken on at Hiram Bridge about 10:00 a.m. and driven through Cornish, Limington Corner, Hollis (Swetts Tavern), arriving at Waterboro the same day.[31] The Portland, Saco, and Parsonsfield Stage Company ran through town about this same time. Arthur McArthur was its secretary, notifying its members in 1829 of its meeting at the hall of Abner Libby in Limington.[32]

Gould was followed by John Smith who drove for twenty-two years without missing a day except when business called him to Washington.[33] He became an excellent driver, having an interest in the route and supplying fine coaches, horses and fittings. Horses were changed about every ten miles. The changes were made at Osgood's Tavern, Fryeburg; Spring's Tavern, Hiram; Dyer's house, East Baldwin and Clement's Tavern, West Gorham.[34]

Another old-time stage driver was Eben Howe, the grandson of Eben Irish, the first carrier of the mail on horseback. He was on the road from 1848-64, driving four and six horses on the Conway and Portland route. He was a famous whip and never had any really serious accidents, but he experienced some hair-breadth escapes. "Once," quoting Mr. Howe,

"I had a narrow escape between Limington and Cornish. I had a new horse who wouldn't hold a pound. I was coming down a steep hill with a stringer bridge at the foot. In order to keep the lead horses out of the way, I set them a-going and kept them a-going. When I was on the steepest part of the hill, an old farmer with a big load came up on the other end of the bridge. It was too late for either of us to do anything. I knew there was not room enough for both, but I gave him all I could spare, and expected to knock him off into the river. Instead, I only slued his wagon over, and landed him high and dry on one of the big log stringers. The butter and eggs were hove in all directions, and it was a pretty bad looking sight. He said about ten dollars would 'fix it up'. I can tell you I was thankful to 'fix it up' so easily. I told him we were both very lucky not to be in the river beyond 'fixing'."[35]

Before the Civil War Levi Clough, nicknamed "Little Levi," ran a stage from Gorham to Freedom, New Hampshire. His route was from Gorham via

West Gorham, Standish, Cornish, Kezar Falls and Porter to Freedom.[36] For two years, Mr. Dyer of East Baldwin ran a line in competition during which time "Little Levi" had no price for carrying passengers. He always told his passengers to step on and if the ride was worth anything to them they could pay, if not it was all the same.[37]

"Little Levi" often had trouble with the opposition, their drivers in his words sometimes used to do things out of sheer ugliness. "One time, old Limington bridge was impassable, and the stages had to cross Chase Parker's bridge a mile or so up the river. We had to make a square turn after coming off the bridge; the road was quite narrow, and it was a little difficult with a six or even a four-horse team to make the turn. It was on my up trip from Portland. I had crossed the bridge, and there, standing in the road about where I wanted to make my turn to go down the road, was a two-horse black vehicle, headed down the river. It was the opposition. It had come down from East Baldwin to take passengers, if there were any, from the opposition that came up from Saco and went to Porter. I said to the driver of the little black vehicle, 'I guess you will have to start down a little, and give me a chance to get into the road.' He demurred, and finally said he would not, and that he had a right to stand there. I said, 'Undoubtedly.' I also said, not very loud I guess, that I thought I had a right to get into the road and go along. I had a six-horse team, and they were pretty good horses. Jake and Dan on the chain, and they were a power in themselves; on the lead were Boots and his mate, and they were a pair of boots; the polers were good ones. I had had a good load of passengers, perhaps not twenty-seven. I drove the team across the road and the leaders up to the fence, swung the team off and backed the coach; then swung to and straightened the team. I had a new snapper on my lash, and I thought this was a good time to see how loud I could make it crack. I was sitting on the wrong side to see the little vehicle and where the hind wheels of my coach were going, and the hind wheel on the right side of my coach — accidentally, of course — locked in with the off hind wheel of the little vehicle, and the wheel, for some reason or other, dropped flat on the ground. The driver began screaming for me to stop, and said, 'Here's damage, here's damage.' But I couldn't stop, as I was in a hurry to make up lost time. A young man that was sitting beside me took up the mail pouch, shook it at the driver and said, 'Keep your old hearse off the way.' Some called that vehicle a hearse on account of its color. I told the driver to call at the office. I guess he didn't call, as I heard nothing more about it."[38]

In 1885, Leonard J. Strout, the executor of Joab Black's estate, sold the mail and stage route from Limington to Steep Falls to Charles E. Emery of North Limington. There were then two mails per day on this route from Limington to Steep Falls.[39] Frank A. Hobson who contracted to carry the mail from South Limington to Hollis Center sold his route in June 1887, to Jerry H. Anderson.[40]

Ezra Miles was Limington's famed veteran stage driver. He was employed in 1891, the same year that Charles E. Emery purchased the stage route from Limington Corner to Steep Falls from the popular stage driver, Charles Yates of South Limington.[41] Ezra Miles was an employee for over twenty years and never had a day's vacation, with the exception of three or four days when his wife was dangerously ill. He drove in the first few years thirty-five miles a day and the remaining years twenty-five miles a day, besides the many trips taken evenings and Sundays to carry passengers to and from the station.[42]

During these years he missed the train but twice, the first time was the morning after the Steamer Portland was lost and the roads were almost impassable, in fact, he encountered one drift on the road from Limington Corner to South Limington where the snow was fourteen feet deep and after a hard struggle managed to turn his team and return to his home until a crew of men could shovel through the drift. The following February thirteenth there was another severe storm during which about eighteen inches of damp snow fell.[43] Mr. Miles started earlier than usual and broke the road, but the train was pulling out of the station just as he drove in.

Just before Mr. Miles began to drive the stage a new road was built on a part of his route, shortening the distance from Limington to Steep Falls quite a good deal; but being built through Pickpole swamp, it was such a rough road that during the spring and fall it was torture to ride over it.

When he had been driving about a year the old wooden covered bridge over the Saco River between the towns of Limington and Standish was removed and a steel bridge put in its place. During the process of construction the mail was carried and passengers walked over narrow planks placed on stringers to the Standish side where a team from Marean's Hotel met them and took them to the station a distance of one-half mile.[44]

Post Offices

Limington Corner postmasters and their dates of appointments have been Jacob Quincy, 1801; Ezra Davis, 1809; Wingate Frost, 1810; James Frost, 1811; Daniel Tyler, 1840; David Otis, 1842; Isaac L. Mitchell, 1844; William Dimock, 1856; Isaac L. Mitchell, 1861; Miss Kate Mitchell, 1872; John T. Lord, 1878; Charles E. Dimmock, 1885; Benjamin Small, 1889; Frank M. Bradbury, 1893; Hardy H. McKenney, 1897; and Charles E. Dimmock, 1914.

East Limington post office was established on January 26, 1838 and discontinued on December 31, 1938. The postmasters and dates of appointments have been Henry Small, 1838; George M. Small, 1876; John F. Chase, 1886; Augustus S. Chick, 1887; Edward L. Chick, 1926; and Mrs. Carrie M. Cotton, 1936.

North Limington post office was established on December 14, 1865 and discontinued on January 15, 1918. The list of postmasters and dates of appointments have been Hiram H. Bragdon, 1865; Israel Boothby, 1873; John A. Hubbard, 1877; Samuel N. Small, 1881; John Seavey, 1886; Leonard Abbott, 1886; Lyman S. Pitts, 1901.

South Limington post office was established on June 30, 1866 and discontinued on January 15, 1921. The postmasters and dates of appointments have been James McArthur, 1866; Joseph Davis, Jr., 1870; Frank A. Hobson, 1877; Emily J. Wentworth, 1886; David Walker, 1889; Truman F. Maxim, 1901; John F. Ridlon, 1902; Everett J. Pattee, 1910; and Rosilla C. Foster, 1917.

West Limington post office was established as North Limington on March 2, 1852 and discontinued on July 6, 1865. It was re-established on November 7, 1865 and changed to West Limington on December 14, 1865. It was discontinued on December 17, 1867. The postmasters and dates of appointments have been John Seavey, 1852; Ezekiel Small, 1862; and Joshua R. Cobb, 1865.

Leonard Abbott House and Post Office, Slabstreet.

Chapter VI — Religious Societies

Limington is "a place somewhat noted at times in consequence of being the field on which have been hard fought battles in the Holy War."[1] The inhabitants of Limington have been a church-going people. The early settlers of the town were not far enough removed from their Puritan and Pilgrim ancestors to have forgotten or neglected their duties in providing for religious worship, and their pious example and veneration of things sacred, have been transmitted as a priceless legacy to their posterities.

From the records of the four churches, Congregational, Free-Will Baptist, Calvinist Baptist, and Quaker, one is able to glean some interesting information and facts revealing the role these churches played in this small community in the early eighteen hundreds. Limington's ecclesiastical records, contained within the existing church books and recorded monthly minutes, recite many incidences where the church tried to right the character of her members. Often, we are told what the sins were that had to be dealt with, and how they, as a church, tried to remedy the situation. Admonitions were often taken as well as given forth-rightly.

The church acted as the overseer of its flock and if any difficulties arose between its brethren, a certain appointed committee on behalf of the church was sent to help remedy the situation. On one occasion concerning difficulties between Mark Manson and William Manson, a committee of three was sent personally to help take up their "stumbling blocks." Their orders were to withdraw the hand of fellowship from the Mansons in behalf of the church unless they found "a returning" in them. At the next conference "the three man committee reported they had been and conversed with the two parties and found them firm in the Shakers' principle and obtained no satisfaction."[2] Upon hearing this report, some brethren in attendance were still not satisfied, concluding that they had not been dealt with according to Scripture. Another committee was chosen to go and visit the Mansons, and if they found no satisfaction to let them know in behalf of the church that it would have no fellowship with them. A report was to be made at the next meeting. One more meeting and five months later the chosen committee reported they found them resolved to pursue their errors and on behalf of the church had cut them off. One might conclude that the church hated to admit defeat.

Insofar as each member kept a watchful eye on the other, different reports on a certain brethren's conduct would be voiced at the monthly conference. On one occasion "from the lips of a loyal sister, a Sister Martha Russel was reported as walking disorderly, and before this has been labored with agreeable to Scripture."[3] A letter of rejection was agreed upon at the next meeting, and it was sent to her.

"At the next meeting the two sisters chosen at that meeting to visit Almira Stevens, reported that they had found but little satisfaction from Sister Stevens. Another committee was chosen to go and see her and if they found no repentance in her to withdraw from her the hand of fellowship in behalf of the church. They soon reported they found Sister Stevens in a penitent state as she confessed that she had wandered out of the way and caused trouble to the brethren, but said she intended to do better."[4]

This was evidently not a satisfactory testament as two months later she was sent a letter of rejection.

Limington Congregational Church

In 1790 the plantation's population had grown to six hundred and seven.[5] However sparse in number, on October 11, 1789, Little Ossipee was the first of the towns in the Ossipees to organize a Congregational Church.[6] This was nearly two and one-half years before the town was incorporated by the name of Limington. No record of the transaction has been preserved except the declaration and covenant, and names of the original members. There were six original members, Francis Small, Isaac Robinson, Amos Chase, Jonathan Boothby, Daniel Dyer and Asa Edmunds. During the first five years only four new members were added, the church having no pastor nor stated preaching. One of the four was a female Mrs. Mary Sawyer, "a most remarkable if not unique record among Maine churches at the time." Her membership was short for she lived but a year, "dying in September, 1790."[7]

The earliest labors in the gospel ministry in this and all of the neighboring Ossipee towns, except Cornish, were by Rev. John Adams, a graduate of Harvard in 1745. In March 1781, Mr. Adams moved from Durham, New Hampshire, where he had been pastor of the Congregational Church for thirty years, and settled at Newfield when there were but five families in that place. Mr. Adams might have been called a circuit preacher traveling from town to town to services every week weather permitting. Prior to the building of any meeting-houses or even school houses in the area, he held preaching services in barns, kitchens and wherever he could.[8] It was from him that Newfield, Limerick and Limington first received the preached gospel.

He was not a man of great physical strength and did not, like so many of the first ministers, draw much from the soil. He had considerable knowledge of the medical art and skill in its practice, so he ministered not only to the spiritual, but also to the physical health of the people. This latter service was not of slight importance to the scattered settlers and their households.[9] Probably Rev. Adams was the doctor for widow Rackliff's husband, who was the first settler to die of disease in Little Ossipee. The record of Mr. Rackliff's estate probated January 7, 1789, indicated a nursing fee of fifteen pounds, a doctor's bill of nine shillings, and a burial cost of a pound and four shillings.[10]

For eleven years Mr. Adams rendered himself useful in both professions to the Ossipee towns and yet the church at Limington was the only religious establishment that he lived to witness before his death at Newfield on June 4, 1792. In 1793 the town began building its "meeting-house," and progressed so as to offer at public sale, April 1794 the "privileges for pews."[11] It was largely through Adams' efforts that the church was organized and by his influence the first meeting-house was built on the present spot. The church was completed in 1794. It was of ancient style, fifty-six by forty-two feet with a main entrance on the south, side entrances on east and west, and porches containing stairways to galleries. By 1822 it had passed into control of "proprietors." It was then proposed to remove the porches and build a belfry.[12]

At the first town meeting held in April 1792, it was voted to hire a minister and to give him for his services fifteen pounds when he came and in September a like sum. On November of that year William Gregg received a call as pastor, but remained only a few months, resigning on account of ill health. Gregg was a graduate of Dartmouth College in 1787, and a classmate of Rev. Atkinson who later accepted the job.

In the autumn of 1793 the town then recently incorporated voted to give a call to Jonathan Atkinson to settle with them in the work of the gospel ministry. The town also voted to give him one hundred twenty pounds for settlement and eighty pounds annually for his support during his ministry. Rev. Atkinson accepted the call on May 1794, and was ordained and installed on October 15, 1794, the first settled minister in the town's first church. On November 12, 1794, Atkinson moved his family from Newbury, Massachusetts to Limington, and in 1798 he began to build a house which he moved into the next spring. Later in 1803 the house was destroyed by fire and the present pastorage was raised and moved into just sixty-one days later.[13] "Soon began a grievous defection from his supporters by reason of the incoming Baptist and Methodist societies. For the years 1811-1813, he was paid a mere part for his services and some of the time nothing at all. One time when he asked for remuneration, the parish was so angry they even refused to let him administer the sacraments, but later the parish relented some and allowed him that privilege."[14] He held the pastoral office for nearly twenty-seven years, though he preached but little for the last six or seven years. He was dismissed in September 1821 and continued to reside at his homestead in Limington until his death on January 16, 1836.[15] During the long term of Mr. Atkinson's ministry forty-two had joined the church.

Soon after Rev. Atkinson's pastoral relation with the church was dissolved, Rev. Robert H. Noyes preached as stated supply for two years before moving to New Gloucester where he died. He was succeeded by Rev. Caleb F. Page, a graduate of Bowdoin in 1820, who was ordained at

Rev. Caleb F. Page, Third Pastor of the Limington Congregational Church.

Limington on November 5, 1823. During his successful ten year pastorate about fifty persons united with the church, nearly all of them on profession of their faith. Mr. Page was dismissed September 24, 1833, going to a pastorate in Bridgton. Few pastors enjoyed as many revivals as he; his aim was to lead souls to Christ. Rev. Hazel Lucas succeeded Mr. Page, and supplied one year before leaving to preach for several years in New Hampshire. A call was then given to Rev. Ivory Kimball, fresh out of Bangor Seminary coming directly on November 12, 1834. During the first year of his settlement the old church was taken down and the present building was erected upon the same spot, at a cost of $2,496.00. This new edifice had the same dimensions, with galleries on the east and west sides as well as on the south end. Those on the sides were reached by stairways on the outside of the church. The building was dedicated on September 14, 1835.[16] A bell tower was then added and a bell weighing fifteen hundred pounds was probably purchased in the autumn of 1836.[17] Rev. Ivory Kimball's labors ceased in January 1840, though his dismissal did not occur until October 24, 1842. He served two years each at Lyndeboro, New Hampshire, and Kennebunkport, finally settling at Edgecomb where he died.

In the new church, there was a large semi-circular pulpit of walnut which was about four feet long in length and height. A fluted wine colored drape extending from near the top to within about six inches of the floor was placed over the pulpit. There were casters on the bottom of the pulpit which made it easy to move about. An organ manufactured by Mr. Paine of Standish was purchased, placed in the present gallery, and played by William Chick who was totally blind. Records show that the walls and pews were painted light brown with darker brown trimmings. The lighting for the church was provided by two oil burning chandeliers over each aisle with small lamps for the organ and pulpit. The floor was covered with a bright red carpet.[18]

Limington Congregational Church built in 1835.

The first heating device was a large box stove in the back of the church. This raised the temperature somewhat but worshipers' feet always were cold. Later a round wood heater was purchased, but only succeeded in roasting the choir while the congregation froze.

The next minister in residence who took charge of the newly built church was an older man, Henry Ambrose Merrill, one of the first graduates of Bangor Theological Seminary. Rev. Merrill was engaged in March 1840, and remained three years. Rev. Franklin Yeaton followed. He was a graduate of Bowdoin in 1831 and of Bangor Theological in 1836. He held the position of classical teacher at Gorham Seminary before accepting the call to Limington on August 1843. He was installed the following month. During his settlement a parsonage was built in 1844-45 on six acres of land on the Shaving Hill Road. Mr. Yeaton was dismissed, to the universal regret of his people, on June 3, 1846.

The pastors of the Limington Congregational Church for the next thirty-two years were young men beginning in the ministry, and all were ordained in town. Rev. John Harper Garman, a graduate of Amherst and Andover Theological Seminary in 1845 was ordained and installed on November 3, 1847. While here, Mr. Garman took an active part in town affairs, being instrumental in starting the academy. Charles Edward Garman, his son, was born in town and became a noted professor of philosophy at Amherst College. Rev. Garman's pastorate closed July 2, 1855.

Rev. John Parsons, a native of Parsonsfield and a graduate of Brown University in 1842 and Andover Theological Seminary in 1848 was ordained and installed on May 14, 1857. He remained for five years. During his pastorate about thirty were added to the church, most of them on profession of faith.

Mr. Albion H. Johnson of Augusta was Mr. Parson's successor and was ordained and installed in the pastoral office on October 31, 1865. Rev. Johnson's labors were very successful and it was to the deep regret of the church and society that he was dismissed in September 1868, after a pastorate of three years. In June 1869, Mr. Samuel W. Pearson, a graduate of Bowdoin in 1862 and of Bangor Theological Seminary in 1866 began as stated supply. He was ordained here in November 1870, and continued to the general satisfaction of al until October 1872. Rev. Reuben D. Osgood, also a Bangor graduate, succeeded Mr. Pearson in November 2, 1873, and remained for six years. Mr. Osgood was a stone-cutter prior to the Civil War and strangely enough experienced religion during the roar of the battle. He resigned on May 1879. The membership during his pastorate was one hundred and eight. The oldest member during his pastorate was William Thompson, who lived to his one hundred and first year.

Rev. Thomas N. Lord commenced his work on November 9, 1879, Limington being his last work in the active ministry. Rev. Lord first studied for the ministry with Rev. David Thurston, D.D., of Winthrop and had more than a dozen different churches to his credit. The next pastor, Edgar Thomas Pitts a graduate of Bates College, was called to serve and stayed until July 1884. The congregation at Limington, joined by the East Baldwin parish then extended a call to Rev. David S. Hibbard. Rev. Hibbard was educated at Bowdoin in 1857 and Bangor Theological Seminary in 1860, a man of ability and culture. He was dismissed July 1885, and immediately left with his family for Kansas where he made his home for several years.

Rev. Charles H. Gates was engaged by the combined parishes in October 1885. He started his long career as a pioneer missionary in the state of Iowa, after finishing his studies at Amherst in 1847 and Andover Seminary in 1850.[19] He returned east because of his mother's illness and resumed his work by preaching at different places in York County. Rev. Gates left Limington after the church's Centennial Anniversary. The whole number enrolled during its first hundred years was two hundred twenty-one.

The anniversary was observed on October 15, 1889. The church was finely decorated and was completely filled on the day of the occasion. The following was the order of exercises: anthem by the choir; invocation by Rev. C. H. Gates, pastor; church history by Prof. Wm. G. Lord; reading of letters from former pastors and others; address by Rev. A. H. Johnson, a former pastor; poems by T. S. Perry of Limerick; centennial ode, written by Fred J. Allen and sung by congregation; addresses made by Abner Chase of Boston, Rev. A. K. P. Small of Portland and others.[20]

Henry Otis Thayer, educated at Bowdoin in 1862 and Bangor in 1865 served from October 1889 to June 1893. Besides his faithful and successful work in the ministry, he gave himself to historic investigations, accounts of which appeared in the public press. He soon gave up the ministry and for a number of years was librarian of the Maine Historical Society.

In 1894 Rev. Charles S. Wilder was installed and continued in the active discharge of his duties here for five years. He returned three years later and supplied the church for another two years. In the meantime, Rev. George K. Goodwin for two and one-half years serving the two churches, eight miles apart, as well as being superintendent of the public schools. He introduced and suggested certain changes that brought the schools to a higher standard of efficiency.

Limington Congregational Roll of Ministers

1. Jonathan Atkinson, b. Newbury, Mass., Dec. 30, 1756; Dartmouth College, 1787; ord. Limington, Oct. 15, '94; p. to Sept. 26, '21; d. Limington, Jan. 16, 1836.

2. Robert Noyes, b. Newbury, Mass., Nov. 10, 1782; council declined to ord.; p. Oct. '21 to '22; d. New Gloucester, Feb. 14, 1854.

3. Caleb Fessenden Page, b. Fryeburg, Feb. 15, 1797; Bowdoin Coll. 1820, studied theology with Rev. David Thurston of Winthrop; ord. Limington Nov. 5, 1823; p. to Sept. 24, '33; d. Milton Mills, N.H., Dec. 6, 1873.

4. Hazel Lucas, b. Carver, Mass., Apr. 16, 1801; studied Bangor Sem. 1830-31, studied theology with Revs. Benjamin Whitmore and Frederic Freeman, of Plymouth, Mass.; ord. Plymouth, Mass., Apr. 1831; p. Oct. '33 to '34; d. Grand Rapids, Mich., Apr. 13, 1876.

5. Ivory Kimball, b. Wells, Sept. 21, 1805; Bangor Sem. 1834; ord. Limington, Nov. 12, '34; p. to Oct. 24, '42; d. Edgecomb, July 24, 1853.

6. Henry Ambrose Merrill, b. Conway, N.H., June 13, 1795; Bangor Sem. 1822; ord. Shapleigh, Apr. 23, '23; p. Mar. '40 to June '43; d. Granville, Ohio, Sept. 24, 1872.

7. Franklin Yeaton, b. Alna, Me., Dec. 26, 1808; Bowdoin Coll. 1831, Bangor Sem. 1836; ord. Perry, Me., Oct. 4, '47; p. Sept. 20, '43 to June 3, '46; d. Naples, Nov. 30, 1864.

8. John Harper Garman, b. Laconia, N.H. Jan. 20, 1811; Amherst, 1832-33, Andover Sem. 1845; ord. Limington, Nov. 3, '47; p. July 2, '55; d. No. Orange, Mass., June 15, 1905.

9. John Parsons, b. Parsonsfield, Sept. 25, 1820; Brown Univ. 1842, Andover Sem. 1848; ord. Limington, May 14, '57; p. Mar. '62; d. Brookline, Mass., Mar. 31, 1910.

10. Albion Henry Johnson, b. Vienna, Me., Oct. 12, 1840; Bowdoin Coll. 1861, Bangor Sem. 1864; ord. Limington, Oct. 31, '65; p. to Sept. '68; d. Acworth, N.H., Jan. 1, 1923.

11. Samuel Wiggin Pearson, b. Alna, Me., Oct. 24, 1836; Bowdoin Coll. 1862, Bangor Sem. 1866; ord. Limington, Nov. 9, '70; p. June '69 to Oct. '72; d. Brunswick, Me., Jan. 2, 1912.

12. Reuben Dodge Osgood, b. Bluehill, Me., Feb. 1, 1836; Bangor Sem. 1869; ord. Eastport, Oct. 24, '71; p. Nov. '73 to May '79; d. Turner, Me., Dec. 31, 1891.

13. Thomas N. Lord, b. Newburyport, Mass., Aug. 19, 1807; Bowdoin Coll. 1835, studied theology with Rev. David Thurston, D.D., of Winthrop and Rev. Thomas Shepard; ord. Topsham, Aug. 10, 1837; p. Nov. '79 to May '81; d. Oshkosh, Wisc., Feb. 25, 1884.

14. Edgar Thomas Pitts, b. New Portland, Aug. 28, 1853; Bates Coll. 1881; ord. Limington, Feb. 8, '82; p. June '81 to July 23, 1884; d. Lisbon Falls, Me., Mar. 30, 1917.

15. David Sutherland Hibbard, b. Lisbon, N.H., Apr. 27, 1831; Bowdoin Coll. 1857; Bangor Sem. 1860; ord. Veazie, Me., July 26, '60; p. Oct. 1, '84 to Aug. 16, '85; d. Gorham, Dec. 7, 1911.

16. Charles Henry Gates, b. Palmer, Mass., Aug. 23, 1823; Amherst Coll. 1847, Andover Sem. 1850; ord. Wilbraham, Mass., Nov. 14, '51; p. Oct. 11, '85 to Sept. 1, '89; d. Auburndale, Mass., Dec. 12, 1914.

17. Henry Otis Thayer, b. So. Paris, Dec. 2, 1832; Bowdoin Coll. 1862; Bangor Sem. 1865; ord. Bangor, Me., July 20, '66; p. Oct. '89 to June 13, '93; d. Jackson Heights, N.Y., Mar. 28, 1927.

18. Charles Samuel Wilder, b. Conway, Mass., Feb. 18, 1860; Colby Univ., Bangor Sem. 1887; ord. Monson, Feb. 18, '90; p. Mar. '94 to '99; also '02 to '04; d. East Longmeadow, Mass., Jan. 22, 1939.

19. George Kittredge Goodwin, b. Groton, Vt., Apr. 12, 1865; Bangor Sem. 1896; Dartmouth Coll., 1909; p. '99 to '02; d. Dale City, Fla., May 17, 1943.

Limington Free-Will Baptist

The founder and progenitor of the denomination called Free-Will Baptist was Benjamin Randall, an ordained evangelist who gathered a church in New Durham, New Hampshire. This was the first church organized in the connexion, laying the foundation for what became a denomination of over 61,000 members in the 1840's,[21] many of whom were then living in Maine. The covenant was adopted the thirtieth of June 1780, signed by Randall and six other members.[22] Two of the signers, Robert Boody and his wife, Margery, six years later moved into Limington. Elder Randall's youngest brother, Shadrack,[23] took a Limington bride and moved to the neighboring town of Limerick, while a sister, Peggy Lyons, lived at South Limington. Once in 1801 Randall visited her, finding her in great trouble having lately buried her husband.[24] Randall and his adherents known as "the Freewillers" held to the freedom of the will, and that men may be regenerated in this life and fitted for heaven through improving the means of grace which God has bestowed upon them. They took the Bible as their rule of faith and practice.

The Free-Will Baptist Church of Limington was organized in 1798, mainly through the efforts of Deacon Andrew Cobb and Elisha Strout,[25] who had migrated from Gorham. The town was then in its infancy, and the population was not large. Settlers, however, were coming in, among them were some that belonged to Free-Will Baptist Churches in other places. These began to associate and soon a few were found who wished to enjoy church privileges. A council was called, which met and formed a small church. Between 1804 and 1810, many of the inhabitants in town were "polled off" and united with the Free-Will Baptist Church in Parsonsfield under Elder John Buzzell.[26]

"The members mostly lived and endeavored to walk in gospel order, with occasional preaching until 1810, when God blessed them with a glorious outpouring of his spirit. It began in October and continued through much of the winter. While it was in progress, a young man named Jeremiah Bullock came to the place and labored as a public exhorter."[27]

He was soon followed by his father, Christopher, who preached here only one season before moving to Week's Corner at Parsonsfield, where he labored until his death in the spring of 1825.[28]

Jeremiah Bullock began appointing meetings and commenced preaching though but recently converted. The people became interested and many professed religion amidst great opposition. In December 1810, young Bullock and fourteen others were baptized and the work continued until one hundred and eighty were numbered among the converts. On May 22, 1811, Jeremiah was ordained at Buxton and became the overseer of the flock. The quarterly meeting that August was held in town in a beautiful grove, and two thousand persons eagerly listened to the preached word. At a meeting for administering the Lord's supper, a few weeks after this, a thousand people were present and two hundred of them partook of the consecrated emblems.[29]

"While many members of the church were humble and devoted there were a number who were favored with good gifts and their testimony in public and private cut like a sharp sword."[30] One of the first of those was James Emery who lived at West Limington at Emery's Corner. At the age of sixteen, he became a subject of the 1810 reformation; until then he had been "powerfully convicted in sin."[31] Upon baptism, he became a member of the church and began to preach about 1816. The services at his ordination in August 23, 1823, were held in a grove a little west of where the old meetinghouse once stood at South Limngton.[32] He traveled and preached intensively in his place of residence and the adjacent town, where he saw many converted to the Lord. "His preaching was decidedly evangelical, simple in structure, though forcible and generally attended by the Holy Spirit. His was such a strong and penetrating mind and so much was he assisted by the Spirit, that he hardly ever failed in his prognostics of a revival."[33] Having spent several years here, seeing that Limington was quite well supplied with preachers, he decided in 1829 to move to Tamworth, New Hampshire.

In 1823, the same year that Elder Emery publicly set apart to the work of the ministry for prayer John Stevens was ordained to preach the gospel of Christ. Preaching all he could, Elder Stevens labored in Limington, Limerick, Waterboro and other places until the spring of 1832 when a gracious outpouring of the Spirit was witnessed among the people. The meetings were thronged with anxious listeners, and he held meetings day and night in the surrounding neighborhoods, with occasional visits and assistance of Elder Jeremiah Bullock and wife, brother James Buck, a Methodist local preacher and brother B.S. Manson.[34] The next few years were spent as a traveling evangelist. During the year of 1828, though most of five months was spent in Limington, he traveled more than 2,000 miles. At another revival in Limington his younger brother Theodore was converted. On September 3, 1834, at the North Limington meeting-house, he helped to ordain Theodore into the ministry.[35]

Rev. John Stevens

A former schoolmate and close friend of Elder Stevens was Benjamin S. Manson, another native son to enter the ministry. First converted at fifteen, B.S. Manson was ordained at a session of the Parsonsfield Quarterly Meeting held at Hiram in August 1825.[36] His first pastorship was in Conway, New Hampshire where he was at the same time engaged in teaching. He continued his labors as pastor in churches at Meredith, Epsom and Candia, New Hampshire, until the spring of 1839, when he was called back to Limington. Elder Manson continued to labor mostly with the second church at South Limington for the next thirteen years excepting for a brief two year span after the spring of 1845, when he was at Westbrook.[37] Glorious revival seasons were enjoyed in 1839, '40, '41, '42, and '43 and the South Limington Church increased from ninety-five to two hundred twenty-three.[38] On July 29, 1844, thirty-seven of its dismissed members organized a church in the west part of Limington called the Limington and Limerick Church.[39]

A good degree of union in sentiment and action prevailed among the ministers at Limington and in the church until the temperance and anti-slavery questions were started. These questions first arose in the Congregational Society at the corner in 1825 when Rev. Asa Meads of Brunswick delivered Limington's first temperance lecture.[40] Up to this time the whole community at public as well as private meetings was in the constant habit of using liquor. Strong drinks were sold in the local taverns and inns and a number of the citizenry had their own cider supplies. Even the town's most influential and senior elder, Jeremiah Bullock, believed liquor made from fruit and not distilled was fit to drink as God intended.

The Free-Will Baptist ministers and people stood aloof for a time and the temperance movement made slow progress. Then an overturn took place, scarcely paralleled in the annals of the past, as the Free-Will Baptists entered the field, "causing the cup of devils to be driven from the lips of thousands thus preparing the church to be filled with the Holy Spirit."

As time went on the Limington Free-Will Baptist Church, having the largest membership and being the most influential, increased its involvement with the temperance cause. Elder John Stevens compelled by the logic of his own reasoning was the first of its ministers to take a position against strong drink, followed by brother Emery.[41] Unfortunately for harmony, Elder Jeremiah Bullock with a considerable part of the church in Limington, especially the First Free-Will Church, took issue and opposed Elders Stevens and Emery.[42] These two views caused hard feelings among the brethren at Limington.

In January 1831 a new church was organized at North Limington by Elder John Stevens, with forty-two of its members taking their letters from the First Church under the care of Elder Bullock.[43] This became known as the Second Free-Will Church of Limington, adopting temperance as one plank of its platform along with Sabbath schools, missions, and the abolition of slavery. Elder Stevens left this church in the fall of 1837. In September 1842, Deacon William Merrill, with Elder James Rand and fifty-one others took their letters and formed the First Free-Will Baptist Church at Cornish.[44] The remaining members voted to disband the church in 1848. This Baptist church was located near the Ralph Bragdon place on the North Road.

The next Free-Will Baptist Church organized in town, mainly through the efforts of Elder John Stevens, was called the Third Church and consisted mostly of members from Emery's Corner at West Limington. It was formed on the sixteenth and seventeenth of January 1833, because the records say "they were so scattered over the country, the members could not become acquainted with each other" and "they could not meet together, as they ought, once a month."[45] The location of this church was at Barbel Creek, about two miles northeast of the old First Church site at the southern end of Quaker Lane. Charles Bean, a young man from Emery's Corner, became its second pastor shortly after becoming ordained November 21, 1833, at Freedom, New Hampshire.[46] Less than six months after his ordination he had baptized a rising number of twenty.[47] Elder Bean with Theodore Stevens, then a licentiate, labored with success in most of the places where revivals were experienced.

A temperance society was organized at Limington Corner in January 5, 1830. The reform spread among the Free-Will Baptists in town, and about

1833 another temperance society was started with twenty-six members in the midst of hard speeches and opposition.[48] In one year the society had grown to two hundred in number. Elder John Stevens assisted by brother Emery became leaders in the movement and organized a society in the southern part of town which in 1834 had about two hundred members.[49] These societies were upon the plan of total abstinence except when indispensable as a medicine.

An anti-slavery society was formed in town in the early spring of 1835. In the spring of 1836 a home mission society was formed among the women and was followed by the formation of a Sabbath school society.[50] These groups brought opposition from the members of the church, but the reformations spread. Many of the opposers of these enterprising societies, styled themselves as Free-Will Baptists of the old stamp.[51]

The importance of giving the young religious instruction was also felt. A Sabbath School Union was instituted in 1833 and in August 1834, a Home Mission Society was formed. These things were condemned by the brethren at Limington under Elder Bullock in a greater or lesser degree.[52] While Elder Bullock and his followers who didn't approve of the Free-Will Baptist reforms condemned them, there were brethren and preachers, namely Elders Stevens and Bean, who were interested in these causes, and some unkind feelings and words were indulged on both sides. Up to this time the Free-Will Baptists of Limington had remained in one church, numbering about three hundred members. Elder Bullock was the leader of the principal one in South Limington numbering one hundred twenty-five, the Second Church in the northern part of town under Elder John Stevens had one hundred twenty-two, and a third in Emery's Corner, had fifty-three members.[53] At this time three meeting-houses in town belonged to the denomination; the First Church situated near the old Taterboro School erected by 1819, the north meeting-house on the North Road, and the west meeting-house at Emery's Corner, constructed by contributions in 1827.

The state of things was becoming bad, and at the quarterly meeting held at Waterboro in October 1834, a council was chosen to visit the churches in Limington and look into their difficulties. On this council were Elder Joseph White, Samuel Burbank, and three others. They convened about the middle of November and made an investigation, and a report in which a number of irregular proceedings were condemned. Elder Bullock's course in publicly and privately taking a stand against various benevolent causes was disapproved. Confessions were recommended. It was also suggested that those who were interested in enterprises should enjoy the privilege of carrying them forward without ridicule, and that those who did not see their way clear to take an active part in them were not to be despised by those who did. This report was made to the quarterly meeting held at Limington in January 1835 and accepted.[54]

Upon hearing the report the First Church thought they had been dealt with unfairly, and stated that they thought there were many errors in the report. They requested the privilege of pointing out some of them, but they were refused the privilege, and recommendations were hurried through by a very small majority.[55]

The members present of the First Church were very much hurt, and its clerk in behalf of the same, requested a dismissal from the quarterly meeting which was refused. Next, the clerk in behalf of the church, declared the First Church of Limington independent of the Free-Will Baptist Connexion. "Elder Bullock at that time was a member of regular standing in the First Church, which, at their next church meeting, (fully attended), unanimously ratified the doings of their clerk in declaring the church independent from said quarterly meeting."[56] The Limington Quarterly Conference was soon after formed by the First Church under the leadership of Elder Bullock. They were called "Bullockites," but they themselves recognized no name but Free-Will Baptist.

The First Church in Limington, having been rejected, the north one became the First, the south one became the Second, and the church at Emery's Corner the Third. After the North Church disbanded in 1848, the South, belonging to the Parsonsfield Quarterly Meeting, became the First, and the one in West Limington the Second.

The Old Free-Will Baptist Church built in 1841 and burned 1959.

A good meeting-house at South Limington was built in 1841 and was the place of the ministry of Elder B.S. Manson before 1845, followed by Elder Andrew Hobson who supplied until about the first of 1846 when Elder Theodore Stevens took charge.[57] In 1847 "Elder Theodore Stevens left to restore new life to the Saco Church, continuing his work there until his iron constitution yielded a year later. He was obliged and over-exertion, the result being that he could neither preach nor work at manual labor for years, on account of vertigo."⁵⁸ For almost ten years he lived in Limington, supplying the pulpit at Limerick, Hollis and some other places, as strength and opportunity availed him. He later held pastorates in Springvale, North Berwick, and Lebanon, moving to Saco in the fall of 1868 where he lived the rest of his days.

The next pastor of the First Free-Will Baptist Church was Uriah Chase, a native of Canterbury, New Hampshire, who began his short tenure after being ordained at East Parsonsfield, on March 13, 1850. He was assisted during the winter of 1851 by Elder Alvin W. Foss and in March started a protracted meeting, converting more than twenty people.⁵⁹ In January 1859 Jeremiah Hayden, a native of Raymond, became the minister. During the early 1860's, Charles Hurlin, an Englishman who had recently migrated to this country, was pastor, followed by Oliver S. Hasty, a local minister, who lived at Limerick, near Gove's Ridge. The church was re-organized on May 17, 1872 and took the name "The Free Baptist Parish of South Limington."⁶⁰

Elder Jeremiah Bullock's main position against the reforms of his day was that all organizations such as temperance and missionary societies should be independent of the church and that the church was under no necessity to form any such societies.

> "His views on temperance were that churches were already a temperate society, and members who had convenanted together to take the scriptures for their only rule of faith and practice, and lived up to their profession did not need any other pledge; but it was well enough for those who did not make any profession, to form themselves into societies, and pledge themselves to be temperate."⁶¹

In his preachings, Elder Bullock universally preached against intemperance, and the church to which he belonged often labored with those members who were reported intemperate, and rejected those that would not reform from what was considered evil practice.⁶²

On December 16, 1849, Elder Bullock died of typhoid fever at his home at South Limington.⁶³

> "His health was poor for some time before he became ill, and he seemed entirely reconciled to the will of the Lord, and would converse upon the subject of death with as much composure as upon any other. A day or two previous to his death his fever raged to such a degree that he was insensible at times. A short time before he died, his mind cleared, and his son told him that he thought he could not live. He replied, 'My greatest desire is that my children walk in the truth.' "⁶⁴

His funeral was held at his own home. Elder Silas Moulton preached his funeral sermon using Second Timothy, the fourth chapter, verses seven and eight.⁶⁵ He was interred at South Limington and later reburied at the Forest City Cemetery at Bridgton.

Elder Bullock has been described as "a very temperate, honest-hearted, and plain-dealing man; he said what he thought without fear or hypocrisy, which sometimes made him enemies. He always held to, and preached, the same doctrine that Randall, Buzzell, Colby and others preached. They universally preached against the hireling system; which is, preaching for hire and divining for money—and against the institutions and inventions of men—which doctrine Elder Bullock promulgated to the day of his death; and by so doing, caused some to become enimical to him, and tried in various ways to injure him—but where he was known, his character stood firm, and they never were able to succeed."[66]

Elder Jeremiah Bullock House, located just north of the Old Nicholas Edgecomb place, South Limington. Pictured is Ebenezer McLellan who last occupied the place.

During his Christian warfare, Elder Bullock saw many hundred souls converted to God as a result of his work and had the privilege of baptizing more than one thousand converts. It was his theme to point souls to Christ as the only refuge and safe hiding place. He never believed that uninspired men were able to write or fix any discipline fit to rule the church by, but that the scriptures of truth were a sufficient rule for the government of the church, and that the church was the highest earthly tribunal. He depended entirely on God's spirit to select his subject or text, believing that God was able to call and qualify his own preachers, and that if they would follow him they never would lack a competent support.[67]

After Elder Bullock's death his widow, Almira, who had even commenced attending and appointing meetings in several towns adjoining Gorham before their marriage in 1817, continued the work of winning souls. She traveled with her husband for many years and saw the cause of God prosper in several states.[68]

"Elder Bullock was a man of unpre-possessing personality; a big course featured, stiff-haired, loud-spoken preacher, and his rather rough-and-tumble method of presenting the truth acquired for him the name of 'breaking-up plow'. Almira was his antipode, and as graceful and fine as silk. She had a pleasant open face, a musical voice, clear articulation, and was ingenious in her exposition and illustration of sacred story and so she was the 'smoothing-plane' in contra-distinction of Jeremiah."[69]

In 1851, the widow Bullock married Deacon Andrew Cobb, a worthy Christian, and one who was willing to travel with her wherever God called. She and her husband moved to Bridgton and still preached Christ. Few preachers could call out and entertain greater audiences. Her preaching was pointed, plain, familiar and instructive. She always depended upon God for her subject, believing that he could assist all those who trusted in him. Through her life, Almira preached in public, and lived in private.[70]

The Bullockites, as they were called, named after their founder, basically adhered to the principles of the Free-Will Baptist. However, they did have certain peculiarities in their mode of worship and belief which seem at least quite unusual to one not acquainted with their manners and customs. Their meetings were marked by informality. A brother or sister rose to speak any time that the urge was felt and might burst into song whenever a bit of music seemed fitting. Older members were especially enthusiastic, walking the aisles shouting praises and telling how the Lord had blessed them.[71] It has been remarked that one could but notice with pleasure the unity of feeling and purpose which seemed to prevail in their meetings. The main points of their belief which follow give evidence that in some ways they differed from most other sects:

"a belief in the scriptures of truth, as the Christian's discipline; that God has the only power to call to preach the gospel, and to support those called; that the church is the highest earthly tribunal of its members; that every person has the privilege of obeying God, for himself, without restraint; that the worship of God must be in spirit and in truth, that God is not worshipped by instrumental singing; that preaching to build up certain sects or parties, is not preaching the gospel, and that note or skeleton preaching is fit only for those who run without being sent or called of God."[72]

Many humorous incidents, some of which are still told are said to have occurred at these old time meetings. Once an elder in the habit of chewing tobacco came down the aisle to greet a visiting elder. As he approached him, his foot caught on the carpet and he stumbled, spewing tobacco juice over the visiting elder's shirt front.[73] Many elders were able to chew tobacco and preach at the same time. Spittoons were accessories to the pulpit.

In 1852 by contribution, the Bullockites of Limington built a new church farther up Quaker Lane next to the district school, at the cost of $1,200.00.[74] The number belonging to the Limington Quarterly Conference at that time was about one thousand, and churches were established in Parsonsfield, Porter, Hiram, Wakefield, Waterboro, Raymond, Standish, Gray, Eaton and Brownfield, Freedom, Bridgton, Naples, Sebago and Tamworth, as well as the mother church at Limington.[75] Later other churches in Baldwin, Hollis, Saco and Biddeford, and Ossipee, New Hampshire became members.

Quarterly Meeting of the Bullockites at Kimball's Corner, Naples, 1890.

Some of the old time Bullockite preachers were Silas Moulton of Parsonsfield, John F. Cooley of Ossipee, Samuel Boothby of Saco, Cyrus K. Ward of Sebago, William H. Cotton of Buxton, Wescott Bullock of Biddeford, Frank Rice of Saco, Loring Staples of Limerick and Joseph Storer and Henry Wentworth both of Limington. All were laboring men being employed in either farming, blacksmithing, or some other trade through the week and devoting the Lord's day to spreading the Gospel. The preached word was as free as the air the worshippers breathed, for a collection was never taken in a Bullockite meeting. At different times, parishioners would make donations to the Elder in farm produce and the like, but they gave very little money.

It is declared that Elder Wentworth possessed such a powerful voice that he could be heard a mile away from where he was preaching.[76] Elder Storer, was known for his fervid talks. Somebody once remarked that when he preached, he preached all over. He sometimes took off his coat and threw it to one side as he strode up and down the aisle, then his vest, and ended up by loosening his shirt collar. It was a habit with him to intersperse his preaching with side remarks to brethren and sisters.[77]

It was the custom of this group of Christians to make pilgrimages, "for to worship and renew the bonds of fellowship with those of like precious faith." These quarterly meetings, as they were called, were held on the third and fourth days in January, May, August and October. The delegates and visiting brethren and sisters who attended these meetings were among the "choicest spirit and gifts" of the Free-Will Baptist denomination.[78]

Several days before the assembling of the looked for ministers and delegates, the necessary preparations for entertainment were attended to in the farm houses around the village where the quarterly session was to be held. The great brick ovens were heated like "a burning fiery furnace" and were filled again and again with puddings, loaves of "rye-and Injun' bread and spareribs. Mince pies, apple-dowdy, Waterboro doughnuts, and caraway-seed cookies were stored away by panfuls.[79] There was always enough in the food to feed the multitude both at noon and suppertime, the meeting extending well into the evening. Those people who came from far away were kept overnight.

After the Bullockite Church at South Limington was destroyed by fire on the night of April 27, 1884,[80] they held their meetings in the old Friends' Church at the head of Quaker Lane. Here the movement in town conducted meetings at different times into the present century. Each year the church had fewer and fewer members as more zealous and devout followers passed on. Finally they became extinct and now the Bullockites remain only a memory in the minds of Limington's older residents.

The pastors of the Free Baptist Parish at South Limington, formerly the First Free-Will Baptist Church, and their dates of service have been Daniel A. Maddox, 1872 to Jan. 1873; George Wilson Howe, Jan. 1873 to Jan. 1875; Oliver S. Hasty, Mar. 1875 to Mar. 1877; Benjamin S. Moody, Dec. 1879 to Mar. 1881; Truman F. Maxim, Oct. 1881 to Nov. 1885, July 1890 to Mar. 1898; Fred A. Palmer, Nov. 1885 to Apr. 1887; Isambert Burnell Stuart, Apr. 1887 to Nov. 1888; and Lemuel A. Jones, May 1899 to May 1900.

Biography of Free-Will Baptist Ministers

Rev. Jeremiah Bullock was born in Royalston, Massachusetts, May 21, 1788. He embraced religion when about twenty years of age. In the first part of his ministry he traveled through the states of Vermont, New Hampshire, Rhode Island, Connecticut, New York and Maine. He finally came to Limington where his preaching was blessed with many conversions though opposition was great. He was a bold, plain, impressive preacher, who was for many years a successful evangelist and pastor. He always preached Christ's gospel free, believing that he who preached the gospel should live of the gospel.[81] He married Almira Wescott of Gorham in 1817.

Rev. Nahum Foss was born at South Limington in 1799. He was a minister for fifty-three years, having entered into the work which he enthusiastically followed when but twenty-eight years of age. He preached in the pulpits of nearly every denomination. He was self-sacrificing, kind and generous and always tried to improve the condition of others. He preached in Hollis from 1841 to 1844 and then went to Sebago for two years. In the spring of 1846 he moved to Effingham, New Hampshire, where he remained until 1864 at which time he took his family to Topeka, Kansas. He died there, March 24, 1880.

Rev. Charles Frost Osborne was born March 12, 1800, in Lee, New Hampshire. In 1818 he was converted and joined the Alton Church, where he was then residing. Later he settled at Scarboro where he was licensed in May 1838, and preached successfully. He was ordained by a council from the Gorham Quarterly Meeting on September 4, 1840. In 1845, after six years in the ministry at Scarboro he removed to West Limington and assumed care of the Limerick and Limington Church where he remained until 1853. During the last three years of his life he had no charge as pastor, but traveled and preached as his health and existing circumstances would permit. A few months before his death on January 23, 1856, he purchased and moved to a farm in Gorham.

Rev. John Stevens was born in South Limington on June 18, 1801. He experienced religion at the age of seventeen, and soon afterward began preaching. He was publicly ordained in June 1823 at the old South Meeting-House. He continued his ministerial work in his native town for ten years during which there were great revivals, and many were brought to Christ. He baptized ninety converts as the result of one of these revivals. In the fall of 1837 he was appointed to missionary work in the Montville Quarterly meetings. In 1843 Elder Stevens settled in Windsor where he remained for eight years. Afterward he served churches in Gardiner, Bath, Augusta and Wayne, North Berwick and Wells Branch. In June 1860 he moved to Biddeford and remained there until his death on April 5, 1878.

"Unlike some of his contemporaries, he early became the ardent champion of education, temperance, the anti-slavery movement, Mission Sabbath School, and many other benevolent enterprises. He was a man of unusual natural ability, possessing a clear judgment, a quickness of perception, and a liberality of sentiment that kept him from anything like bigotry or narrow-mindedness. Firm in his convictions and unswerving in the last degree in what he believed to be right, he was, nevertheless, lenient in judgment, charitable towards those differed from himself in point of doctrine."[82]

Rev. Benjamin Small Manson was born in Limington on March 5, 1802. He was converted at the age of fifteen, and the year following became a member of the church. He studied at the Academy at Effingham, New Hampshire, and afterwards taught. At the age of twenty he began to conduct religious services, and at twenty-two he was licensed by the Parsonsfield Quarterly Meeting. He was ordained at a session of the Parsonsfield Quarterly Meeting held at Hiram in August 1825. He preached for two years in Conway, five years in Meredith and later went to Epsom, New Hampshire. From 1836 to 1839 he was at Candia and then was called to his native town, Limington, where he was very successful and remained for thirteen years. Next he went to Parsonsfield and then to Lisbon, New Hampshire. After this he resided in New Hampton for two years so that his children could attend school. Age and infirmities then forced him to retire from pastoral work, and he bought a farm in Newmarket, New Hampshire. The deaths of his wife and daughter in

January 1866 left him entirely alone. He decided to preach again, and settled at Kittery, Maine, where he remained five years.[83] In the spring of 1871 he retired to spend the rest of his days in Raymond, New Hampshire, dying December 7, 1879.

Rev. Theodore Stevens was born in Limington, October 11, 1812. He was converted at the age of nineteen and began to preach when about twenty-one years of age. In September 3, 1834, he was ordained at North Limington. He first settled in Lebanon and preached half of the time in Acton. After three years he settled in Springvale and was there for four years after which he moved to his native town. He never entirely recovered from the arduous work of these years. In 1847-48 he made a strenuous effort to restore the Saco Church to new life. He returned home, and for years he could neither preach nor labor. When strength began to return, he supplied at Limerick, Hollis and other places and had preached for a year and a half at Springvale when he was forced to retire again. After three years on a farm in Somersworth, New Hampshire, his health improved so that in 1860 he became pastor of the North Berwick Church. After preaching in Lebanon for six years he moved to Saco where he lived the rest of his life. During this time he supplied at Carver's Harbor a season, two years at Doughty's Falls, two years at Cape Elizabeth and two years at Kennebunkport.[84] He died October 21, 1880 at Saco.

Rev. Charles Bean was born in Limerick on January 3, 1811. In May 1828, when seventeen years old, he became a Christian, and the following autumn was baptized by Elder James Emery and was united with the church in Limington. He was ordained by a council of the Parsonsfield Quarterly Meeting on November 21, 1833, at Freedom, New Hampshire. After a short tenure at South Limington, Elder Bean held pastorates in the west part of Standish and Standish Neck, Lisbon, Saco, Brunswick, Topsham, Bowdoinham, Richmond, South Parsonsfield, Gray and Buxton.[85] Sixty years of ministrial work made his name familiar in western Maine. He died at Scarboro, June 18, 1889.

Limington has furnished the Free Baptist denomination with a large number of native born ministers, other than those mentioned. They have been James Sawyer, ordained 1822; Samuel V. Nason; Edenezer Cobb, 1868; James Stevens; John Chadbourne Sawyer, 1840; James Strout, 1839; Joseph M. Foss; Joseph Edgecomb; Stephen Sawyer; Nathaniel Strout; Alvah Strout; Alvin W. Foss; Wescott Bullock, 1856; Henry Wentworth, 1869; Loring T. Staples, 1869; B. Franklin McKenney and John F. Lord, 1878.

Calvinist Baptist Church at North Limington

Rev. John Chadbourne, pastor of the Baptist Church in Cornish began about 1798 to visit Limington and preach the gospel to the people. "Now came a conflict between baptism and sprinkling; but God gave the victory to the Baptists in a few cases of conversion, and those who became Baptists united immediately with the church in Cornish, under the pastoral care of the Rev. Mr. Chadbourne."[86] The church numbers at Limington increased, and in 1802 they withdrew from the church in Cornish and formed the church at Limington. Elder Chadbourne by an urgent request of the new membership left the church in Cornish and became their pastor. With this church he labored successfully for one year, then resigned and moved to Dixmont. Mr. Chadbourne was succeeded the same year by Rev. Stephen Webber, who continued in the office until 1809 when he resigned.[87]

When it was first organized the church numbered thirteen, six males and seven females, who at first adopted the Articles of Faith used by the New Hampshire Association. They later changed them for those prepared by the York Baptist Association. In 1803 the church and society built a meetinghouse, and worshipped in it in an unfinished state for a number of years. In 1840 it was enlarged and finished, costing about $1200.00.[88]

From 1809 to 1814 the church was destitute of a pastor. Then John Seavey, an active member in the church, served in the capacity of a Licentiate until 1816 when he was ordained its pastor, working successfully in the church. During the year previous to the ordination of Mr. Seavey, the church excluded one-third of its members after having problems with a portion of its members who refused aid in sustaining the poor of the church. This greatly diminished the church but brought peace and prosperity as the encouraging result. Although their number was greatly diminished, yet the Lord did not forget the small congregation for in the two succeeding years more than twenty were added to the church.[89]

In 1823 another revival followed in which twenty-one more members were added to their number. From that time to 1840 there were frequent revivals and almost yearly additions to the church. In 1840 there was a more general and extensive reformation than ever before, thirty-eight were added to the church, and there were many others probably converted who did not publicly profess their faith in Christ. The beloved pastor, Brother Seavey, had been laboring with interest, and for a long time previous to the commencement of this work of God he had seen but little fruit of his labors or much to encourage him. The church was in a lukewarm state, the meetings often thin and the pastor himself nearly worn out in the service making him feel that his usefulness was nearly at an end.

"However, about the twentieth of April it was discovered that there were anxious souls in the vicinity; the church began to awake, prayer-meetings were commenced and attended with interest, which continued through the season. In September following a protracted meeting was commenced, and the result was beyond anticipation. People of all classes left their worldly affairs and went to meetings, and appeared to feel a great interest in the salvation of their souls."[90]

From 1840 to 1844 the church passed along in love and union; and there were frequent conversions and baptisms. In 1844 the church received a heavy blow by the death of its pastor. Brother Seavey had been the regular pastor since his ordination in 1816 and had preached to them two years as a licentiate, making in all thirty years as a constant leader of the church. After the death of Elder Seavey the church procured the labors of the Rev. Abner Flanders for three months. In December 1845, Rev. Leander S. Tripp took the pastoral care of the church for one year. He was succeeded by the Rev. Larkin L. Jordan, who continued his pastorate for two years and was succeeded by the Rev. M. Byrne, who remained four months. From March 1850, to April 1852, the church had no settled pastor. In 1852 the Rev. Gideon Cook commenced his labor and continued for one year. Rev. Levi Burnham came to the church in the spring of 1853 and left some time in 1854. It was at this time that the church was at a low point toward which it had been gradually sinking since the death of Elder Seavey. Brother Seavey had been the leader for so long that changing from a pastorate of thirty years to those of two years and less was like "following the voice of strangers."[91]

In 1855 Rev. Augustus Hubbard began his pastorate under very discouraging circumstances. Some of the church members said they would be happy to have him preach if it would be of any use, but interest was so low that they could not sustain even a prayer meeting. This nearly discouraged him from beginning his labors, but he put his trust in God and did not let the opportunity pass without doing something for his Lord.[92]

One of the first things he did was to start the prayer meeting. This was long attended with a good degree of interest, backsliders began to return, and the few that had been struggling through the long difficult period began to rejoice. In the following October a protracted meeting commenced to which a number of ministers and laymen of churches abroad were invited.[93] The people left their work and attended with interest. Upwards of twenty were added to the church, and a goodly number of others were hopefully converted who did not make a public profession of their faith. Brother Hubbard continued his labors with unfailing enthusiasm until his death on October 5, 1857.[94] Again the church was left without a leader until the following spring when the Rev. Thomas J. Swett took the pastoral charge of the church, and continued his pastorate for about eighteen months. After this the church had but little preaching until June 1860, when Brother John C. Sawyer, a member of the Christian order, having changed his views and become a Baptist, joined the church, and was recognized as the pastor of the church.[95]

John C. Sawyer resigned in December 1862, and left his native town to preach at West Hampden. He was followed by Brother Snyder who resigned in 1863. It was during this time that the church groaned under the weight of pro-slavery sentiment that existed among some of its members. The membership was then at forty-one.

In January 1867, Rev. Ransom Dunham, after laboring with the society for three months enjoyed an interesting revival of religion, and there were some twenty or thirty cases of hopeful conversions.[96] He was followed on June 1869 by the long pastorate of Rev. Nathaniel Whittemore.

On June 7, 1871, the church was struck by lightning and damaged so that it was taken down soon after.[97] A question arose as to where the new building was to be located, and a division resulted. Fifteen members who lived at East Limington received their letters on September 21, 1872, and other subsequently joined them by letters or baptism and formed a new church in their part of town. A house of worship was erected and on August 21, 1873 was dedicated. The membership of this church was at that time thirty-seven.[98]

Baptist Church, Ruin Corner.

East Limington Church and School.

In 1876 the north branch at Ruin Corner, left with a membership of nine, began to rebuild a new meeting-house on the old site. It was not completed until 1880 shortly before the resignation of Rev. Nathaniel Whittemore who for the last several years had supplied both parishes. The church was not able to find anyone to replace their lost minister, and its membership continued to drop.

In December 1881, Rev. Eben C. Stover, a graduate of Colby College was installed the new pastor at the East Limington church. A parsonage was being built but because Rev. Stover accepted a new position at Belvedere, Illinois, it was sold in 1883.[99]

Quaker Church

Among the first of the Society of Friends in Limington were Samuel Brackett, Reuben Brackett, Jedediah Allen, Robert Boody, Jacob Clark, Stephen Purington, Wingate Frost, Nicholas Cobb, Elisha Richardson and Simeon Strout. Many settled on and near the section known as Quaker Lane.

The early elders were Robert Boody, Jacob Clark and Stephen Purington. Their first meeting-house was built by Samuel Brackett in 1807.[100] The building was rebuilt, and reduced in size in 1858. It was used for regular worship until the small band of Friends that remained in town sold it in 1887 to the Bullockites and held their meetings at Parsonsfield. The families belonging to the order here at the time were Joshua Cobb, Edwin Allen, William Pillsbury, Abram Winslow, Oliver Allen, and Josiah Marston.[101]

The Quakers in town originally belonged to the Windham Monthly

Friends' Church located at head of Quaker Lane. It was later taken down and used as a barn on the Foss farm.

Meeting, but they broke away in 1846 to form the Limington Monthly. The members connected with this monthly meeting would alternate their meetings between Limington and Parsonsfield.

The Friends Church located on Quaker Lane had a partition through the center of it, men sitting on one side and women on the other. The Elders sat on what was called the High Seat. The order of worship was to sit in perfect silence for one hour on the hard plank seats, get up, all shake hands and go home.

The Friends held their members to a rigid moral code, seeming to be firm and as personal in their watchfullness as were the sternest sects. Historical records relate that Brother John Purington once sold Josiah Marston a butchered hog taking the leaf lard out. At the next Sunday meeting Brother Purington was called before the bar of justice and received the following reprimand, "Brother Purington I want thee to return the leaf lard taken from the hog thee sold Brother Marston at once in order that the conscience may be clear and thy soul saved from eternal damnation."

Brick House on Pine Hill built by Wingate Frost in 1800. He was a Quaker.

Chapter VII — Education

The first settlers took early measures for the education of their children. They were from educated communities and felt the importance of giving their children an education that would fit them to cope with the stern realities of life. "Hannah, wife of Captain James Small, not only with her own hands helped to cut down the trees and build a house, but taught her little boys the alphabet and the figures making the letters and the numbers on birch bark using a charred end of a stick for a pencil."[1] Most of the early settlers came as newlyweds or with few school age children and those who did have children that age were busy erecting themselves log cabins and clearing the unbroken forest.

An early settler named John Kennison had many children, but little else. A Bible was the only book in the house. Mrs. Kennison was the only member of the family who could read, and her reading was limited to easy words and guesses at the hard ones.

"Each Sunday morning Mrs. Kennison guessed her way through a chapter in the Bible, and stout Mr. Kennison explained the knotty points to his numerous youngsters as she stumbled onward - and very knotty indeed were some of her guesses. On one unlucky Sunday as she was guessing her way through the twenty-second chapter of Genesis, she read the names of the eight children of Nabor and his wife Melicab, calling them names never heard followed by the words, 'These eight Melicab did bear unto Nabor,' which she read, 'these eight did milk a bear at Nabor.

As bears were then plentiful in Limington and the young Kennisons knew something about them, the father felt called upon to explain the case and did so in these words; said Mr. Kennison thoughtfully, 'I spuz Nabor is somewhuz up in New Hampshire, where the durned bears is thick, and I spuz it took several of them to hold the peaky bear while t'other one milked.' "[2]

When the town was incorporated in 1792, the one hundred forty families organized themselves into school districts. Those families located near each other in the following sections of town made up the following seven districts:[3]

76

District one: Jacob Small, Isaac Dyer, Abraham Parker, Nathaniel Sawyer, Joshua Sawyer, Amos Chase, William Whitmore, Daniel Small, Jesse Libby, Josiah Black, Joseph Tyler, Joshua Small, Esquire, Joshua Small, Jr., John Small, Isaac Small, Jonathan Boothby, Aaron Libby, Jonathan Sparrow, John Weeman. These nineteen families took in East Limington, the area along the Little Ossipee River from Alvah Weeman's running northerly by the old road to the top of Pine Hill, Cutler Row and Slabstreet.

District two: Joshua Brackett, Abraham Brackett, Humphrey McKenney, Henry Small, Lt. Daniel Small, Harvey Libby, Abraham Tyler, George Meserve, Thaddeus Richardson, Elisha Richardson, Wingate Frost, Jonathan Nason, David Nason, Ephraim Clark, Philemon Libby, Abner Libby, Nathan Chick, William Small, Nathan Wing, Obediah Irish, Ebenezer Irish, Ebenezer Morton, Joseph Morton, John Douglass, Elias Foss, Edward Kennard, George Foss, Benjamin Small, Samuel Strout, Simeon Strout, David Richardson, Sarah Rackliff, Jonathan B. Ordway, Nathaniel Meserve, Ephraim Clark. The village district consisting of thirty-five families covered the road to Pine Hill, the Shaving Hill Road, the North Road to the town farm, south to Elson Norton's, and west to the bottom of the Strout's Hill.

District three: Job Foss, Elisha Strout, Robert Boody, David Hasty, Robert Staples, Azariah Boody, Robert Hasty, James Berry, Robert Jackson, Samuel Brackett, James Randall, Isaac Frost, Thomas Miller. These thirteen families covered the area from Strout's Hill to the Limerick line, including Quaker Lane and west of Gilkey Brook Bridge.

District four: Ezra Davis, William Johnson, Samuel Berry, Nicholas Davis, David Young, Daniel Dyer, John McArthur, James Gilkey, Peletiah Marr, John Ellis, Enoch Strout, Richard Strout, John Nason, John Nason Sr., Captain Nicholas Edgecomb, Nicholas Edgecomb, William Edgecomb, Joseph Libby, Thomas Rumery, John Foss, Reuben Brackett, William Strout, Gilbert Strout, Dennis Mulloy, Daniel Ridlon, William Manson, Joseph Rose, John Strout, Enoch Staple, Richard Berry, John Strout, Jr., Moses Frost, Isaac Strout, Mark Manson. These thirty-four families were located in South Limington, east of Gilkey Brook Bridge, south to Edgecomb's Bridge and west on the Holmes Road to the Limerick line. It also included all of Hardscrabble south from the Johnson Cemetery.

District five: Daniel Hanscom, Isaac Marr, Joseph Meserve, Samuel Sawyer, Ebenezer Sawyer, Ebenezer Clark, James Small, John Sutton, Samuel Larrabee, Isaac Larrabee, Reuben Small, Phineas Milliken, James Marr, John Andrews, David Boothby, William Bragdon, Walter Hagens, George Fogg, Daniel Fogg, Robert Libby, William Anderson, Elisha Bragdon, Charles Fogg, Joseph Fogg. These twenty-four families were found in northeastern Limington, including Ruin Corner, Christian Hill, the Marr Road, and the Steep Falls section.

District six: William Wentworth, George Stone, James McKenney, Luther Lumbard, Joshua Adams, Dominicus McKenney, Daniel Mitchell, Isaac Hurd, John Stone, John Wentworth. These ten families were found in the northwestern part of town, including the North Road starting at the town farm, and all of Bradbury's Grant now known as the Bean neighborhood.

District seven: Andrew Cobb, Nathan Cobb, John Greenlaw, William Whitney, Paul Lombard. These five families were at Emery's Corner west of Paul Lombard's hill.

A school house at the village was erected and used for the first town meeting in April 1792. Thirty pounds was appropriated for the support of schools. This was nineteen years after the first settler came to town. In 1794, forty-five pounds was raised and in three years time the sum was one hundred pounds. The town voted that the school money be distributed according to the population of each district, the larger, more populous districts got a larger sum and thus had more terms than those with a small number of pupils.[4] In many cases the mothers and other children acted as teachers, some out-building serving as a schoolroom for the time being.

Limington Village School.

The number of school districts in 1809 was twelve. In 1815 the number had increased to eighteen district schools, and the town raised $800.00 for their support. After Maine became a separate state in 1820, the state legislature enacted that every town of whatever size should raise annually for the support of schools, a sum equal at least to forty cents for each person in town and distribute this sum among the several districts, in proportion to the respective number of inhabitants in each. This gave four and a half months schooling. The schools were also required to be established in convenient districts and to be invested with corporate powers to build and repair school houses and for other purposes of minor consequence. The parents were required to furnish their children with such books as may be prescribed by the superintending school committee of the town, and all were equally entitled to the benefits of the school.[5]

Each school district was a separate legal organization within the town, and each owned and cared for its own properties. The districts differed in population and extent. The school was built by levying a tax upon the property within the limits of the school district, and each had its agent who engaged the teacher and cared for the school accommodations. The general idea applicable to popular education was simple. It was regarded as a public duty to give to each child an education in the branches of knowledge requisite for general business transactions. Reading, writing, arithmetic and the so-called common branches were taught to all. The person who could not read and write was looked down upon as an object to be spoken of with contempt.

The first school district in town encompassed the area that is East Limington. This district had what was known as Hamblen School which was located near Wheelwright Corner by Hamblen's Brook, so named because one of two brothers by that name lived opposite the old school site. The scholars ranged from four to twenty-one years of age, all receiving their due share of attention from the one teacher. The district was large, and most of the families had a goodly number of children in the 1830's. In winter the room was filled to its utmost capacity. There were Hamblens, Sawyers, Chases, Smalls, Stockins, Chicks, Bensons, McLellans, and others. A few of the boys, after leaving the old schoolhouse, prepared for college, but most of them received their entire education at the Hamblen School and made men of worth and integrity in their various pursuits of life, as merchants, sea captains, railroad men, teachers, printers, tanners, farmers, and ministers.

All those who went there, so full of life and hope have fallen by the wayside, but what stories they could tell if alive. Let us go back to the Hamblen School days as told by Mary Susan Small, one who long ago went there. We look upon the long row of scholars in the reading class and hear their voices as of yore. Henry C. Small gave particular satisfaction to the teachers for his loud reading. He could often be heard in the street, especially when reading 'Damon and Pythias' or a speech of Patrick Henry, from the old English Reader, and in times of political excitement, or rumors of war, read the Eastern Argus to the elderly men who gathered at the country store to hear the news. At the close of school on stormy days, there came into the school-yard the yellow tub-bottomed sleigh of Peter Chick, and the low square backed sleigh of Mr. Haskell.[6]

In the summer the children were early at the schoolhouse and often took time to go to the brook to wade in its cool, clear waters. They were not always particular to be in their seats at nine o'clock, much to the annoyance of the teacher whose reprimands did not have a very lasting effect, for the offense was often repeated. At noon those who went home for their dinners, hurried back to get a little time under the large oak tree in the Wheelwright pasture with those who remained to weave the leaves into trimming for decorating the school room. From the same pasture the boys gathered sweet fern to make brooms for the girls to sweep the floor, by clasping as many as they could hold in their hands.

The school was also the place of religious meeting for all denominations. Services were held sometimes on the Sabbath, but usually during evenings, beginning at early candle light. One good deacon never let any time go unimproved. He was always ready to speak, and shook hands several times over with the same person. Occasionally a good sister sang a solo, perhaps not quite up to the modern style of singing, but well enunciated, and in a high key.[7]

The Hanscom Schoolhouse located at North Limington was one of about the last examples of the old type district school in town. The old schoolhouse was nearly in the center of the district which had a radius of a mile and a half each way on four roads. It was the first school built in the district. Excellent materials were used in its frame and trimmings, with immense sills, and boards that ran the whole length of the house. Its timbers were hewed with broad axe and adz, the shingles were reeved out by hand and the clayboards were split from great pine logs.[8] The furniture, old time benches and desks, were also made of the best pine from the old forests, and these were occupied even to the very front bench. Those were the days of big families of six, to a dozen living in the old fashioned farm houses. When the town dwindled in population, forty-seven percent in fifty years from 2116 in 1850 to 1001 in 1900, children became too few to form a school and were transported to a nearby school.

Hanscom School, Hanscom Corner.

From 1816 to 1845, there was but one college graduate from Limington. During this long period it appears that the people were directing their attention almost entirely to business pursuits, and a very interesting chapter of the town's history belongs to that period. A generation of substantial farmers was starting then. Many of the merchants and tradesmen later found the country over, whose early home was Limington learned their trade in that period. Among the prominent families in the town during this period were the Smalls, Chases, Davises, Boothbys, Frosts, Marrs, Meserves, Edgecombs, Hagens, McKenneys, Boodys, Lords, Bracketts, Strouts, Libbys, Blacks, Blakes, Richardsons, Atkinsons, Bullocks, Emerys, Mansons and Fosses.[9]

In 1883 a committee of the old residents of Limington living at New York and Boston decided to have a reunion of the people who were born in and had gone from this town to other towns, or states. Programs were forwarded to at least two hundred and fifty nonresidents, and on the appointed date, July Fourth, three thousand came for the all day occasion.[10]

Limington's population in 1840 was 2,210 and it had eighteen school districts. The number of children between four and twenty one years was seven hundred twenty-four. The avg. number usually attended by a master was six hundred thirteen and by a mistress, five hundred twenty-three. The number of weeks all were in operation during the year was twenty-four. The average wage per month including board was $16.25 for a master and $7.94 for a mistress.[11] In the spring of 1847 there were eight hundred eighty-five children in town between four and twenty-one, with only four hundred fifty attending school in summer, and five hundred seventy-five in winter. This left four hundred thirty-five who were deprived of school in summer, and three hundred ten in winter.[12] The number of pupils reported in the 1850 census was seven hundred sixty; 1860 reported six hundred eighty-eight and in 1870 the report was four hundred fifty.

The town has been known for its many fine teachers. "A Limington teacher is above reproach" is a proverb.[13] Many competent teachers have been furnished not only for local use in town and state, but for other states as well. During the winter of 1879-80, Limington furnished sixteen male teachers in public schools in different parts of the state from York to Aroostook Counties, besides employing seven or eight in its own town.[14] In 1885 by school report there were twenty-six teachers employed in town and only one of that number lived out of town; that one was a former resident.

In 1894 an important change was brought about when an act of Legislature entitled, "an act to abolish school districts and to provide for more efficient supervision of Public Schools," became law. This made a radical change in the management of the common schools. In that year the town dispensed with school districts number five, seven, twelve, fourteen, fifteen and sixteen. The remaining nine districts were then renumbered. The village district became number nine and the Bean district was changed to seven. School district eleven was renumbered six and number thirteen was called five.[15]

District No. & Name in 1878	Old Location	1878	1880	1882	1884	1886	1888	1890	1892
1. Steep Falls	Opposite Mineral Spring	47	48	41	34	43	44	36	37
2. East Limington	Site of the Old Lincoln	67	60	50	54	32	29	21	20
3. Nason Mills	Across Ed Dixon's place	38	35	33	27	30	21	22	23
4. Manson	Later Whittier School	33	27	18	20	19	19	25	20
5. Young or Moody	On Corner south of Johnson Cem.	33	34	24	16	18	18	17	18
6. Pine Hill	Pine Hill Corner	Discontinued in 1882.							
7. Hanscom	Hanscom Corner	35	27	26	26	27	16	15	14
8. North Limington	In Harry Boothby's yard	37	43	41	50	54	47	45	42
9. Bean	Lane near Falker McKenney's	24	21	16	18	23	20	18	18
10. Merrifield	Near brook by Levi Merrifield's	14	12	Annexed to No. 11 in 1882					
11. Wentworth	Half-mile North of Ben Webster's	20	17	26	24	16	12	15	20
12. Foss or Taterboro	Bottom of Quaker Lane	14	12	12	10	11	11	10	9
13. Strout	Opposite Emerson School	21	24	24	22	22	19	16	17
14. Boody	Site of Fulton Gammon's place	16	16	9	7	10	11	6	8
15. Gove Ridge	Across Will Durgin's place	10	10	12	6	8	6	5	5
16. Shaving Hill	Beyond Anna Larrabee's place	11	14	10	8	11	10	9	8
17. Village	Later Longfellow School	80	77	76	64	70	62	54	55
Total number of scholars for year.		503	480	421	388	396	345	314	315
Money voted by town for year		$1305	$1350	$1200	$1200	$1200	$1200	$1200	$1200

Rapids School, Hardscrabble.

Grant School, North Limington.

Limington Academy:

In 1848 Arthur McArthur, Dr. Samuel M. Bradbury and Walter Higgins made up the school committee in Limington. They met Saturday afternoons in the fall at McArthur's office to examine applicants for teaching, etc.; and while at one of his meetings the idea of building an academy was originated. This small group of prominent townsmen drew up a subscription paper, each donated and others followed.[16] In March 1848, a list was made of the twenty-nine men present, and the amount which each promised to donate to the building fund.[17] A board of trustees was elected in April 1848, after some difficulty in obtaining subscriptions and in deciding upon a suitable site. It was the duty of this board to petition the state legislature for an Act of Incorporation, and it was expected that thereafter all powers should be vested in this board. The Act of Incorporation was approved by the state legislature and by the governor on August 8, 1848.

The first term of instruction began in the spring of 1851 with John M. Eveleth, A. M., as principal. It was held in the district schoolhouse at the village and was really a continuation of that school. More definite arrangements were made for the fall term of 1851. William G. Lord had graduated from Waterville College, now Colby College, and was called back to town by the trustees to be principal of the Academy. Some of the early terms of school were held in the hall of the Free-masons, the McArthur house and the red store which stood at the corner between the north and east roads. At a meeting on April 18, 1853, the trustees voted to buy a lot from Rev. John Garman in the village and elected a drafting committee and a committee to superintend the building.[18] It was not until 1854 that the present building was erected, and in the spring term teachers and pupils moved to their new quarters. The total amount paid out for erecting the two story high building was $2,102.05.[19]

The original board of fifteen trustees was made up of representatives of various occupations of the town. Most of the members were farmers who had become leaders in town affairs. Professional men were also usually included on the board. Samuel M. Bradbury, Moses E. Sweat, and Richard Meserve were physicians, John H. Garman was pastor of the village church, and Arthur McArthur, the first mover in the effort to establish the Academy, was a lawyer. George Small was the proprietor of a store and Robert Brackett was a carpenter. They had stated their object in the by-laws of the board at a meeting held on November 20, 1848. It was "to establish an institution for the promotion of Science and Literature and wherein youth may be in-

Limington Academy

structed in the higher branches of education usually taught in the Academies of this state."[20]

The course of instruction for the first year was divided into four departments: the Primary, the General and Higher English, and the Classical.[21] The curriculum remained much the same during the next forty years, except for the addition of modern languages in 1854.

The curriculum was typical of that found in other small academies during this period. It included the subjects which were considered necessary for meeting the needs of the youth who desired the more advanced training. There was no graded system; the student attended the school until the principal felt that he was ready for teaching, college, or whatever occupation he might have in mind. Many who did not plan to go to college carried on advanced study beyond the ordinary length of time.

William G. Lord retained a whole hearted devotion to his pupils and the welfare of Limington Academy from 1851 to 1894, with the exception of nine scattered terms and three terms in the year 1877-78 when the school was administered as a free high school without surrendering its corporate rights.[22] It was during Mr. Lord's tenure that the school reached the height of its prosperity, due in great measure to his ability as a teacher. There were then no high schools in the neighboring towns and pupils came from far and near to sit at the feet of this great teacher. The attendance was frequently more than a hundred, and often Mr. Lord was without an assistant teacher. In other years when Mr. Lord did not feel that one teacher could satisfactorily accomplish the required work, he had assistance whenever possible. During the last years of his teaching, his daughter, Inez, after studying for a time at Smith College, came back to assist in the languages, while Lillian and Kate

Limington Academy, 1889
Front row—John Cassin, Walter Taylor, Frank Ilsley, Frank Moulton, Allen Hubbard, Arthur Moulton, Gertrude Tufts,———, Benjamin Wentworth, Percy Waldron, Lewis Cousins.
Middle row— Fannie Fitch, Helen Tufts, Carrie Ridlon, Marjorie Stone, Belle Weston, Louise Waldron, Lillian Tufts, Cora Libby, Fannie Stone, Blanche Bracket, Lou Chase, Evelyn Small.
Back row—Avery Brooks, Oliver Christie, ———, James C. Richardson, Roland Gove, ———, William G. Lord, principal, Sarah Blake, Fred Meserve, Addie Walker, Esther Tufts, Isabel Christie, Lizzie Greenlaw, Jennie Blake.

Small taught all students who wished to sing songs and play on instruments. Leila Thayer taught the art of drawing and painting pictures.

In the fall of 1894, Charles L. Orton of Vermont became principal of the school and proved himself a competent successor to Mr. Lord in the two years of his connection with the school. The increase of pupils rendered assistance necessary so Annie Strout, Limington Academy 1892, and also a graduate of Abbott Academy, returned to her Alma Mater as teacher. It was during Mr. Orton's tenure that a step was taken in the democratization of the school in

1895. The trustees voted to receive all qualified scholars of the town into the Academy on their application.

Colby College sent Herbert L. Whitman who acted as principal with Mary Brackett as his assistant. Mr. Whitman likewise stayed two years. During his management the system of ranking and examinations was inaugurated. The students hoped they would end when he left, but they were not destined to be so short lived.

Limington Academy, 1901
Front row—Frost Pillsbury, Pearle Hayes, John Moulton, Harold Emery, Hattie Chase, Abbie Small, Evelyn Taylor, Bessie Chase, Maude Boothby, Belle Maxim, Ethel Mulloy.
Second row—Sidney Chaplin, Jamie Drost, Hazel Bray, Mae Miles, Alice Boothby, Blanche Cole, asst., Charles Spiller, William Small, William Meserve, Clara Caswell, John Boothby.
Third row—Ada Strout, Marion Small, Blanche Quinn, Janet Small, Ethel Caswell, Ava Meserve, Roy Brackett, Emery McKenney, Falker McKenney, Chester Tibbets, Elmer Ridlon, Thomas Winslow.
Back row—Edith Rounds, Burton M. Clough, Prin., Alice Pillsbury, Harold Small, Howard Hobson, Grover Emery.

In the fall of 1898, Charles Cogswell Smith, a graduate of Bowdoin College, proceeded to instruct the students of Limington Academy. His labors ended with the school year, but in that time he had formed some lasting friendships. In the spring term of that year Miss Martha Dunnells, Kents' Hill 1896, came back to teach where once she had been taught.

The following autumn Mr. Orton, after an absence of three years, was welcomed back to his old position.

During the decade of 1890 to 1900 some important innovations had taken place; the ranking system and examinations; public graduations startting with the class of 1892, and a complete renovation of the Academy building and long-needed improvements had been made. The walls were dressed in a fresh coat of paint and comfortable seats replaced the battered benches. The schoolroom walls were decorated by busts and pictures, the gifts of out-going classes.

South Limington Seminary

This long-gone institution was situated in the southern part of town, at Barbel Creek next to the old store on the corner. Located entirely in a rural district, it was peculiarly adapted for those who wished for a retired and quiet school.[23] It was a desirable school for young gentlemen preparing for college, where good moral and religious influences predominated.

The seminary was built and put in operation as a public school in 1852 by the generous contributions of the friends of education residing exclusively in South Limington.[24] The seminary movement was lead by James M. Hopkinson, James McArthur, Silas Moulton, Henry Wentworth and others. The trustees tried to importune the Legislature for a grant of wild land for private speculation or other purposes, but failed and had to rely entirely upon the moral character and usefulness of the institution to obtain substantial funds. Financed by public patronage, the school maintained an honorable rank among academical institutions for over a decade.[25] In the fall of 1861 the school numbered between forty and fifty. The institution offered a spring, fall and winter term continuing eleven weeks in common English, higher English and language.[26]

Henry Dunlap, A.M. of Brunswick served as one of its early principals until the fall of 1855.[27] He was followed by J. W. Weston, A.B. for one term. In 1855 John McPerkins was principal, serving until October 1861, when he enlisted in the Civil War. He was followed by Albert G. Manson and Charles S. McArthur, both natives of this town.

Chapter VIII — Industries

Due to the fact that it is bordered on three sides by rivers, Limington had numerous mill privileges and stream mills. The peak of its mill industry came about 1840 when the town had one gristmill, seven sawmills and three fulling mills. In 1859 the mechanical establishments consisted of five sawmills, three gristmills, three shingle machines, and one carriage manufacturer.[1]

In available water powers Limington ranks among the most highly favored in the State. "Among the principal falls are Nason's Falls, on the Little Ossipee, in the southeast part of the town. They have a descent of seventy-five feet in width, flowing through lands especially adapted to the location of industries."[2] It was occupied by a stave, a shingle, sawmill and gristmill. Three miles below, Chase's Falls has a descent of thirty-five feet through a channel one hundred and sixty feet wide. This, the site of the first mill in the town, was occupied by a sawmill, box and shingle-mills.[3]

At the northeast corner of Limington, Steep Falls on Saco River have a fall of forty feet in three-quarters of a mile. The river at this point is one hundred and fifty feet wide and ten feet deep. A mile below, at Limington Falls, its width increases to two hundred and fifty feet, and it takes a further descent of sixty-five feet in one-third of a mile. At this point there were a box-machine, a sawmill, and a shingle-mill. On Webster's Pond, at the outlet of Horn Pond, there were saw and gristmills. Salmon Brook had a tannery and gristmill, and Kellock Pond a sawmill, shingle-mill, and clapboard mill.[4]

According to old deeds mill privileges were purchased in fractional parts. It was quite common for the farmers to own mills in that way. Many of them did not have the capital and could not give their whole attention to milling, and the mills on many small streams did not have the power to run during most of the year. If the farmer could have the use of a good mill one day in eight he could cut quite a pile of lumber for his fencing, etc., and at least make enough to pay his taxes. There was an advantage in having such property divided into eighths, instead of sixths, or other fractional parts because some days were better for sawing than others. A man owning two shares or "days" would the first week have Monday and Tuesday, the second

Wednesday and Thursday, the third Friday and Saturday. On the fourth week he would have no "turn". At the beginning of the year each owner would take his old Farmers Almanac and work his turns in the mill on the margin of the calender of each month. In this way no mistakes would occur as to the right an owner would have to occupy the mill when there happened to be an unusual fall of rain or if spring opened early.

Considerable quantities of boards were sawed in town from timber grown on the land and used in the local area. Some were hauled by oxen to Portland, although some went to Saco, Kennebunk and Kennebunkport. Those who sawed boards generally sent them to market by their own teams, and they brought back cash, West-India produce or manufactured goods. Cash was usually obtained for boards.[5]

The several mechanics, blacksmiths, shoemakers, and others were paid for their services chiefly in produce or mechanical articles; and farmers exchanged their produce chiefly for what their families consumed. In winter sleigh loads of butter and pork were carried to market by single horses. In the spring, summer and fall, butter was bartered in neighboring stores. Traders also bartered grain, especially Indian corn at the market.[6]

Mills on the Little Ossipee at East Limington

The first mill in town was built by Amos and his father Deacon Amos Chase soon after their arrival in 1773 on the Little Ossipee River near its mouth at East Limington.[7] Before his death in 1825, Amos Chase had deeded much of his mill to his heirs. This sawmill and privilege on the lower falls was described in early deeds as a twenty-four day mill.

One of the quarter-owners of the Chase sawmill was Amos' eldest son, Abner Chase. One day in April 1816, young Chase decided to go out on the river near the lower falls to break a jam of logs. A log strewed, knocking Abner into the water and in spite of his attempts to escape he was carried over the falls. His body was found about fifteen minutes later under a log a short distance from the falls.[8]

Chases' mill continued to operate and was the principal supplier of lumber for the area. As the business expanded new additions were built. In 1836 a new building was erected at the southwest side of the sawmill for a shingle machine.[9] Later a box machine was added.[10]

On July 13, 1847, the owners and proprietors of Chases' sawmill, entered into an agreement, made by and between subscribers; Asa Boothby, John D. Boothby, Nathaniel C. Small, Joshua Small, Peter Chick, John Chick, William F. Haskell, James M. Chase and John Chase all of Limington. It was agreed that each owner could use and occupy the mill during certain stated periods of time, each and every month.[11] This mutual agreement remained in effect until all the owners had sold out their two-twenty-fourths parts to Colonel John Chase by 1861.[12] In 1880, John Chase sold one-half of his sawmill with a shingle machine to his two sons, John F. and Amos Howard Chase.[13] John's brother, Josiah E. Chase, a part owner, sold out the remaining share a year later to John F. and Amos H. Chase,[14] his two nephews, who continued to occupy the mill well into the present century.

After having built a sawmill on the southern bank of the Little Ossipee River, Amos Chase constructed an eighteen day gristmill on the opposite bank using the same dam. When the town was surveyed and mapped in May 1795, Chases' gristmill was drawn on the plan and stood a little east of Chases' bridge just above the falls.

Chases' sawmill on Little Ossipee River now in ruins, East Limington.

In 1807 Amos Chase sold to his neighbor Peter Chick, one-third part of this mill and privilege then standing,[15] and two years later deeded the same amount, six-eighteenths, to his sons, John and Daniel Chase, merchants of Saco, for one hundred sixty-six dollars.[16] Shortly after this the gristmill either was torn down or burned, leaving only a privilege site.[17]

Located on the northwest corner of the old gristmill was once a fulling mill privilege. This piece of land was first sold to Josiah Morse of Gorham "for a fulling mill and clothiers works and privileges for tender bars."[18] Later in February 1797 Josiah and his wife sold their new business consisting of a fulling mill standing on the Little Ossipee River with a privilege for setting up tender bars for drying cloth, all within forty rods and six feet from the north end of the Little Ossipee bridge to Josiah Chase Jr. of York, also a clothier.[19]

Josiah Chase Jr. the new owner continued to carry on a clothiers business alone until 1806 when he took Rufus Chase on as a partner.[20] In 1810 Josiah and Rufus Chase sold out their fulling mill and dwelling house to a cousin, Josiah Chase who had two years previously married a daughter of old Amos Chase.[21] This Chase family lived in the house near the river until the evening of February 27, 1814, when a tragic event occurred. On that evening Josiah and his wife Deborah went to the village to celebrate the good news of America's second victory over England, leaving their home and three children in the care of a young woman. The housekeeper soon put all the children to bed, except John the youngest who wanted to stay up. Thinking that she had taken care of the fires, she went with the child to a friends' house to visit at about eight o'clock. An hour later the house caught fire and was entirely consumed with all of its contents, including the two small Chase children.[22] The heartbroken parents rebuilt a good two story dwelling house on the same site, now the house of George Chase.

Josiah Chase advertised for sale his situation near Chase's bridge several years later consisting of a house, also twelve acres lying near part under improvement and his fulling mill with a first-rate water privilege, one and a half acres belonging. However, he did not sell and continued in the clothing business up to the time of his death in 1851.

Carding mills and privileges were started early at East Limington in conjunction with Chases' fulling mills. Wingate Frost in 1804 purchased from Amos Chase, a site three rods north of the Chase gristmill and established a carding mill and privilege,[23] selling four years later to the Mayall family who had long established mills at Gray.[24] Robert Mayall, the first of that family to appear in town, had by 1806 erected one more machine for carding wool at his carding mill at East Limington and advertised that he "was able to card for those who live at a distance the day they bring the wool in."[25] In 1817, Mayall sold his carding business and store to George Small and Josiah Chase,[26] both of Limington, and moved to Ohio where he died in 1826.

During the latter period that Robert Mayall was transacting business, Levi Stone Libby, who had worked for one of the Mayall's in Gray, came to Limington and married Lydia, a daughter of Peter Chick, and started to woolcard on the Little Ossipee River. Libby continued in business with two machines until about 1820 when he moved to Cornish. In 1825, Moses, the youngest son of Amos Chase, sold this mill privilege to James C. Hill of North Yarmouth. Hill sold the privilege three years later to James Stockin formerly of Monmouth together with buildings, and two carding machines.[27]

James Stockin in 1831 sold one half of the privilege for five hundred dollars to Thomas B. Stockin[28] and later the other half to James Madison Chase, the brother of Thomas Stockin's wife. These two partners were the last to occupy the business until its end in the late 1850's.

Henry Small's Store, East Limington

As early as 1800 Daniel Chase owned a store near the site of the present one at East Limington.[29] The store with a shed was sold by John Elden Chase to Robert Mayall who had established the clothiers works on the nearby river.[30] Mayall sold the store in 1817 to George Small who had recently arrived from Gray.[31] Small sold to his brother, Henry Small in 1821[32] and moved to a place in the village now on the site of the present library.

Colonel Henry Small remained at East Limington and built a house that he ran as an Inn up to the time of his death in 1875. In the days before the Mountain Division of the Maine Central Railroad, a stage coach made a trip each way daily between Freedom, New Hampshire, and Portland. The inn was a stopping place on the run. Here the Stanley brothers, Moses and Lorenzo, nicknamed "Dow", drivers of a Concord coach for years over the route and known far and wide as two of the best men in the southwestern Maine behind "Hosses," tied up as they drove over the stage route daily. Here, too, in the days which saw fifty to sixty million feet of lumber driven down the Saco River and its tributaries on each spring's head of water, a half hundred hardy river drivers annually made their headquarters, "boarding out." But the advance of the iron horse and the gradual decline of the long lumber industry changed all that. There were dozens of sawmills on the Saco River and its tributaries in those robust days. However, even in the failing days of Colonel Small, who was the neighborhood's first postmaster, the business at the tavern faded and he ceased to operate it as such.[33]

The next two generations occupied it merely as a family homestead, a rambling frame house with two spacious ells and an adjoining shed, at the Ossipee Trail and South Road. It burned on Labor Day weekend 1931, two years after it was sold upon the death of Miss Lillian H. Small, granddaughter of Colonel Henry Small.

Colonel Henry Small Tavern last owned by granddaughter, Lillian H. Small, before it burned in 1931.

The store formerly owned and operated by Colonel Henry Small was entirely destroyed by fire on the afternoon of May 8, 1892. The store was owned by his son, Melville Small and occupied by the Chick brothers. The post office was also consumed along with the mail bags and mail.[34] The east side of the general store came within twenty-five feet of the end of the shed adjoining the inn.

Mills on the Saco at East Limington

The second earliest mill and the first to be constructed on the Saco River at Limington was built by Jonathan Norris in 1792.[35] It was a forty-eight day double sawmill located at Limington Falls on the western side of the river about one half mile below the site of the old bridge site at Parker's Rips. Norris occupied the mill and privilege with his co-owners Abraham Parker, and Nathaniel Sawyer until he sold out his interest to Ebenezer Irish in 1798[36] and moved to Limerick.

In 1802 the mill fell into the hands of several of the Small Proprietors who resided in town and was called, "the Proprietors Mill." This standing double mill with its privileges was sold in September 1806 by the Proprietors soon after they disbanded, to William and Abner Woodsum, owners of mills in Buxton.[37] The mill remained Woodsums' Mill and was so called until 1821 when Abiather Woodsum sold his nineteen forty-eight interest that he had received from his brother William, to Isaac Cole before moving to Clinton.[38] Isaac Cole, a millman from Buxton, in the same year purchased the remaining days and privilege rights from Thomas Spencer,[39] John Sawyer, Abijiah Woodsum, Benjamin T. Chase, Benjamin Poland and John Weeman.[40]

The old double sawmill formerly occupied by the Woodsums' was destroyed in the fall of 1821 and was in the process of being replaced that November by Isaac Cole, the new owner.[41] This was a single sawmill built on the falls at the head of Bolden Creek so named for John Bolden who once owned the island between the creek and the river. The island was formerly called Small's Island and is now crossed by bridges connecting Standish with Limington.

By 1825 Cole had built a dam and clapboard mill between Small's Island and the western bank[42] which he soon sold.[43] In 1854 the privilege was sold to John Chick[44] and he built a shingle mill on the southwest corner of the present bridge leading to the island.

In 1825 Isaac Cole sold his interest where Woodsums' mill formerly stood[45] along with five acres with buildings opposite his new mill to Colonel Isaac Lane of Hollis,[46] reserving the store on his land built by Isaac Merrill. Cole also sold a twelve twenty-fourths part of his newly built single sawmill, with its privilege rights to Joseph Woodman,[47] who in turn sold it in 1830 to Joel and Nicholas S. Burnham of Standish.[48] The mill called Cole's remained owned by the Lanes, and Joel Burnham up to the 1840's.[49] The mill later took the name of its principal owner and was known as Burnham's Mill.[50]

In January 1878, Burnham's mill was sold when Isaac Sawyer, Randall Foss, Perley and John Burnham deeded their one-half combined with the one-half interest of Samuel Sawyer and Luther Whitney to Mrs. Sarah A. Wood and Leroy S. Mayo.[51] A stave and heading mill together with all machinery and fixtures occupied the site at the time. Later the Mayo mill went out of business.

Industry at North Limington
Located farther up on the old stage road from East Limington to Cornish is a hamlet known as Slabstreet. It was named because the land before 1890 was fenced in with slabs from the mills.

The earliest mill in this part of town was a corn mill built on the northeast corner of lot number 3 on range G, before March 1797 by Amaziah Goodwin.[52] This was on the site of the present mill using the same dam location. Goodwin, a short time resident of the town, sold in January 1799 for thirty pounds to Israel and James Small,[53] who constructed a sawmill. In two years time they sold one-half of their interest in the mills to their brothers, Ezekiel and Isaac Small.[54] James Small soon moved to Limerick, selling his one-fourth share to a brother in 1804. In the same year Ezekiel, Israel and Barzillai sold the gristmill to their brother, Isaac Small.[55] Isaac operated the mill for many years and by 1837 had sold it for $1,460 to George Wheelwright.[56] The gristmill described as being on the east side of a mill stream known as "Wheelwright Mill" was sold by Wheelwright's only child, Elizabeth G. Schermerhorn to Walter Higgins in 1853.[57]

The sawmill, meanwhile, continued to be owned and operated by the Small brothers until 1833 when Ezekiel Small sold out his one-fourth interest.[58] Israel Small kept his interest, and willed it to his sons, Ezekiel and Asahel.[59] In 1869 Asahel Small sold his one-eighth to his brother, Ezekiel.[60] Isaac Small, a quarter owner, sold out his share about 1830 and moved to Ossipee, New Hampshire. Barzillai died in 1842 and his quarter went to his son, James M. Small.

In 1849, Walter Higgins started to acquire a major share in the sawmill known as "Small Mills",[61] and with what was purchased of Samuel Hopkinson and James M. Small owned over one-half by 1854. It was during this time that Limington Academy was being built and Higgins, being one of the trustees, supplied the lumber for its construction. In 1856, Higgins moved to Fryeburg and proceeded to sell his mills at Limington. First he sold his gristmill in 1860 for $1500,[62] and in 1862 for $500, deeded his fourteen twenty-fourths interest in the sawmill, both to John W. Lane of Portland.[63]

Josiah E. Chase of East Limington purchased Lane's interest in Small Mills for $1200[64] in 1865 and sold it in 1872 for $1600 to John F. Parkhurst of Gorham.[65] Parkhurst then proceeded to buy remaining outstanding shares, one-eighteenth from John Seavey,[66] one-twelfth from Sewall S. Black[67] and one-quarter part of a shingle sawmill from Ezekiel Small.[68]

The Saco Water Power Company purchased the mill, mill bridge and pond known as Small's Mill from Parkhurst in 1876. They in turn leased the mills to John and Silas Hubbard, who did a thriving business, threshing in the season of 1882 with their water power thresher, eighty-nine bushels of rye, four hundred fifty bushels wheat, two thousand five hundred fifteen bushels of oats and barley.[69] The mills were consumed by fire on the evening of January 30, 1884. The gristmill department was carried on by Edmund Black. The Hubbards who had leased the other part of the mill lost considerable machinery and a good deal of carriage lumber which they had on hand to saw boards and shingles. Their loss was about one thousand five hundred dollars.[70] In March 1885, the Hubbards had rebuilt their mills and ran saw, grist and shingle mills at full speed.[71]

Hubbard Mills continued to operate at North Limington up to the turn of the century when the water rights to the pond were acquired by the Webster Brothers, and Silas Hubbard was forced to move. Hubbard relocated himself at East Limington and in 1901 had built a new sawmill on the bank of the Little Ossipee.

Webster's Old Mill, Slabstreet. Site of Small's mills.

The Webster Brothers, R. Scott, James and Joseph then established themselves at Small's Mills and carried on the trade first started by their father, James D. S. Webster. Their father was a native of Gray who came to

Limington with a wife and three small children after a fire had burned their house and belongings. He bought and cleared a small property on the road between the ball field and Ruin Corner. Later by New England thrift and energy Webster purchased a piece of land and built a fair example of farm buildings at Slabstreet. In May 1869 he had a shingle machine that was burned at a loss of one thousand dollars.[72] James D. S. Webster and his sons built a sawmill a little below Small's Mill Pond on a small stream at the outlet of Ward's Pond which soon became his principal asset. He and his wife reared a family of nine children. Four of his sons dealt in land and by thrift had accumulated more than 3000 acres of timberland in three counties. Their large holdings were left to their nephew, Howard M. Blake who continued to carry on the family business.

There was located near the post office run by Leonard Abbott at Slabstreet a building where Henry Cutler and his sons first began manufacturing carriages in the 1850's. After the Cutlers moved their place of business near their homes on Meserve's Brook, the shop was purchased by Silas Hubbard for a workshop. In 1882 it was sold to Samuel N. Small who used it for a blacksmith shop.[73]

Mial and William Cutler continued their father's vocation most of their lives and become diligent and approved carriage makers. William, the younger brother, did both the woodwork and the iron work and the various kind of carriages he turned out at his place of business were unexcelled for looks and service. He did an extensive business, in one year making fifty-two carriages. Some of his single vehicles sold for about one hundred fifty dollars. After his carriage shop located at Cutler row was destroyed by fire in May 1879, William sold and moved to Denmark. The carriage shop was rebuilt on the brook and occupied by Mial and his son, Charles Henry Cutler.

James Nason in his blacksmith shop, Slabstreet.

Ruin Corner

Ruin Corner at North Limington is said to have received its name after several buildings in the place had burned, whereupon a local resident was quoted as saying, "now the corner is ruined."[74] Like other hamlets found within town, it once claimed several dwellings, a district school, several shops, a church and two stores.

The earliest settlers in the immediate area were Captain James Small, Thomas Boothby, John Sutton and Samuel Larrabee. Captain James Small, the earliest settler, came to the locality in 1776 and built on the road to Horn Pond. Samuel Larrabee was the next settler and built the old house taken down by Dr. Edmond Bragdon many years ago.[75] Larrabee soon left this area and cleared a farm about a mile west of Limington Village. Thomas Boothby soon after his arrival was killed by a falling tree while clearing his farm in 1789.[76] His son Thomas was a cobbler and lived on a half acre piece opposite the C. Y. Boothby place. John Sutton, a Revolutionary War veteran settled on Sutton's Hill, now owned by the Boothbys.

The first store was built at the corner on land sold to Zenus Elliot by Israel Small in 1823. Elliot in 1829 sold for six hundred dollars his one and a half acres, including a store to Ezekial Small,[77] a son of Israel. Small kept it only one year. George Wheelwright purchased the store for three hundred sixty-five dollars, and had John Higgins run it until the spring of 1834"[78] Hooper Chase and John D. Boothby then carried on the business until it was sold in 1848 to John Seavey who continued to operate it as a store and post office until his death in 1894.

Since the history of any area is found in the works of its people, accounts should be given of the lives of three men who had much to do with the early development of Ruin Corner.

The first was David Strout a native of the town who in 1829 purchased land at the corner and soon established a blacksmith shop. He continued his trade at his shop, selling out to Rufus Small in 1838[79] and moving to a place below Limington Corner. Soon after he left town and went to Auburn, upon the special invitation of Edward Little, who had found out that this young artisan was an upright, industrous, Sabbath keeping man. "His steady habits, his integrity, his interest in Christian worship might have made him the subject of Longfellow's picture of the village blacksmith."[80]

Rufus Small, another selfmade man, was born in 1816 in Limington. When seventeen years of age he apprenticed himself for two years to David Strout who agreed to teach him the blacksmith trade, give him three months schooling each year, allow him seventy-five dollars in cash to use as he pleased and to furnish him with clothes, and a freedom suit. He learned his trade, which he followed for a time in Limington and afterwards as a journeyman in Boston. Returning to Limington in August 1838,[81] he bought the shop in which he had served his apprenticeship. "He later gave his blacksmith shop to his brother, Asa, and began an unusually industrious and varied business career. He first built and ran a country store, in which he was prospering when the store and stock of goods were destroyed by fire, in 1844. He immediately built a new store and hotel which he operated for a time. This failed because he trusted his customers too liberally. Finding no money in running a country hotel, he procured a peddler's wagon on credit, procured a stock of goods and notions in Portland, and started out to do business on the road. In four days he was home again with quite a stock of goods left, and with over fifty dollars in cash profits, out of which he paid for his cart. Then starting out among his neighbors, who patronized him well, he continued the business so successfully that at the end of the first year he had saved enough to cancel his indebtedness to Portland creditors resulting from his store failure, and to leave him with a surplus of several hundred dollars. Then adding another horse and a new cart and increasing his stock of goods, he was soon supplying with yankee notions all the country stores and many in the cities from New Hampshire to Eastern Maine, making his trip about once in two months. Before long he was carrying a stock worth ten thousand dollars, which required a new peddler's wagon costing two hundred dollars, and a third horse for which he paid a hundred and twenty five dollars. With this splendid turnout called a "spike team," he carried on a most successful business, becoming known and respected by the merchants of Maine and New Hampshire. After some four years on the road he retired with about ten thousand dollars. In 1850 he sold his property in Limington at a sacrifice, and moved to Biddeford where he had in the meantime bought land and built a house. He went into the blacksmithing business but in 1855 became an insurance agent.[82]

John Seavey's Store and Post Office, Ruin Corner.

The third man, also highly respected by all who knew him was John Seavey. He came to Limington as a small child with his father, Rev. John Seavey, an ordained minister of the Calvinist Baptist Church at Ruin Corner for nearly thirty years. In early life John studied law with Ira T. Drew of Alfred and practiced for some years in his own town where he did a good business, especially in connection with probate work. He also preformed many useful services for his town and fellow citizens and was considered an able counsel in matters of law. He possessed a good moral character and was strictly honest in his business transactions and enjoyed the confidence and esteem of many friends. For many years he had a post office and grocery business.[83]

Bean Neighborhood

In the northwestern part of town was a tract of five hundred acres called the Bradbury Grant. It was named for Theophilas Bradbury, Esquire, who was granted the land in 1777 for legal advice given the Small Proprietors in connection with the settlement of their claims. Bradbury received his education at Harvard College from which he graduated in 1757. He studied law, and settled in Portland in 1761. Soon after the Revolution began, he returned to Newburyport; and resided there with a good share of practice, and with a high reputation both for his integrity and legal knowledge. He died in 1803, at the age of sixty-six.[84] Bradbury sold his grant in 1783.[85]

The first settlers on this tract were Reuben Chaney, John Greenlaw, and Christopher Cole. Cole came from Sanford in 1798[86] and settled on what was later the farm on the eastern side of the country road.[87] Before his death which occurred in 1848 he had managed to acquire the entire five hundred acre tract.[88] The original Christopher Cole place burnt and was rebuilt by Lewis Libby. Christopher Cole Jr., his son, lived on the other side of the road in a place built in 1825, known as the Jim Cole farm. This house once served as a tavern, the first stop for ox teams leaving Freedom, New Hampshire, fifteen miles to the north. Both places had a beautiful view across the Saco River to the high range of mountains, beginning with Mt. Cutler in Hiram, and extending the whole length of West Baldwin, leveling off to East Baldwin and Steep Falls.

Descending the high hill going toward Cornish Village is Salmon Brook, forming the boundary line between Cornish and Limington. On this brook below the bridge was a mill occupied by Christopher and his son, William Cole, as early as 1818[89] when Christopher sold the land around it to John Hopkinson, his son-in-law. On this piece, Hopkinson built a house. About 1832,[90] he entered partnership with Cotton Lincoln of Cornish and built a dam and gristmill, known as Hopkinson Mill. Above the mill was sold one acre together with a bark mill thereon, to Henry Marshall of Saco,[91] who in June 1835 had buildings thereon, being a shop or mill erected for a tanning establishment and went into debt.[92] In October 1835, Cotton Lincoln for five hundred seventy-five dollars sold one-half interest of the mill with one-half of a rock dam, with the privilege of flooding land to Ivory Cole,[93] a son-in-law to John Hopkinson. Ivory Cole sold this share for two hundred twenty-five dollars to Christopher Cole Jr., in 1847.[94] John Hopkinson finally sold his one-half owned in common with Christopher Cole to Abner Sanborn of Cornish in 1850.[95]

In 1859, Isaac G. Meserve of Limington purchased both halves of the gristmill from Abner Sanborn and Christopher Cole.[96] Meserve soon moved to Naples and sold the mill with the stone dam known as the Hopkinson Mill in 1862 to Oliver P. Allen, who a year later erected a tannery in conjunction with the gristmill.[97]

In 1867 Allen sold to his brother-in-law, Joshua G. Cobb, his new tannery for three thousand dollars and moved to Limington Corner.[98] The tannery occupied by J. G. Cobb was sold at auction, March 15, 1871.[99] The tannery and gristmill continued to operate into the present century. It was finally run by the Walper Brothers of Cornish.

"The grist and tannery mill sat on the edge of a large pond formed by a huge dam across the brook, to get the water power necessary for turning the wheels of industry. In the tannery would be watched, the process of a hairy cowhide as it went from vat to vat of liquid until it came out a finished piece of leather from the last one. In the gristmill two round heavy stones ground back and forth on each other, and because of the hopping motion, this compartment was called the hopper. The yellow home raised corn was thrown into the hopper where it was ground between the stones into golden yellow meal which then dropped down into a huge bin on the floor below. Here it was picked up by a series of metal pockets fastened to a long vertical belt which worked exactly as a snowloader. The sifted meal was carried along to its final resting place for delivery to owners who gave a certain percentage of the output to the miller for his service. Then the miller sold his part to the stores or neighbors."[100]

The Bradbury Grant became known as the Bean neighborhood. The William Bean place burned and is now the site of Phillip Mayo's house. Daniel R. Bean, a son, built a house nearby, which was later torn down, and Charles Waterhouse built the present dwelling bounded on two sides by roads. Across the North Road stood Daniel R. Bean's blacksmith shop, which had a hall above it used for special occasions.

On the outskirts of the Bean neighborhood is Davis Brook, named for Ezra Davis who before 1807 had built a sawmill near the present bridge. Nearby are the stone cellar ruins of "Twin Mills", built about 1852 by Charles W. and Edwin W. Meserve.[101] The dam of the mill was on the site of the present bridge going towards Hanscom's Corner. Overflow water came from the dams, and followed a canal on a high bank west of the main stream then hitting an over-shot waterwheel. The twins carried on sawing and carriage work at their mill. In 1870 the output was one hundred m. shingles, twelve coffins, three carriages, and ten stair posts, a total value of $2500.[102] The deserted buildings were taken down by C. Y. Boothby about 1900 to be used for his second shingle mill on Stone's Brook.[103]

Farther up on Davis Brook at the bridge on the North Road was an early mill for grinding corn constructed by William Manning about 1808.[104] In 1836 Manning sold what was described as three acres of land and water power to his son. The mill was eight or ten rods behind his house, and the old sills are still buried in the mud near the brook.

Benjamin Wentworth, (1793-1870) blacksmith who lived on the North Road and father to Benjamin, Emery, Henry and Ivory, who were also blacksmiths in town.

Steep Falls on Limington Side
   The mill privilege site on the Saco at Steep Falls on the Limington side was first purchased in January 1831 by Daniel Heath and John L. Atkinson,[105] two of six proprietors who improved the water power and built the saw mills in 1827 on the opposite bank.[106] In the fall of 1831 a double sawmill was built on the Limington side.[107]
   In 1833, Jabez Hobson came into town from Buxton and soon purchased a six-eighth interest in the sawmill, and in conjunction with James and Abner Chase Warren who owned the other two-eighths, operated the mill.[108] The two-story Hobson place was one of the first buildings built in the area. A store which was owned and occupied by Hobson,[109] was constructed near the house on the south end of the bridge. In 1853 it was sold to Tobias Lord who owned and ran the mills on the other side of the river for many years.
   Next to the sawmill with its two saws Hobson built a gristmill, taking its water through the same dam.[110] This gristmill was described as having two runs of stones, two bolts, a stove and other fixtures. It was sold in 1839 to Samuel Burbank of Limerick for $2150. Both of these mills were destroyed by fire in 1847, as reported in the following article in a local paper:

> "A fire broke out last Sunday (Feb. 16th) morning at Steep Falls, on the Limington side in a sawmill owned by Tobias Lord and Jabez Hobson, which destroyed the above sawmill, a gristmill and several contiguous buildings with machinery in them. The gristmill was owned by Stephen Wood. Probable loss $5000 or $6000, part of which was covered by insurance. In consequence of this loss, some thirty or forty men were put out of employment."[111]

   The mills were rebuilt; the new gristmill stood within thirty-five feet from the foot of the sawmill.[112] It was divided into parcels and sold by the administrator of the Burbank estate, one half in 1851 to Stephen W. Wood for $1000[113] and the other half in 1853 to Edmond Mann for $865.[114] Soon after this partnership was formed[115] both mills were again consumed by fire.[116] In 1852 prior to the fire a Kimball and Robinson had started to manufacture knives and forks in the mill. Wood and Mann rebuilt and went into manufacturing looking glass and backs.[117] In 1856 Edmond Mann sold his one-half interest owned in common with Wood to Levi Sanborn.[118] Sanborn was succeeded by his son Andrew F. Sanborn, who took on a partner, Bradbury B. Merrill. In 1873 Giedon M. Tucker bought the one-fourth interest of Merrill[119] in the A. F. Sanborn Lumber Company and was a member of that firm until the mill burnt on November 24, 1875. One month after this incident Stephen Wood sold out his interest to Stephen H. Cousins and Samuel Banks,[120] already part owners.[121] The water privilege was divided and Wood built a new mill on the old site while the other co-owners built a little further down the river next to the ledges,[122] and soon were doing a snug business in the manufacture of packing cases and headings.[123] After Mr. Banks' death in 1886, Gideon Tucker bought out the heirs and again became a member of the A. F. Sanborn Lumber company. In 1892 they built a gristmill run by a gasoline engine, and in 1902 the company moved to Steep Falls Village.

Meanwhile, Jabez Hobson continued to own his lumber mill and extensive interests as an independent operator. Hobson's firm sawed out eight hundred million feet valued at $4,800 and produced $525 worth of shingles from two mills in 1860. Hobson later went into partnership with his son, and continued to do business until they went out in the early eighties.

Nason's Mills

The small hamlet nestling on the bank of the Little Ossipee River was Nason's Mills a hundred years ago, but to the residents who occupied it and to the locals it was known as "Hardscrabble." The name is said to have come about after one of the natives fell into the river. When asked how he got out, he said that he first hit bottom and then had to scrabble on the hard rocky bottom to get out.[124] Hardscrabble, now a deserted and abandoned part of town, was once a prosperous area covered with timber before the turn of the century.

Today there is little left to indicate what in Civil War times was a busy hustling village furnishing homes and occupations for a score of families. The buildings that once housed Jacob Dearborn; Atkinson Seavey; Benjamin Haley, the village blacksmith and Melville Bradeen, the local storekeeper, are all gone as are the structures that were once busy marts of trade. The rough built and rambling shacks in which hummed the water driven machinery that helped manufacture finished lumber have rotted away. The little story and a half building that was the "little red school" and the unpretentious store that served for a post office are a passing memory.

Most of the Hardscrabble area lies between the Little Ossipee and Saco River, comprising of about 2300 acres of principally plain's land. This was annexed from Little Falls, now Hollis, by the Massachusetts Legislature on

February 27, 1798, upon the petition of Abner Chase, John Gilkey, James Davis, Elisha Cobb, and Edward and Nicholas Nason, inhabitants of the area. The tract at the time was covered by tall white pine, a forest wilderness.

The first settlers were Abel Hardy and Isaac Robinson, brothers-in-law of Amos Chase whose farm lay just across the river. They came in 1774[125] and would have been considered very early settlers of the town had this area not been part of Hollis. The Hardy farm consisted of two hundred seventeen acres lying opposite Abner Chase's land in the most northerly part bordering the Little Ossipee River. Robinson and Hardy and their families moved to Hampden, Maine, in 1798.

David and Thomas Young first stopping to visit Amos Chase in 1773 ran out lines [126] in the eastern district near the present Limington and Hollis town line on the bank of the Saco. John Davis came early, settling in 1776 and was followed by his brother James Davis. Abner Chase, a son of Amos, was a major land owner of the area which comprised over five hundred acres. The Chase lands were bounded by the two hundred acres owned by James Davis, and by large pieces held by John Gilkey and Abel Hardy.

In 1780, Deacon John Nason came from Buxton and settled on a six hundred acre piece of land on the Little Ossipee. This was later named Nason's Mills. By 1792 a dam, a gristmill and a saw-mill had been built at Nason's Falls. They were owned and operated by Nason's sons.[127] Edward Nason owned the gristmill and four twenty-fourths of the sawmill at the time. The remaining principal parts were held by his brother Moses Nason, with John Nason, Jonathan Rumery, and Thomas Ridlon each owning a one twenty-fourth share. In 1798 John Nasons Jr. owned the gristmill valued at one hundred dollars.[128] Soon after Nason's death his widow and son, Benjamin E. Nason, in 1811 sold the six hundred acre farm with three-quarters of a cornmill and five twenty-fourths of a sawmill standing on the premises to Nicholas Edgecomb Jr. for six hundred fifteen dollars.[129] Enoch Strout, a step-son of the widow Nason, purchased part of the gristmill, a double and single sawmill and operated them under the name, Strout Mills, until his death in 1825. The mill was then purchased by Benjamin Elwell and a one-half interest was deeded to Albion P. Strout, alias, Sally Strout.[130] In a newspaper printed at Limington, Strout advertised for sale his gristmill at Nason's Falls in 1833, describing it as being in good repair and situated in a good place for custom. [131]

Oliver Dow purchased Strout mills and entered a partnership with George W. Lord, another mill owner at West Buxton,[132] operating under the former name, Nason's Mills. In 1845 Oliver Dow conveyed to David Sawyer one half of all booms used for mills and lathe machines along with logs in the pond and boards sawed out.[133] A store was built and occupied by Sawyer in 1848. In the same year the mill privilege and a gristmill, having gates for two runs of stones, was sold for seven hundred dollars to Isaac Rand of Limington.[134] After operating the mills for nine years Isaac Rand deeded his gristmill, then having three runs of stones, to Dr. Samuel M. Bradbury of

Limington. In 1857, the same year the mill changed hands, the mill burned.[135] Alfred H. Watson, the last owner, had purchased the mill from Dr. Bradbury in December 1864 for one thousand dollars.[136]

Meanwhile, David Sawyer sold his one-half of the mill and lot together with two dwelling houses on the lot occupied by Alherton Usher and Erastus Berry in 1850 to Oliver Dow, the former owner.[137] During the Civil War the saw privilege was owned in part by Isaac E. Edgecomb and Henry C. Moore, succeeded in 1864 by Rev. Carleton Small[138] who sold the sawmill, boom, chain and sawmill fixtures in 1867 to Ruhamah S. Richardson.[139] After an unsuccessful business venture with their mill and store the Richardsons moved to Baldwin and soon lost their Limington property in taxes. The town acquired the mill privilege and in 1872 it was conveyed to Alfred H. Watson, the owner of the other parcel on the falls.[140]

Alfred Watson was a blacksmith from Kennebunk where he had placed iron on wooden ships. He eventually acquired nearly the whole section around Nason's Falls where he carried on the blacksmithing trade while his son George operated the mills.[141] After his death in 1893, the mill property was run for two or three years by George Watson until he left Hardscrabble. Then the business was carried on by his brother, Roscoe. Roscoe Watson was a poor business man, and at the end of the century he gave his extensive property at Hardscrabble to Royal Scott Webster to settle a three hundred dollar mortgage, outstanding since 1884, and moved west.[142] Thus ended the industry at Hardscrabble which had begun in the 1850's and 1860's producing at the time three cooper shops, a post office, a school, a blacksmith shop, a store and a number of dwellings.

Barbel Creek

South Limington was the home of the town's earlier settlers, Ezra Davis, John McArthur, Joseph Libby, Nicholas Edgecomb and Dennis Mulloy. The heart of the settlement centered on a junction adjoining two county roads on Barbel Creek, thus giving the small village the nickname, "The Creek." The land found on the eastern side of the road leading from the Edgecomb place to Limington Village was originally owned by Ezra Davis, the first settler of Limington. The property was conveyed to his son Robert Davis who lived in the old Davis place situated on the Creek going towards Young's Corner just east of the store lot. Robert was succeeded in the occupancy of the house by his son Joseph and later by two grandson's Joseph Jr. and Jeremiah.

The old community store building can still be seen at the junction located on the one-fourth acre Ezra Davis sold[143] to Joseph Larrabee in 1839.[144] Larrabee sold in 1845 for four hundred seventy-five dollars to Edward Mulloy, but remained to live on the premises until 1849 when it was purchased by Irving Small.[145] In the same year Small sold a half interest to David Moore[146] and operated under the name of Small and Moore until 1852 when Small sold out his interest to Henry C. Moore, son of his partner.[147] The store was purchased in 1857 by Isaac E. Edgecomb and resold two years later to its former owner, Henry C. Moore.[148] In 1866 three years after Henry C.

Moore's death the store was sold by his widow and Samuel M. Boothby to George Moulton. Moulton operated the store until 1872 when he conveyed it to David Walker and Frank A. Hobson.[149] Later Hobson went to Montana, but Walker continued to use the building as a store up to the turn of the century.

Barbel Creek, South Limington.

Near the Creek bridge soon after May 1821, a mill and mill privilege were built on a four acre piece by James Staples, Junior.[150] Josiah Marston, a clothier, purchased the mill in 1825 from the widow Staples and operated it for nearly a decade.[151] Aaron C. Waldron, a sleigh and cabinet maker purchased the property and had a sleigh mill in 1838, when he sold. Three years later it was bought by his son Henry P. Waldron.[152] Shortly afterwards the mill privilege was converted into a gristmill and occupied by Joseph Davis up to 1885.

In 1866 Alvin C. Moulton moved to the creek from Parsonsfield and purchased a mill frame standing on the old mill pond privilege[153] and established a carriage shop which he operated, except for three years, until his death in 1880.[154]

Near the northeast corner of A. C. Moulton's carriage shop was the blacksmith shop of John C. Wentworth, one of a number who carried on that trade at the creek. In 1856 Andrew Staples bought the house facing the store lot and for three years had his shop on the bank of the creek. He was succeeded by Henry Wentworth,[155] a local Baptist minister, who continued to carry on blacksmithing in the shop until his death. Rev. Truman Maxim then purchased the place.

A tannery was located east of the South Limington community on Black Brook, a branch of Barbel Creek. It was erected by Joshua Small soon after his settlement in 1775. He was succeeded by his son Isaac and grandsons Isaac and Joshua. Isaac Small died in 1832 and the trade was carried on by his brother, Joshua until his death in 1847.

Isaac Small House located near Pine Hill. Pictured is Scott Small and family.

Isaac Small known to all men as old Uncle Isaac, was a most whimsical man, as the following story that took place in 1824 will convey.

"Once when it was the correct thing for young men to be married in heavy long-legged boots, a young man from Cornish named Greenlief Smith appeared at Uncle Isaac's to buy calfskin.

He made his errand known to Uncle Isaac, whereupon the latter exclaimed in seeming surprise, 'Calf skins? Good gracious! Calf skins. There is nothing so scarce about here as calf skins. We haven't one in the shop, and shall not have one these two years. When you go home, you tell all the Cornish people and save them the trouble of coming down.' Then he insisted upon putting Mr. Smith's horse in the barn and liberally feeding him. After talking awhile, and as though suddenly struck with a new thought, he abruptly said: 'we've got a plenty of thin sole-leather, if you can make that do. Could you be married in a pair of sole-leather boots, Mr. Smith?' The youngster thought he could not, and then the old gentleman said, as though a new ray of hope had dawned, 'Let us go down to the shop and hunt, for it may that an old calf skin has got in with the sole-leather somehow.'

When they entered the shop the young man was astounded, for there before his eyes were more calf-skins than a cart would hold. Uncle Isaac took down a beautiful one and softly caressing it with his hand said: 'Did you ever see a finer skin that that, Mr. Smith? It is as soft as a lady's glove and will cling to the foot just like the skin.' The young man eagerly assented and said he would take that one, but the old gentleman put it back and took down another. More than a dozen skins were taken down and praised and all were put back, and the anxious Smith thought that for some reason connected with his father, to him unknown, Uncle Isaac would not sell him a skin. There was further talk on indifferent subjects, and then Uncle Isaac very abruptly said, as though another idea had suddenly entered his mind without knocking, 'I wonder what is in that old closet? It has been a long time since I saw the inside of it.' He tried the door, and it was locked. He then hunted a long time for the key, and at last found it hanging where he knew it was all the time and where he had put it the previous day no doubt, and unlocked the door, and there were a half-hundred of his finest calf-skins. Deftly and rapidly selecting the softest and finest one, he kindly, and with the courtly grace of an old-school gentleman, presented it to the dazed man, shyly remarking that his horse was probably done eating by that time. Young Smith, who then knew nothing of Uncle Isaac's whimsical ways, went home in confused frame of mind, but tightly hugging the wedding calfskin."[156]

Limington Corner

All of the property at the village or the corner as it is called came from four one hundred acre lots centering at the junction of two roads. Limington Corner lies near the center of the town and is located on a point of land extending into a broad valley, surrounded by broken farming lands to the west and timberlands to the east. The site of Limington Village is elevated, and much of the lower level country may be seen from its streets. The village

Limington Village from Richardson's Hill, 1905.

offers a pretty collection of neat houses, and the streets were once adorned with beautiful shade trees—elms and maples—which greatly added beauty to its appearance. The horse chestnut, both the white and red flowering varieties, grew well here and there were several beautiful specimens standing before the McArthur house, but they too are now gone as are the businesses that once flourished there.

The land lying on the northern side of the road leading to Limerick and west of the North Road was given to Philemon Libby by his wife's father Deacon Samuel Small in 1777.[157] Libby settled on the land and in 1794 built a large gambrel roof dwelling which remained his home up to the time of his death and in 1836 was sold to Arthur McArthur.[158] Philemon Libby was for many years a licensed innholder in town. James Libby, a son, built a large spacious dwelling on a part of the Libby farm. After moving to Bridgton he sold the farm to Peter Strout[159] who operated it as an Inn. In 1837, Ebenezer I. Larrabee purchased the house and is still occupied by a descendant.[160]

Philemon and Abner Libby Jr. owned a store at the junction which was sold to James McArthur in 1814.[161] McArthur constructed a new building in the summer of 1818 at the cost of five hundred forty dollars, designing the building exclusively for the use of the newly formed Masonic Lodge which occupied the third floor. The bottom two floors were used, excepting a few years, for McArthur's store up to the 1850's. Adoniram Lodge, A.F. and A.M., purchased the building in 1859 and immediately rented the bottom floors to Clark and Brackett for a store.[162] Lewis Clark rented up to 1872 when his goods were sold at auction. The next to rent was Samuel T. Bickford in 1876. He paid fifty dollars per year and remained in the grocery and millinery business until shortly before his death in 1884.

Adoniram Lodge, A.F. & A.M.

The hundred acre lot, just east of Philemon Libby's land and bounded on the west and south by roads was purchased and settled in 1778 by Thaddeus Richardson. While living at the village he gave the parish the land on which the Congregational meeting-house now stands. In 1795, Richardson sold the quarter south-west of his farm to Abner Libby[163] and the remaining part to Joseph Moody in 1800.[164]

Simon Moody House located in village, owned by William Brunk when it burned in 1927.

Abner Libby was a blacksmith and engaged in the trade for many years. Libby built a dwelling next to the church which he used as a public house. Later he erected a building cornered by two roads a little west of his house which he operated as a store. After his death in 1843, the store business was carried on by his son Isaac H. Libby, until he sold to Erving Small in 1855.[165] Lewis Clark purchased the building and remained two years. He then sold to Eliza Chick who used it for her millinery shop.[166] Elias Libby, the eldest son of Abner, learned the blacksmith trade by working in his father's shop before moving to Limerick. Parmenio Libby, his next son, learned the trade and settled on the north part of the home farm where he built a house and shop.

Aaron C. Waldron, an enterprising man, came to town about 1824 and brought with him the town's first iron stove.[167] A.C. Waldron established himself as a cabinet maker in his shop[168] and later joined by his son, Leonard, made sleighs and carriages.[169] The number of sleighs made by them in 1860 was thirty.[170] The census ten years later shows that twelve wagons and forty coffins were made as well as eighteen carriages.[171] Their large sleigh and carriage factory was destroyed by fire on April 8, 1870.[172] The Waldron's then established themselves in the paint shop erected by Aaron's son, Henry in 1855 on the bank of the brook east of the church.

The land on the southern part of the country road was owned by Ephraim Clark, a crewman under Captain John Paul Jones, who settled on this one hundred acre lot after the war. He first sold a small parcel on the northerly end of his farm in 1797. Jacob Quincy bought the piece and built a house.[173] In 1800 Clark conveyed to John McDonald a small lot nearly opposite the church where McDonald established a business as a cobbler of boots and shoes with a few groceries and rum. He moved to Limerick in 1805.[174] The store was next occupied by the partnership of John Small and Robert Edgecomb and then Edward Small and Nathaniel Sawyer, Junior.[175] Mrs. Harriet Boody purchased the store property in 1843[176] and in five years sold to Isaac Mitchell.[177] Mitchell and his wife ran the store and post office in the building until his death.[178] In 1876 Dr. John F. Moulton purchased the building and used it for his office.[179]

By a vote at the 1794 town meeting the town pound was constructed in the northwestern corner of Clark's land north of the district school. This piece of land where the old pound formerly stood was later the site of the town house built in 1826 for two hundred fifty-five dollars. In December 1869 the town became dissatisfied with the old town house. A meeting was held and it was voted to build a new house with a sum money not exceeding $3,000. There was a great deal of trouble in town over building the town house, but at last it was completed and on October 14, 1871, and it was voted to accept the building as built by Jacob Black and Ivory Fogg.[180] The present town hall is situated on the site of Eben I. Larrabee's harness shop first established in 1840. The old shop was moved next to the Larrabee home and later used as a building for the town's first library.

Ebenezer I. Larrabee House and the old Library.

Nathan Chick, one of the town's Proprietors, drew lot number 8 on range E, and moved from Falmouth to the corner in the early 1780's.[181] After Chick's death in 1808, one-third of the land went to Sarah, his widow, and the remaining acreage along the road running towards Limerick given equally to his ten children. Nathan Chick, Jr. continued in his father's trade and by 1825 had a blacksmith shop.

Aaron C. Waldron
[1792-1878]

A large baronial type house was built on the north east corner that Nathan Chick sold to Jacob Quincy in 1802.[182] Captain David Otis occupied the house for a number of years[183] followed by General George Small who moved from East Limington in 1822. General Small opened a store and remained in business until his death in 1850. Small's trade was carried on by Charles Libby; who had a well stocked store and a good run of customers.[184] The Small homestead in the 1890's was occupied by Charles Henry Small of New York as a summer residence. The house was torn down in 1911 in order to build on that site the Davis Library.

The building west of the library was used as the private residence of John T. Lord, a civil war veteran. Mr. Lord was appointed postmaster at the village in 1878 and had the post office and harness business in the same building. In 1885 the house was purchased by Cyrus H. Moody and opened to the public. Moody sold in April 1893 to Charles E. Emery who remodeled the house and added the annex. Emery called his hotel the "Limington House."[185]

William Dimock established a store at the village in 1864. Dimock was joined by his son Charles and in 1877 established a clothing salework shop in the present Grange Hall, employing fifteen to twenty people. This was also where Charles Dimock ran the post office.

Situated about one-half mile east of the village was Oliver Allen's tannery. The business was first established by Abram Winslow, a Quaker who came from Windham after his wife's death. He married a daughter of his new neighbor, Wingate Frost, and began the tannery in 1832. A pottery had previously occupied the same ground. In 1869 Oliver P. Allen, a son-in-law, continued the trade until the last week of May 1882, when the tannery was burned to the ground. The fire was first discovered a little past eleven on a

Saturday night by Dr. Moulton. All the fixtures, together with about $1000 worth of green hides and a quantity of leathers were burned.[186]

Limington Corner was the home of the town's first newspaper called "The Maine Recorder." It was printed weekly on a hand press on the second floor of Captain Abner Libby's store. The paper was owned by James McArthur and commenced in April 1832.[187] It was of Whig origin and was used as a campaign paper. Moses A. Dow was publisher and Gamaliel E. Smith of Newfield was the first editor, holding that position for less than a year. Henry B. Pratt next filled the editorial chair from June to October 1832. Pratt afterward married Maria Dimock of Limington, and moved to Calais where he published "The Calais Times and Boundary Gazette." The third and last editor was Arthur M. Baker, an alias name for James McArthur. The paper ceased publication on December 31, 1835, and was nicknamed by the townspeople the "Smut Mill."[188]

Limington Town Hall, built in 1871.

Limington Village at the turn of the century.

Chapter IX — Prominient Citizens

Walter Hagens

Walter Hagens was born in Scarboro, November 26, 1765 and died in Limington, September 27, 1847. He was brought up by his grandfather Fergus Hagens. When Fergus died, his property was divided and Walter took his share in money. In 1785 he bought a place about a mile west of Ruin Corner where he settled and resided until his death.

"From 1794 till 1827, Walter Hagens served in the most important offices of his town. He represented his district in the General Court, at Boston in 1812 and 1813. He was obliged to journey to Boston on horseback, carrying the money for the town taxes, etc., in saddlebags, a dangerous undertaking in that sparsely settled country. On one of his journeys he stopped at a tavern overnight, bringing his saddlebags into the general sitting room and laying them down in the room. During the evening he saw the landlord lift the saddlebags and put them down in another part of the room. Soon after he went to his chamber, taking his saddlebags with him. There was no fastening on the door; so putting out his candle, he lay down on the outside of the bed, unable to sleep. In the middle of the night he heard footsteps softly creeping up the stairs and along the hall to his door. He rose, and as the latch was gently raised he shouted: 'Whoever opens that door is a dead man!' The latch was dropped and the steps quickly retreated. At daybreak he saddled his horse and proceeded on his journey, delivering his money safely to the authorities in Boston.

Uncle Walter, as he was called, was held in high regard for his wisdom, and general sense of justice. The neighbors, far and near, brought their disputes to him for settlement. He asked few questions and made no comments. He sat silent for a long time, rubbing his forefinger and thumb together; after which he gave his decision which was accepted as final.

He had no patience with hypocrisy and deceit. A member of the church, whom he knew to be dishonest, often prayed in the 'experience meetings' that usually followed the sermon. On such occasions Uncle Walter would rise, put on his triple-caped drab broadcloth cloak, and saying to his wife: 'Come, woman, it's time for us to go, walk with dignity out of the church.' "[1]

Aaron Hagens, the fourth child of Walter, succeeded him in possession of the homestead on Christian Hill, and was for many years the recipient of civic honors from his townsmen. He was noted in military affairs and was captain of the first military company in Limington. He represented his town in the Legislature in Portland in 1827. In 1836, by an act of the Legislature on his petition, his name was changed to Higgins. He died a young man in his native town on August 18, 1837, age forty-three years.

Samuel Greenlaw and family on Christian Hill in 1882. The farm was sold to him by Walter Higgins, grandson of Walter Hagens.

Abner Libby, Esquire

Abner Libby was born in Scarboro, December 27, 1766, and died there May 5, 1843. He was what would be termed an "all around" man and could turn his hand to anything that required his attention. For many years he filled a large place in the community. In 1792 he settled at Limington Corner, on a farm and built a shop where for years he worked at blacksmithing. Subsequently he carried on a general store and kept a tavern. The first school in town was taught by him. From 1793 to 1800 he was town clerk; 1794 to 1802 selectman; and 1804 to 1809 town treasurer. For about forty years he was a justice of the peace, and as there was no lawyer in town for many years, he did much business of a legal nature.[2]

Arthur McArthur, Esquire

Arthur McArthur was born in the old homestead at South Limington, January 14, 1790. He graduated from Bowdoin College in 1810 and was admitted to the bar at Alfred in 1815. In 1817, he began his law practice in town which he successfully carried on for more than half a century.

He filled a large place in his town, and in all matters affecting its welfare he took a keen interest. It was largely through his efforts that the Academy was established. He was also one of the builders of the Congregational meeting-house. He served on the school board, and was always most active in educational and religious affairs of the town.[3]

Extremely interested in antiquarian research, he had collected much and valuable material for a history of Limington. Genial and scholarly, and gifted with rare conversational powers, he interested all who approached him and attracted their friendship. He was an honest man and true to every obligation in life. He died sincerely mourned on the 29th day of November, 1874.[4]

Mr. McArthur was always noted for a certain sprightliness of manner and for a veracity of spirit that made his companionship and conversation delightful. He was noted for his wit and humor as evidenced by the number of stories about him that were passed from one generation to the next. One of the best of these is as follows:

"A few years after his graduation he received a communication in usual form, from the President of Bowdoin College, informing him that the faculty had conferred upon him the degree of A.M.; and that the parchment evidence thereof would be forwarded to him upon the payment of the customary fee of ten dollars. Mr. McArthur made no response to the letter at the time, but nearly if not quite, half a century afterwards, took it down from the pigeon hole where he had carefully deposited it and addressed a polite note to the President of the college in his official capacity, acknowledging the receipt of his letter of fifty years before, in the same terms he would have done had it been a matter of weeks previous; thanking the faculty for their honorable remembrance of him, and enclosing the ten dollars with a request that his own example of promptness in attending to his correspondence, might be copied, and the parchment forwarded to his address without delay."[5]

David Boyd, Esquire

David Boyd was born in South Berwick, May 20, 1781.

"He was an esteemed Christian man, a good citizen, in him was generally found much to admire—his tact for business was above mediocrity; his prayers and exhortations generally sympathetic and earnest. He was a man who didn't easily change his judgment after conclusions had been drawn. He was a fast friend, and a determined opponent, with an even disposition."[6]

In 1803 he moved to South Limington, settling near Boyd's Pond which bears his name. He was frequently called to posts of public trust. He was a member of the Massachusetts Legislature, when this state was an appendage to that state, and a delegate from Limington to help frame the state constitution.

"He was versed in the routine of probate matters and other technicalities of law, ready to counsel, safe in advice, a friend to the widow and the fatherless. His house was always the pilgrim's resting and refreshing place — none were ever turned from his door hungry."[7]

In 1821 he moved to South Berwick, his native town and became a Free-Will Baptist preacher. He died there December 11, 1855.

Nathaniel Clark, Esquire

Nathaniel Clark, was born in Limington, February 4, 1783, and died in Auburn, December 4, 1850.[8] He was prominent in the political life of his town, serving as selectman and a Justice of the Peace for many years. In the fall of 1819 he was delegate to the convention called to frame a constitution for the state. Mr. Clark was a State Representative and was nominated for the State Senate. He moved to Danville in 1838. In 1806, he married Mary, a daughter of Edward Small.

James Warren Joy, Esquire

James W. Joy was born in Limington, February 17, 1811.

"He was a justice for more than fifty years with all varieties of the commission—notary public, dectimus, trial, justice of the peace and quorum, and never advised parties to their injury. Squire Joy was widely known in York County and was looked to by his townsmen as an advisor on all matters where legal questions were concerned. He was better acquainted with the reported decisions of the several courts than most lawyers, and could readily cite a case in hand. Very rarely did his townsmen act contrary to his advice."[9]

Mr. Joy was an officer of the town in more capacities and longer than any other man and was always esteemed and respected by all parties. Though a life-long and unswerving Democrat, he had on all occasions votes from the other side. In addition to holding town and county offices he represented the district in the Legislature. He was a fast friend to education, believing in the common school, and an early friend to the Academy, serving in the early years of its existence on the board of trustees. A severe cold with pneumonia resulting was the cause of his death, which occurred on March 30, 1892.

William G. Davis

Honorable William Goodwin Davis was born in South Limington, June 16, 1825 and died in Portland, April 19, 1903.

"His parents were blessed with but very little of this world's goods and his boyhood was spent amidst poverty and toil. When fourteen years old, he went to Portland where he entered the canning business. Success followed his efforts and he died a wealthy man. Sometime before his death he expressed a desire to furnish the town of Limington with a library building. Years later, Walter Davis, Sr., of Portland carried out his father's wishes giving the town the present brick building and its furnishings."[10]

The son purchased the house and lot known as the General Small homestead from Charles Small of New York.

When the Library Association of Limington was incorporated in 1895, the greater part of the books catalogued were given by William G. Davis and Edward Adams, a son of Dr. Clement J. Adams, who was a practicing physician in the town for a number of years. Mr. Adams and Mr. Davis were intimate friends.[11]

William G. Lord

William Godding Lord was born in Hiram, December 31, 1827 and died at Limington, August 26, 1898. He received degrees from Colby University, 1854, and from Dartmouth in 1885. He was principal of Limington Academy from 1851 to 1894, excepting twelve terms. Mr. Lord was a student and reader, and his lectures were highly instructive. He was active in town politics, holding almost every office—selectman, town clerk, town treasurer and supervisor of schools. He was a trial justice for twenty-one years. Mr. Lord held the highest office in Adoniram Lodge, A.F. and A.M. and served as a deacon of the Congregational Church from 1876 to 1898. In 1854 he married Mary Clark and made his residence in the Clark homestead across from the Academy.

James M. Hopkinson

James Monroe Hopkinson was born in Limington May 5, 1828 and died there on February 22, 1889. He was a leader in town affairs and held various offices. He represented his district in the State Legislature and was a pillar of the South Limington Free Baptist Church. Mr. Hopkinson took an interest in school matters and was one of the leaders in the "South Limington Seminary" movement. For nearly forty years he was one of the leading businessmen in the town.

Colonel William Miltmore McArthur

Colonel McArthur was born in Limington, July 7, 1832. After preparing for college at North Yarmouth Academy he entered Bowdoin College, graduating in 1853. He read law with his father and was admitted to the York County Bar in May, 1860.

He entered the military service of the United States on September 7, 1861, as a captain in the 8th Maine Volunteers and advanced through the various grades until he commanded the regiment. Twice he was brevetted Brigadier General, but he declined the title.[12] Returning home to Limington surrounded by all the glory of a hero, he was elected to represent his district in the State Legislature of 1867, and his county in the Legislature of 1869.

Colonel McArthur inherited a large farm from his father and devoted much time to its management. He cultivated an extensive apple orchard. He would walk through the fields with a cane and wherever the cane touched the ground, there he would plant a tree. He gave but little time to the practice of law, though he kept his office until a few years before his death.

In 1885 Colonel McArthur won the $50,000 prize in the Louisiana State lottery and the news of his good fortune spread like wildfire. He won numerous other lesser prizes in the same lottery, the sum total being in the vicinity of $75,000.[13]

Something of the peculiarities of the man may be gathered from an incident that happened during the time he was seeking an overseer for his farm.

Colonel William McArthur.

"The job carried a fat salary, for General McArthur spent with a lavish hand in the upkeep of his property. There were many applicants and they were hired and fired almost as fast as they made application. Finally one man who sought the position was taken down into a field on the farm by the general, where there lay a heap of large rocks.

'I want you to take all those rocks and build a continuation of that stone wall,' he told the applicant. The man asked no questions but went to work. Two days later he reported that the job was done.

'Well, pull the wall down again and pile the rocks up where you found them,' was McArthur's next order. Again the man applied himself to his task without question, and when he had finished McArthur called him to the house and said: 'You're the man I want. You know how to do what you're told to do.' "[14]

James F. Brackett

Honorable James F. Brackett was born in Limington, March 16, 1833, and died there, August 30, 1921. He served his town as treasurer, auditor, collector, agent and was for years the president of the board of trustees of Limington Academy. He was elected to the State Legislature and held the office of county commissioner for nine years. "Mr. Brackett was actively concerned in all public affairs and in every public enterprise."[15]

Frank S. Black

Frank Swett Black was born on Libby Mountain in Limington, March 8, 1853. He obtained such education as the town could afford before moving with his parents to Alfred in 1864, where his father became keeper of the county jail. In 1875 he graduated from Dartmouth College after working to earn expenses. He was admitted to the New York bar and became one of its leading attorneys. He served New York state as a Congressman one term and was governor from 1897 to 1899. As a public speaker he ranked with the foremost men in the country. He died at Troy, New Hampshire, March 22, 1913.

Gov. Frank S. Black's Birthplace, Libby Mountain, now gone.

Doctors

Thomas Foster

Thomas Foster was the first doctor to settle in town about 1796. He came from Wentworth, New Hampshire, where he had started his practice four years before.[16] He was part Indian and probably only an herb doctor. He lived in a place on what is now a vacant lot north of Longfellow School at the village. He was an early innholder and for a short time had a store. He died January 18, 1849, at Limington. Dr. Foster was twice married and had eight children.

James Cochran

Dr. James Cochran was born in Windham, New Hampshire, October 23, 1777, and died at Monmouth, October, 1860.[17] He came to Limington in 1801 and a year later built a house located on the site of the present library at the village. In 1806 he moved to Monmouth where he soon became successful in the practice of his profession. He married Jane Moore who bore fourteen children.

Henry Dimock

Dr. Henry Dimock was born in Durham, Connecticut, July 6, 1780. He came to Limington Corner in 1808 and remained there except for a few years in the late twenties. His granddaughter Susan Dimock of Washington, D.C. was a noted female physician and surgeon when women doctors were rare. On September 25, 1803, he married Nancy Whitmore and they had nine children. He died May 23, 1852.

Henry Tufts

Henry Tufts was born in Newmarket, New Hampshire, June 25, 1748, and died in Limerick, January 21, 1831. When he was about twenty-four, he severely injured himself and was advised to visit an Indian tribe living at Bethel. For three years (1772-75) he remained with them, and at first was visited daily by Molly Orcut, whose name is still preserved in memory as the most noted of Indian doctors. He observed her methods and took her medicines. There were also other renowned doctors such as Sabattus and Old Philips; and Tufts took great pains to study what he called "Indian botany and physic," and thus gained a knowledge on which he frequently traded for the rest of his life.[18] His name appears in Limington town books as having practiced his trade on local paupers. The story of his life is told in a book entitled, *A Narrative of the Life, Adventures, Travels and Sufferings of Henry Tufts, Now Residing at Limington, in The District of Maine*. It was printed by Samuel Bragg, Jr. at Dover, New Hampshire in 1807. The story of Colonel T.W. Higginson's New England Vagabond in "Harper's Magazine" of March, 1888, is founded on the vagaries of Henry Tufts' autobiography.

"Henry Tufts was famous in his day and in his field, which extended from Maine to Virginia, for a reprobate life under many disguises and marvelous escapes, hearing assumed names, appearing as rake, tramp, bully wrestler, burglar, horse-thief, freebooter, bounty-jumper, fortune teller, Indian herb doctor, religious enthusiast, and New Light preacher. He was nearly a score of times in a score and a half of years sentenced to prisons, dungeons, and chains at Falmouth and York, Dover, Exeter, eight times, Newburyport, Ipswich, Salem and Castle William in Boston Harbor.[19]

In 1798 the fortress at Castle William where he was imprisoned was ceded to the National Government, and he was removed to Salem, whereas he soon escaped, and joined his first wife and family at Limington.

His wife was Lydia Bickford, some years his senior but a very notable and discreet woman contributing more to the support of the family than her husband. She and her son Simeon moved to Limington with Richard Edgerly's family.

Ward Bassett

Dr. Ward Bassett came to town about 1811 and by 1813 left to serve in the U.S. Navy. Before coming here he lived in Poland where he was jailed for debt and later at Pownal where he shared the same fate, "Having bought medicines not paid for at Freeport."[20] He left Dartmouth Medical School as a non-graduate in 1815 and went to Randolph, Vermont, where he served about four years. He later became a surgeon of considerable reputation.

Clement Jackson Adams

Clement Jackson Adams was born in Limerick, March 10, 1795, and died in Bridgton, October 4, 1853.[21] He studied medicine with Dr. Alexander Ramsey of Fryeburg, a distinguished lecturer on anatomy and physiology.[22] Dr. Adams began practice at Limington Village in 1819, living in the Arthur Boothby place next to the Masonic Hall. He left town about 1844 for a practice in Bridgton. He was a genial courteous gentleman. He and his family are buried in Fryeburg.

Dr. Adams first wife died at Limington on August 20, 1839. His second wife was the widow of General James Steele of Brownfield.

Jesse Frederic Locke

Dr. Jesse Frederic Locke was born in Hollis, June 2, 1810. He attended Bowdoin Medical School (1834) and Dartmouth Medical School. He first set up an office in Abner Libby's store, opposite the present MasonicHall. His tenure in Limington was short, a period from June 20, to October 10, 1834.[23] He later resided at Biddeford and died of congestion of the lungs at Tonawanda, New York, March 12, 1861.[24]

Lewis Whitney

Dr. Lewis Whitney was born in Gorham, September 21, 1806, and died at North Yarmouth, May 18, 1857.[25] He graduated from Bowdoin Medical School in 1830. In October 1834, he moved into town from Baldwin and took an office over James McArthur's store in the Masonic Hall.[26] He left in the winter of 1835 to return to Baldwin.

He married Mary A., daughter of David and Mary G. Small of Limington, on November 16, 1836.

Cyrus Jordan

Dr. Cyrus Jordan was born in Raymond, January 1, 1803, and died at Raymond, September 28, 1881.[27] He graduated from Dartmouth Medical School in 1832 and by the spring of the next year was in town. In 1849 he returned to Limington for two years. His other practices were at Raymond, Fayette and Weston. Dr. Jordan was buried at New Gloucester.

Samuel Moulton Bradbury

Dr. Samuel Moulton Bradbury was born in Parsonsfield, August 22, 1805, and died of pneumonia in Limington, September 22, 1888. He began the study of medicine with his father, graduated from Bowdoin Medical School in 1831 and began the practice of his profession in Parsonsfield. In

Dr. Samuel M. Bradbury

1836 he moved to Limington where he resided for more than fifty years, regularly attending to his practice until a few days before his death.[28]

"In the profession he was a successful practitioner, sound in his judgment, cautious in his treatment, conservative in his habits of thought and action as regarded plausible, and remedial agents as well-ever maintaining a good standing in the profession—honored by his townsmen and respected by all."[29]

Dr. Bradbury served terms as town clerk, selectman and State Representative. He was one of the founders of Limington Academy and served as president of its board of trustees for thirty years. He was a member of Adoniram Lodge of Masons, and one of the principal supporters of the Baptist Church.[30]

He was first married in 1831 to Susan Brackett of Parsonsfield and secondly to Elizabeth Brackett, sister of his first wife. Dr. Bradbury's first wife bore him two children and the second five children.

Moses Erastus Sweat

Dr. Moses Erastus Sweat, eldest son of Dr. Moses Sweat was born in Parsonsfield, January 16, 1816, and died there on January 1, 1892.[31] He graduated from Bowdoin College in 1833, and

"commenced the study of medicine with his father, attending one course of lectures at Dartmouth, and three at Bowdoin, graduating at the latter institution in 1840. He then practiced with his father one year, moving to Limington in 1841, where he remained until after the death of his mother. In 1862, he returned to his old home at Parsonsfield, to be with his father in his declining years, and there resided. While in Limington he held the various offices, representing the district in the Legislature of 1857. Retiring, quiet, courteous, sound in judgment, logical, firm and steadfast, resolute in an emergency, his success was marked, and had the confidence and esteem of all."[32]

John Thatcher Wedgewood

Dr. John Thatcher Wedgewood was born at Parsonsfield, April 17, 1832, and died at Cornish, March 26, 1889. He studied medicine with Dr. Moses E. Sweat, and graduated from Dartmouth in 1862. In May 1862, he began practice in Limington, taking over the field just vacated by Dr. Moses E. Sweat. He remained in Limington Village until 1867, when he moved to Cornish Village.[33] "The doctor was widely known in musical circles, having kept many singing schools in his younger days. He was a wonderfully energetic, and active businessman, closely devoted to his profession and a successful financier."[34]

In January 1862, he married Ruth, daughter of Dr. Calvin Topliff of Freedom, New Hampshire by whom he had two daughters.

Richard Hunnewell Meserve

Dr. Richard Hunnewell Meserve, was born in Limington, December 4,

1819, and died at Waterville, November 9, 1904. He received his education at Limerick Academy and was engaged in teaching for several years. In 1851 he began the study of medicine with Dr. Moses E. Sweat of Limington, and attended three courses of medical lectures; the second at Dartmouth, the first and third at Bowdoin where he received his degree in 1853. He at once started to practice in Limington and remained until 1862 when he entered the service of the United States as assistant surgeon in the First Regiment, Louisiana Volunteers. After the close of the war he moved to Milan, New Hampshire, where he practiced for sixteen years, ending in 1881. Returning to Maine he continued professional work at Limerick. The closing years of his life were spent at Vassalboro and Waterville. He was a good man and highly esteemed in the communities in which he lived.[35]

On May 26, 1852, Dr. Meserve married Sarah B., daughter of Josiah Marston of Limington.

John Lord

Dr. John Lord was born in Porter, June 25, 1843, and died at Biddeford, January 21, 1903. As a young man he enlisted in the Civil War and on receiving his discharge entered the hospital at Washington as an attendant. On leaving the hospital service in the latter part of 1864 he went into the office of Dr. Jesse P. Sweat in Brownfield and pursued the study of medicine and surgery until 1866. In that year he passed his examination and received the degree of doctor of medicine at Bowdoin Medical School.[36]

Dr. Lord established himself at Limington in 1867 and remained until 1873 when accompanied by his new wife, Helen Dimock of Limington, he went to California to open an office. He returned to Maine and settled in Biddeford where he remained from 1881 to the time of his death.[37]

John Fairfield Moulton

Dr. John Fairfield Moulton was born in Parsonsfield, April 1850, and died in Limington, April 14, 1911. He attended Limerick Academy and Parsonsfield Seminary and studied medicine with Dr. Moses E. Sweat of Parsonsfield. He attended two courses of lectures at Bowdoin, and graduated from Long Island Hospital College, New York in 1874. In August of that year he began practice at Durham, New Hampshire. He moved to Gilmanton Iron Works in December 1875 and in July 1876 he came to Limington where he remained. Here he had a large field of practice. Dr. Moulton was not only looked upon as an excellent physician, but as a man who took a great interest in the affairs of the town.[38]

He was one of the charter members of Cresent Lodge K. of P. and was a member of the board of trustees of Limington Academy, for many years serving as president. Dr. Moulton was a member of Adoniram Lodge of Masons, and a member of the Limington Grange. He married Martha Parsons of Somersworth, New Hampshire. They had seven children.[39]

George Walter Weeks

Dr. George Walter Weeks was born in Cornish, September 1, 1861, and died there September 20, 1938. He taught school in Cornish and Scarboro for a few years then entered Bowdoin Medical School from which he graduated in 1888. He began the practice of medicine in Limington where he took Stella Libby as his bride in 1889. He left in April 1892, for a more extensive practice in Cornish.

John Newton Plaisted

Dr. John Newton Plaisted was born in Limington, June 11, 1854, and died at Gorham, March 14, 1929. He received his early education in the local schools and attended Limington Academy. For several years he taught school and later entered Bowdoin Medical School from which he received a degree in 1881. Dr. Plaisted's first four years of practice were in the town of Pownal where he was successful. In June 1885, he moved to Limerick, leasing the stand then owned by Mrs. Cotton Bean which was centrally located in the village.[39] Five years later he located himself at Sanford and Springvale where he had an extensive practice. It was during his tenure there that his only surviving son was drowned at Mousam Lake.

In 1904 he moved back to Limington town and opened an office next to the church at the village. He ended his profession here in 1927 and moved to Gorham where he died. He was a member of Adoniram Lodge of Masons and was a trustee of Limington Academy.

He was married, December 25, 1879, to Carrie Luella Small, a daughter of Benjamin Small of Limington.

Limington born doctors:

George Dennett Staples (Bowdoin Med. 1838), Stephen Meserve Libby, John Megquire Small (Bowdoin Med. 1847), Ebenezer B. Bangs (Worcester Med. 1847), Friend Drake Lord (Bowdoin Med. 1847), Sumner Burnham Chase (Bowdoin Med.), Alexander Boothby (attended lectures at Bowdoin also N.Y. Grad. 1846), David Small Clark, Isaac P. Hurd, Daniel Moody (Dartmouth Med. 1877), Melville Harrison Manson (Bowdoin Med. 1863), Stephen E. Wentworth, (Bowdoin Med. 1865), John Albert Fellows, Hiram Brackett Haskell (Bowdoin Med. 1873), Henry Audubon Small (Bowdoin Med. 1872), Charles A. Libby (N.Y. Homeopatnic Med. 1873), Charles Lincoln Randall (Phys. & Surgeons, Baltimore 1889), John Moore Boothby (N.Y. Post Grad. Med. 1889), Fred Augustus Bragdon (Bowdoin Med. 1888), Jesse Andrew Randall (Bowdoin Med. 1888), Frank George Manson (Dartmouth Med. 1887), Edward Norton Libby (Dartmouth Med. 1892), Benjamin Franklin Wentworth (Bowdoin Med. 1897), Roland Sumner Gove (Bowdoin Med. 1897), Samuel Guy Sawyer (Bowdoin Med. 1900), Fitz Elmer Small (Bowdoin Med. 1899).

Aged Persons

Lazarus Rowe

Lazarus Rowe was born January 1725 in Greenland, New Hampshire. At the age of eighteen he married Molly Webber, and they consequently lived together eighty-six years.[40] They reared a large family, and saw their descendants to the fifth generation. In early life he was a soldier in the French and

Indian War and was present at the taking of Louisburg in 1745. Afterwards he belonged to Roger's Rangers in New Hampshire and was often in Indian battles.[41] Once he was taken captive, and was on the point of being burned at the stake by the savages, when he escaped by almost superhuman effort.[42] He was engaged near Lake George in 1755 and at Fort William Henry in 1757. He was also a soldier during the greater part of the Revolutionary War. Lazarus and wife came to North Limington from Baldwin, where they had been early settlers, to live the last two years with their youngest daughter, Martha, the widow of Samuel Goodwin.[43] His wife died June 27, and he died September 14, 1829, both were in their one hundredth and fourth year. They were buried on the Old Ben Clay place.

William Thompson

William Thompson was born October 4, 1775, in the town of Falmouth. Fourteen days later, the word came from Mowatt that the town would be destroyed, and twenty-four hours was given to provide for the safety of the women and children.[44] He was hastily taken in a cradle to Windham, where he remained until he was eleven years of age. During this time his mother died, and he never saw his father who was lost at sea. When eleven he bound himself out to Captain Joseph S. Tyler coming to Limington from Standish with that family in 1786. Mr. Thompson married Mary Small in 1801 and moved on the old Henry Small farm where he lived for over seventy years. A birthday party was given on his hundredth year with five generations present, along with one hundred thirty-five other kinfolk.[45] A photographer from Portland arrived but by the time the group had gathered, the aged man tired by the occasion had left his chair and was napping in the house when the picture was taken. At the time Mr. Thompson was physically and mentally in good health. He died at his farm on the Shaving Hill Road, May 27, 1876, at the age of one hundred years, seven months.

William Thompson and his birthday Party at his place on Shaving Hill Road, Oct. 4, 1875.

Years later the Thompson place was where the "Small Clan" would gather for annual picnics. They were held on a four acre grown-up field on the northeast corner of the place called Dundee, so named by Humphrey Small because of its extreme rockiness.

The first picnic was held at Dundee on the fifteenth of September 1892, to celebrate the centennial of the town and the two hundred twenty-fourth anniversary of the purchase of the Ossipee lands by Francis Small. Lauriston Ward Small put out the notices in the Portland Press and thirty-nine of the Small family appeared for the reunion. The next year ninety-seven clansmen appeared upon historical Dundee loaded down with the "food of the fathers" -baked beans and other edibles. The Dundee picnics proved to be very successful occasions and were held years afterward with kinsmen coming from Gorham, Cornish, Limerick, Fryeburg, New York and Massachusetts.

Small Family Annual Picnic held at Dundee on the Shaving Hill Road, August 1911. The picnic grounds had remained in possession of Francis Small's descendants from the time he purchased the Ossipee Tract in 1668.

Jemima Bradeen

Jemima, widow of Henry Bradeen was born December 11, 1782, in Limington, a daughter of John Nason. She was a devout christian, and for eighty years was a staunch member of the Methodist Episcopal Church. When she had reached the age of one hundred years, she had full possession of her faculties and read her Bible aloud without difficulty.[46] She died at Nason Mills, September 8, 1883, age one hundred years, nine months. She left five generations.

Ruth Jewell

Ruth Jewell was born February 2, 1789, in Baldwin, the youngest daughter of Lt. Benjamin Ingalls. She married Enoch Jewell and settled in

Cornish where she lived about seventy-five years. After her husband's death she was kindly cared for by her son-in-law, Ammi Rowe and in the last year and a half by her grand-daughter, Mrs. Theophilus W. Bean at North Limington[47] where she died May 7, 1890, at the age of one hundred and one years, three months. "Aunt" Ruth, as she was called for many years, retained her faculties to a remarkable degree and in her hundredth year drove a horse and chaise around the Cornish Trotting Park at the annual fair.

Elizabeth Moody

Mrs. Elizabeth Moody, the widow of Major Moses Moody lived longer than any other person born in town. "Mrs. Moody was born February 28, 1783, in Limington and came of the hardy stock of the 'first settlers' who were men and women of remarkable physical vigor."[48] Her father, Aaron Libby, was a very athletic man.

She and her husband moved to Cape Elizabeth about 1818. "She was a woman of strong convictions, giving to doing acts of kindness and was noted for her plain common sense and for having a knack of making the best of everything."[49] At the age of one hundred and two, she enjoyed perfect health and except for slight defects in hearing and eyesight, had possession of her faculties.[50] Mrs. Moody died at Cape Elizabeth at the age of one hundred and three years, four months.

Other aged persons who died in town were the following: Mrs. Isaac Marr's mother, (1741-1840); Mary, widow of Robert Davis, (1779-1878); Robert Hasty, (1714-1810); Anna, widow of Levi Merrifield, Jr., (1802-1899); John Babb, (1794-1890); Anna, widow of Levi Merrifield, Sr. (1767-1863); Mary, widow of Joshua McKenney, (1784-1879); Abigail, widow of William Merserve, (1797-1892); Caleb Hopkinson, (1746-1841); Hannah, widow of Christopher Cole, (1773-1867); Nathaniel Staples, (1777-1872); Josiah Black, (1750-1843) Hannah, widow of Christopher Bullock, (1754-1847); Samuel Brackett, (1757-1850); Samuel Manson, (1775-1869); Edward Norton, (1783-1876); Martha, widow of Isaac Mitchell, (1783-1877); Susannah, wife of David Richardson, (1799-1892); Samuel Greenlaw, (1806-1899); Mary, widow of Captian John Small, (1731-1823); Shuah, widow of Nathaniel Sawyer, (1765-1857); Hannah, widow of Soloman Stone, (1774-1867); Eunice, widow of Humphrey McKenney, (1785-1878); Watson Dyer, (1786-1879); Sarah, widow of John Davis, (1796-1889); Noah Deshon, (1799-1891); Soloman Stone, (1739-1830); Sarah, widow of Ebenezer Morton, (1739-1831); Ephraim Clark, (1756-1847); Mary, widow of Francis Meeds, (1770-1862); Charlotte, widow of Daniel Rounds, (1777-1868); George Robinson, (1783-1875); Betsey, widow of Dennis Gilkey, (1792-1883) Anna, widow of Elias Foss, (1770-1861); Abigail, widow of Richard Edgerly, (1759-1849) Joshua McKenney, (1775-1865); Josiah Marston, (1796-1886); Miss Polly Collomy, (1797-1887); Anna, widow of John M. Staples, (1803-1894); Mary, widow of Samuel Brackett, (1762-1852).

Death Statistics

The number of deaths in town over a twenty-eight year period beginning with 1816 were six hundred ninety-seven, with about one third of the number being children. The highest mortality rate occurred in 1825 with fifty deaths, followed by forty-seven deaths in 1843.[51]

The average number of deaths in Limington from 1821 to 1830 inclusive averaged twenty-five, with one death yearly to about eighty-nine inhabitants. The yearly count for the next ten year span averaged twenty-seven deaths yearly. The population was 2320 in 1830, and 2210 in 1840, making one death yearly to about eighty-four inhabitants. The deaths in one years' time, ending June 1850 numbered forty, of which nine were of persons aged sixty-five years or more.

In 1880 the number of inhabitants in town was 1431, with a voting population of fewer than 400. The number living over seventy years at that time was one hundred twelve, and about one-third of that number were past eighty.[52]

Number of deaths in Limington in certain years:

1816—15 adults, 13 children
1817—11 adults, 5 children
1818— 6 adults, 11 children
1819—10 adults, 8 children
1820—19 adults, 8 children
1821—11 adults, 9 children
1822—13 adults, 13 children
1823— 9 adults, 9 children
1824— 9 adults, 11 children
1825—21 adults, 21 children
1826—26 adults, 9 children
1827—11 adults, 3 children
1828— 9 adults, 7 children
1829—14 adults, 5 children
1830—21 adults, 13 children
1831—16 adults, 7 children
1832—22 adults, 12 children
1833—21 adults, 12 children
1834—16 adults, 10 children
1835—19 adults, 14 children
1836—21 adults, 8 children
1837—20 adults, 6 children
1838—21 adults, 7 children
1839— 7 adults, 6 children
1840—19 adults, 4 children
1841—23 adults, 6 children
1842—Lacking
1843—30 adults, 14 children
1844—13 adults, 5 children

Chapter X — Military

A number of the settlers of Limington had been soldiers of the Revolution. Most of them had enlisted from the Scarboro, Cape Elizabeth area, their place of residence at the time. After the war they came to Limington looking for a home in the wilderness. In 1833 there were in town twenty-one Revolutionary veterans who had served a sufficient term to be entitled to a pension. At that time this was the residence of more Revolutionary veterans according to population than any other town in the state.[1]

A number served the cause with distinction and daring. The Clark brothers who in the 1780's settled in Limington were examples.

Ephraim Clark first enlisted at Kittery on November 17, 1776, as seaman on the privateer "Dalton." He was captured and taken to Plymouth, England, and put in Mill Prison where he remained until March 15, 1779, when with other prisoners he was taken to Nantes, France, to be exchanged. He enlisted again on April 5, 1779, for one year's service, on the Continental frigate "Alliance," in the fleet under Commodore Paul Jones. He was in the fight on September 23, 1779, when the "Serapis" and "Countess of Scarboro," British frigates, were captured. He was taken prisoner October 9, 1779, and taken to Fortune prison at Portsmouth, England. He escaped and went to Cherbourg, France, May 3, 1780. He was on the cutter "Marquis Maibeck," a privateer under American colors sailing from Dunkirk, France, when she was captured September 9, 1781, by a British vessel, and he was taken again to Mill Prison in England. He was exchanged and arrived at Marblehead, Massachusetts, August, 1782. In 1785 he came to Limington Corner and settled on the farm across from the present Academy.

He was pensioned July 4, 1820, and again in 1832. His grandsons spent many happy hours at the old homestead listening to the stories of his hairbreadth escapes and adventures by sea and land. It is told that when almost ninety years old he offered to teach one of his grandchildren to dance, saying: "When I was young I gave dancing lessons in France."[2]

Ebenezer Clark was a soldier of the Revolution, afterward following his brother Ephraim to Limington. He served in Colonel Scammans regiment of

Infantry and was at the memorable battle of Bunker Hill. "He led a long life of unwavering moral rectitude and strict integrity."[3]

Limington's Revolutionary Soldiers

William Bragdon, (1754-1802); Joshua Small, (1725-1803); Calvin Lombard, (1748-1808); Benjamin Norton, (—-1810); Elisha Strout, (1746-1811); James McKenney, (1742-1812); Captain James Small, (1734-1812); John Bolden, (—-1813); Robert Boody, (1743-1814); Nicholas Edgecomb, (1741-1815); Humphrey McKenney, (1742-1815); Abraham Brackett, (1760-1815); Daniel Dyer, (1756-1817); Isaac Strout, (1752-1818); John Gove, (1766-1818); John Sutton, (1754-1819); William Manson, (1750-1819); Dennis Mulloy, (1750-1821); James Randall, (1758-1821); Nathaniel Sawyer, (1749-1821); John Miller, (1753-1825); Eli Jackson, (1759-1825); Captain Joseph S. Tyler, (1761-1826); John Robinson, (1759-1826); Henry Small, (1757-1826); Lazarus Rowe, (1725-1829); Soloman Stone, (1739-1830); James Gilkey, (1756-1831); Nathaniel Norton, (1764-1831); Nicholas Davis, (1753-1832); James Marr, (1753-1832); Josiah Milliken, (1758-1833); David Durrell, (1757-1833); Ebenezer Clark, (1752-1833); Isaac Small, (1752-1834); Joseph Libby, (1750-1835); William Small, (1759-1835); Samuel Larrabee, (1753-1836); David Hasty, (1756-1836); Thomas Cumming, (1754-1837); John Foss, (1750-1837); George Moody, (1761-1838); Stephen Purington, (1748-1838); George Stone, (1755-1839); Richard Edgerly, (1762-1840); Joseph Rose, (1761-1841); Caleb Hopkinson, (1746-1841); Ebenezer Sawyer, (1757-1842); Josiah Black, (1750-1843); John Jacobs,(1755-1843); Isaac Dyer, (1760-1843); James Emery, (1763-1844); Major Daniel Small, (1759-1844); Major Joseph Meserve, (1763-1845); Thomas Spencer, (1764-1845); Ephraim Clark, (1756-1847); Walter Hagens, (1765-1847); Major Elias Foss, (1766-1848); Harvey Libby, (1763-1849); Joshua Brackett, (1762-1849); Samuel Brackett, (1757-1850).

Other Revolutionary Soldiers once residents of Limington were: Charles Fogg, George Fogg, Daniel Fogg, John Greenlaw, John Douglass, Nathaniel Meserve, John O'rion, Amaziah Delano, Robert Hasty, William Johnson, Andrew Rankins, Prince Strout, Samuel Sawyer, John Andrews, Jacob Clark, Heard Hubbard, Samuel Sawyer, Edward Kennard, William Spencer, William Irish, Bartholomew Jackson, George Foss, Robert Libby and John Stone.

On March 30, 1809, a group of thirty-seven young inhabitants of Limington petitioned the Massachusetts Senate and House of Representatives to raise by voluntary enlistment a company of light infantry, in the Fifth Regiment, first Brigade and Sixth Division of Militia. The petition was signed by the following people: Nathaniel Sawyer, Abraham Cousins, Thomas Mulloy, John N. Small, Joseph Brackett, Samuel Larrabee Jr., Benjamin Blake, Isaac Small, Jr., David Otis, John Staples, Gideon Libby, Simon McKenney, Isaac Small Jr., William Staples, Edward Mulloy, Peter McArthur, Benjamin Small, Isaiah Morrison, John Black, Seth Blake, Arthur Bragdon, John Douglass Jr., Enoch Staples, James Staples, Humphrey

McKenney Jr., Abner Libby Jr., Daniel Libby, Harvey Libby, John Libby, David Meserve, Thomas Richardson, Enoch Staples Jr., Silas Meserve, Benjamin Hasty, William Thompson, John Small Jr., Elias Libby.[4]

Limington Light Artillery Company
(Service on seacoast at Kennebunk from September 20th to October 17, 1814. Raised at Limington)[5]

RANK AND NAME: Edward Small, Captain; Benjamin Small, Lieutenant; David Otis, Ensign; James Staples, Sergeant; William Staples, Sergeant; Samuel Larrabee, Sergeant; James Libby, Sergeant; Humphrey Small, Corporal; Jonathan Atkinson, Corporal; David Small, Corporal; Joshua Small, Corporal; Isaac Small, Musician; Francis Small, Musician. PRIVATES: Aaron Black, Benjamin Blake, Seth Blake, Arthur Boothby, Asa Boothby, Joseph Brackett, Arthur Bragdon, Nathaniel Clark, Abraham Cousins, Elisha Douglass, John Douglass, Benjamin Hasty, Dominicus Hasty, James Libby, Jr., Parmenio Libby, Stephen Libby, William Libby, Isaac Marr, Humphrey McKenney, Silas Meserve, Daniel Moody, Simon Moody, Edward Mulloy, Thomas Mulloy, Kendall Parker, Isaac Richardson, Thomas Richardson, Nathaniel C. Small, Samuel Small, William Small, William Thompson.

Muster Roll of Captain Soloman Strout's Company
(Service at Saco, from October 30 to November 13, 1814. Raised at Limington)[6]

RANK AND NAME: Soloman Strout, Captain; William P. Marr, Sergeant; Elisha Strout, Sergeant; Soloman McKenney, Musician; Moses Chase, Musician. PRIVATES: William Anderson, Sylvanus Bangs, James Chase, Benjamin Grant, Aaron Hagens, John Heard, John Hopkinson, Samuel Hopkinson, Joseph Manson, Joseph Meserve, Rufus Meserve, Simon Nason, William Randell, James Richardson, Thomas Robinson, Michael Sawyer, Ebenezer Small, Ephraim Small, John Smith, 2nd, Joseph Strout, Samuel Strout, George Sutton.

Muster Roll of Sergeant James Marr's, Jr.
(Service at Biddeford from August 25, to September 23, 1814)[7]

RANK AND NAME: James Marr Jr., Sergeant. PRIVATES: James S. Chick, Ezra Davis, 3rd, John Edgecomb, Artemas Meeds, George Robinson, George Strout.

After the War of 1812 it was determined that the country must thereafter be prepared and kept prepared for defense and a system of universal military training was adopted.[8] Able bodied males from the age of eighteen to forty-five were enrolled, and required to meet and drill four times a year in companies, with an annual muster in the fall season.[9] The companies in town held their meetings at East Limington across from Colonel Henry Small's tavern.

Once a year the companies in other neighboring towns were brought together for general musters which were great social gatherings. Most of the companies and many spectators were on the ground by sunrise. Then commenced marching and counter-marching of the companies, headed by their captains and the music of the fife, and tin or brass drum.[10]

There would be cakes, pies and gingerbread, with new and old cider to wash it down.[11] Tin pails filled to the brim with rum, molasses and water were brought out to "treat" the men, and to strengthen them to bear the fatigues of the day.

Many stories were told as a result of the scrimmages at these gatherings where New England rum was plentiful. One such incident involved a one-armed man named Black. "A man known for his exaggerations told Henry Small of a scrimmage saying that 'Black hitched Boody by the throat with his left hand and gave him wust cuffings with his right hand you ever see.' When asked how a one-armed man could do that, the story teller thought a moment, and then said: 'when Jim Black gets into a fight he forgets he hasn't got two arms.' "[12]

Record of Musters

September 27, 1814 general muster, September 23, 1818 general muster, October 5, 1820 muster, September 13, 1821 muster, October 10, 1822 muster at Limerick, October 19, 1823 muster at Limington, September 16, 1824 muster at Waterboro, September 29, 1825 muster at Limerick, October 5, 1826 muster at Limerick, October 4, 1827 muster at Limington, October 2, 1828 mustered at Waterboro, October 15, 1829 muster at Limington, October 7, 1830 muster at Limerick, October 13, 1831 muster at Waterboro, October 4, 1832 muster at Limington, October 13, 1836 general muster, September 27, 1838 at Limington, September 25, 1839 muster at Limerick, September 23, 1840 muster at Waterboro.[13]

Old Boynton

After the War of 1812, a cannon from a privateer was dismantled at Portland and dragged into town by Simon Moody. Nathaniel Boynton fortified by a "certain kind of spirit" made a speech concerning it, and the six pounder[14] afterwards was known as Old Byington (properly pronounced Byin'ton). In 1836 the Whig town committee obtained the cannon for a celebration, and it spoke for the first time to the people of this town from Shaving Hill. It continued as a Whig gun until the breaking up of that party when it came into the ranks of he local Republican Party. The rights of the Republicans to own it were disputed and on the occasion of a Republican rally in September 1860, a Deputy Sheriff, Mr. Cyrus Small, armed with a replevin writ and backed by a large posse, attempted to take the gun from a torch light procession of wide-awakes. The outcome of that affair is best told by the following parody, composed at the time by one of the participants, who afterwards in the service during the Civil War must have improved his practice in gunnery:

The Burial of Old Byin'ton

Not a drum was heard, tho' many an oath,
as we hurried him on the wagon;
and Cyrus turned back, tho' very lath,
as we started to drive Sewall's nag on.

We buried him darkly, as dead of night,
The leaves with our torch staff turning,
By the struggling moonbeam's misty light,
and with nary "ile-jug" burning.

Thus narrowly having escaped an arrest,
and saf's tho' they never had found him,
We thankfully laid him where none can molest,
With a wide-awake cape wrapt' round him.

Few and short were the words we spoke
as we paused at the grave to place on
a memento,—when waiting our long Nines to smoke,
We wondered where then was John Nason.

We thought as we put the old gun in his bed,
And tucked him up nicely to rest,
How the foe on the morrow might tread on his head,
while we might be under arrest.

Profanely they'll talk of the gun that is gone;
They'll curse and perhaps they'll indict us;
But nothing we'll reck;—let them indict on;
They'll find it a job to affright us.

We knew, as we solemnly laid him down,
(Old Byin'ton brave, so famous in story)
His peals our November's vict'ry would crown,
His grum voice booming in it's glory.[15]

The above was so faulty in metre that after vain attempts to set it to song, Henry Waldron wrote one all about the same affair, prodying "Abe Lincoln is the man". This had greater merit as a campaign song and was sung until after the November election. Suffice it to say the gun spoke in November, and continued to do service in the cause until about the close of the war when the other party got hold of it. From that time it had a varied existence, traveling through neighboring towns and even falling into Greenback hands. But the Republicans got it back, and on the evening of November 2, 1880 it was fired under the charge of Captain Gilman L. Ilsley on

Shaving Hill. It was alternately seized by contending parties and was lowered into cellars, wells, hid in hay lofts and camouflaged in as many diverse ways as tested the wit of the party who had it.[16] Finally, it was stored in a dry well on the Frank Ilsley place and given in 1895 to Charles Emery, the father of the present owner. The gun was last fired when Woodrow Wilson was elected.

The Civil War probably more than any other factor affected the prosperity and growth of the town. By July 4, 1862, some forty-seven from this town had enlisted. In all, Limington sent seventy-three men for three years, fifty-three for one year and twenty-seven for nine months. The town expended $51,150 in payment of war expenses of various calls for troops.

In April 1861, in response to President Lincoln's call for men, William McArthur a young lawyer in town responded with patriotism. He quickly organized and equipped a full company in and about Limington, but it was never mustered into the service since it was offered after the call had been over subscribed. McArthur went out in Company I, the Eighth Maine Regiment, and was promoted to Captain in recognition of brilliant service. Early in the following year, for the same reason, he was promoted again; and finally he was made Colonel of the 8th Maine, a command he held for nearly a year and a half.

Bibliography

CHAPTER I
GEOGRAPHY

1. W.W. Clayton, **History of York County, Maine** (Philadelphia: Everts and Pects, 1880), p. 401.
2. Interview with Bert Sawyer, 1969
3. **Register of Deeds,** (Alfred), Vol. 107:107.
4. **Biddeford Journal,** (Biddeford), November 6, 1885.
5. William Dimock; a poem, 1925.
6. **Daily Evening Times,** (Biddeford) Jan. 30, 1873
7. Stanley Attwood, **Length and Breadth of Maine,** (Augusta: Kennebec Print Shop, 1946), p. 114.
8. Interview with Minot Holmes, 1971.
9. Interview with Lowell Gammon, 1969.
10. Stanley Attwood, **Length and Breadth of Maine,** (Augusta: Kennebec Print Shop, 1946), p. 167.
11. Altine Woodbury Underhill, **Descendants of Edward Small of New England,** (Cambridge, Mass.; The Riverside Press, 1910), p. 1531.
12. **Register of Deeds,** (Alfred), Vol. 61:153.
13. **Portland Transcript,** (Portland), May 25, 1872.
14. **Biddeford Journal,** (Biddeford), Dec. 15, 1881.
15. **Portland Transcript,** (Portland), July 8, 1882.
16. **Portland Transcript,** (Portland), Aug. 5, 1882.
17. Altine Woodbury Underhill, **Descendants of Edward Small of New England,** p. 56.
18. **Union and Journal,** (Biddeford), Jan. 24, 1868.
19. **Maine Democrat,** (Saco), Aug. 1847.
20. **Register of Deeds,** (Alfred), Vol. 76:139.
21. **Maine Democrat,** (Saco), Aug. 1847.
22. **Lewiston Journal,** (Lewiston), Sept. 1, 1923.
23. **Maine Democrat,** (Saco), Aug. 1847.
24. **Lewiston Journal,** (Lewiston), Sept. 1, 1923.
25. **Lewiston Journal,** (Lewiston), April 18, 1908.
26. **Ibid.**
27. **Maine Democrat,** (Saco), Aug. 1847.
28. East Limington Bridge, **Limington Academy Yearbook,** 1941.
29. **Ibid**

CHAPTER II
LAND TITLES

1. Altine Woodbury Underhill, **Descendants of Edward Small of New England,** (Cambridge, Mass.: The Riverside Press, 1910), p. 24
2. **Ibid.,** p. 33.
3. **Ibid.,** p. 33, 34.
4. **Ibid.,** p. 34.
5. **Ibid.,** p. 34, 35.
6. **Lewiston Journal,** (Lewiston), July 9, 1921.
7. Underhill, **Descendants of Edward Small of New England,** p. 8.
8. **Lewiston Journal,** July 9, 1921.
9. Underhill, **Descendants of Edward Small of New England,** p. 37-38.

10. **Ibid.**, p. 41.
11. **Ibid.**, p. 39.
12. **Ibid.**, p. 42.
13. **Ibid.**, p. 1595.
14. **Ibid.**, p. 57-58.
15. **Ibid.**, p. 146.
16. **Ibid.**, p. 44.
17. **Ibid.**, p. 1598-1599.
18. **Ibid.**, p. 1599.
19. **Ibid.**, p. 57.
20. **Ibid.**, p. 127.
21. Proprietor's Map made by Joshua Small, Alfred Court House.
22. **Ibid.**, p. 58.
23. **Ibid.**, p. 58-59.
24. A typed copy of the Proprietor's Records, owned by Phyllis Spraker.
25. **Ibid.**, p. 57.
26. **Ibid.**, p. 1600.
27. **Ibid.**, p. 59.
28. **Ibid.**, p. 60.
29. **Ibid.**
30. **Ibid.**, p. 61.
31. **Ibid.**, p. 65-66.
32. **Ibid.**, p. 58.
33. **Oxford County Record**, (Kezar Falls), October 20, 1883.

CHAPTER III
INDIANS

1. **Narragansett Sun**, (Gorham), January 21, 1909.
2. **Biddeford Journal**, (Biddeford), May 16, 1885.
3. **Ibid.**
4. Benjamin G. Wiley, **Incidents in White Mountain History**, (Portland; Francis Blake, 1856), p. 49.
5. **Ibid.**, p. 50.
6. **Lewiston Journal**, (Lewiston), September 1, 1923.
7. **Eastern Star**, (Portland), August 17, 1894.
8. **Weekly Standard**, (Biddeford), May 13, 1891.
9. **Ibid.**
10. Interview with Perley Burnham, 1968.
11. **Diary of Catherine McArthur**, October 1845.
12. Interview with Ralph Weston, as told to him by his grandfather, Leonard P. Thompson, 1968.
13. Interview with John Hanscom, Waterboro, 1970.
14. Interview with Mrs. Florence Day, Waterboro, 1970.
15. William Teg, **Almuchicoitt**, (Boston: The Christopher Publishing House, 1950), p. 80.
16. **Suffolk County Court Files**, Deposition of Elijah Ward, No. 138379.
17. Interview with Harold Emery, 1971.
18. Interview with Ralph Weston, 1969.
19. **Register of Deeds**, (Alfred), Vol. 120:75.
20. **Narragansett Sun**, January 21, 1909.
21. **Ibid.**
22. **Eastern Argus**, (Portland), June 1901.
23. **Maine Democrat**, (Saco), Sept. 5, 1843.
24. Fannie M. Hilton, **The Mulloy Family**, (South Berwick, Me.: Chronicle Print Shop, 1969), p. 8-9.
25. Interview with George Haley, as told by his grandmother, Mrs. Hannah Foss Cluff, 1969.
26. Interview with Lena Cobb McKenney, 1971.
27. Interview with Harry Boothby, 1972.

CHAPTER IV
EARLY SETTLERS

1. **Kennebunk Gazette**, (Kennebunk), January 14, 1832.
2. **Ossipee Valley News**, (Limerick), February 10, 1883.
3. **Suffolk County Court Files**, Deposition of Philemon Libby, No. 138379.
4. **Ibid.**, Deposition of Daniel Meserve, No. 138379.
5. Walter Goodwin Davis, **The Ancestry of Nicholas Davis of Limington, Maine**, (Portland: The Anthoensen Press, 1956), p. 30.
6. **Suffolk County Court Files**, Deposition of Amos Chase, No. 138378.

7. **Register of Deeds,** (Alfred), Vol. 51:65.
8. Underhill, **Descendants of Edward Small,** p. 1600.
9. **Suffolk County Court Files,** Deposition of Amos Chase, No. 138378.
10. **Morning Star,** (Dover, N.H.), May 4, 1836.
11. Letter from Joseph Davis to Arthur McArthur, April 23, 1868.
12. Davis, **Ancestry of Nicholas Davis,** p. 31.
13. Ibid.
14. Ibid.
15. **Suffolk County Court Files,** Deposition of John Davis, No. 137848.
16. Davis, **Ancestry of Nicholas Davis,** p. 31.
17. John C. Chase, George W. Chamberlain, **Seven Generations of Descendants of Aquila and Thomas Chase,** (Derry, N.H.: Record Publishing Company, 1928), p. 95.
18. Interview with George Chase, 1970.
19. **Manual of Limington Congregational Church,** (Portland: Southworth Press, 1893), p 9.
20. **Suffolk County Court Files,** Deposition of Elijah Ward, No. 138094.
21. **The Records of the Church of Christ in Buxton, Me.,** (Cambridge, Mass.: Press of John Wilson and Son, 1868), p. 22.
22. **Maine Recorder,** (Limington), June 1, 1832.
23. **Suffolk County Court Files,** Deposition of Amos Chase, No. 138379.
24. Ibid.
25. **Suffolk County Court Files,** Small Proprietors vs. Joshua Sawyer, No. 138379.
26. **Family Record,** owned by Mrs. Edmund Sawyer.
27. **Suffolk County Court Files,** Deposition of Samuel Berry, No. 137848.
28. Ibid., Deposition of Elijah Ward, No. 138379.
29. **Bible Record,** owned by Russell Boothby.
30. Arthur McArthur's note, paper at Davis Library, Limington.
31. Charles T. Libby, **The Libby Family in America 1602-1881.** (Portland: B. Thurston and Co., 1882), p. 356.
32. Gideon T. Ridlon, **Saco Valley Settlements and Families,** (Portland: Lakeside Press, 1895), p. 134.
33. Ibid.
34. Underhill, **Descendants of Edward Small of New England,** p. 160.
35. Ibid., p. 159.
36. **Eastern Argus,** clipping by Lauriston W. Small, no date.
37. Letter from Lauriston W. Small to Charles Thorton Libby, January 1, 1891.
38. **Suffolk County Court Files,** Deposition of Amos Chase, No. 138379.
39. **Register of Deeds,** (Alfred), Vol. 56:122.
40. **Men of Progress: Biographical Sketches and Portraits of Leaders in Business and Professional Life in State of Maine,** New England Magazine, 1897, p. 339-40.
41. **Register of Deeds,** (Alfred), Vol. 108:55.
42. **Manual of Limington Congregational Church,** (Portland: Southworth Press, 1893), p. 22.
43. **Suffolk County Court Files,** Deposition of Samuel Berry, No. 137848.
44. Letter from Benjamin C. Libby to Arthur McArthur, 1868.
45. Davis, **Ancestry of Nicholas Davis,** p. 92.
46. **Suffolk County Court Files,** Deposition of Philemon Libby, No. 137848.
47. Ibid., Deposition of Philemon Libby, No. 137779.
48. Ibid., Deposition of Bartholomew Jackson and Jesse Libby, No. 137576.
49. **Register of Deeds,** (Alfred), Vol. 62:154.
50. Underhill, **Descendants of Edward Small of New England,** p. 47.
51. Ibid., p. 49.
52. **Register of Deeds,** (Alfred), Vol. 44:7.
53. Underhill, **Descendants of Edward Small of New England,** p. 50-51.
54. Ibid., p. 51-52
55. **Register of Deeds,** (Portland), Vol. 59:153.
56. **Paper Against Limington's Incorporation,** (Mass. Archives), May 20, 1791.
57. Letter of Lauriston W. Small to Charles Thorton Libby, July 29, 1890.

CHAPTER V
EARLY DAYS

1. **Paper Against Limington's Incorporation,** (Mass. Archives), May 20, 1791.
2. Ibid.
3. Interview with Mrs. Clarence Wentworth, 1967.
4. Interview with Ruth Meserve, 1972.
5. **Oxford County Record,** (Kezar Falls), November 21, 1885.
6. Interview with Clifton Tufts, Alfred, 1967.
7. **The Weekly Visitor,** (Kennebunk), Feb. 6, 1819.
8. **Oxford County Record,** October 3, 1885.

9. **Ibid.**
10. Lauriston W. Small, **Collection and Proceedings of Maine Historical Society,** The Small Family in America, (Portland; Brown Thurston Co., 1892) Second Series, Vol. IV.
11. **Limington Evaluation Poll and Estates,** Nov. 1792.
12. **Ossipee Valley News,** (Limerick), Sept. 2, 1882.
13. **Oxford County Record,** (Kezar Falls), October 3, 1885.
14. **Ibid.**
15. **Paper Against Limington's Incorporation,** (Mass. Archives), May 20, 1791.
16. **Oxford County Record,** (Kezar Falls), April 24, 1886.
17. Underhill, **Descendants of Edward Small,** p. 1559.
18. Letter written by Altine Underhill to Mrs. Francis N. Peloubet, September 1911.
19. Interview with Harry Thorne, 1968.
20. **Ossipee Valley News,** (Limerick), September 23, 1882.
21. **Ibid.**
22. **Portland Express and Advisor** (Portland) Mar. 14, 1914
23. **Deering News,** (Portland), March 4, 1899.
24. **Ossipee Valley News,** September 30, 1882.
25. Interview with Mrs. Ruth Brackett McGrath, 1968.
26. Letter of Stephen M. Watson to Charles T. Libby, 1915.
27. Interview with George Haley, 1968.
28. **Lewiston Journal,** November 4, 1911.
29. **Oxford County Record,** (Kezar Falls) May 8, 1886.
30. **Lewiston Journal,** November 4, 1911.
31. **Maine Recorder,** (Limington), August 24, 1832.
32. **Portland Advertiser,** (Portland), December 29, 1829.
33. **Lewiston Journal,** November 4, 1911.
34. **Ibid.**
35. **Oxford County Record,** (Kezar Falls), April 16, 1887.
36. **Ibid.**
37. **Ibid.**
38. **Ibid.**
39. **Biddeford Journal,** (Biddeford), March 26, 1885.
40. **Ibid.,** June 3, 1887.
41. **Ibid.,** October 23, 1891.
42. **Lewiston Journal,** March 9, 1912.
43. **Ibid.**
44. **Ibid.**

CHAPTER VI
CHURCHES

1. **Morning Star,** (Dover, N.H.), March 24, 1847.
2. **Free-Will Baptist Church Records,** Vol. I, March 4, 1814.
3. **Ibid.,** April 7, 1814.
4. **Ibid.,** June 2, 1814.
5. U.S. Bureau of Census, **First Census of U.S., 1790 Head of Families for Province of Maine.**
6. Calvin M. Clark, **The Congregational Churches in Maine,** (Portland: Southworth Press, 1935) Vol. II, p. 248.
7. **Manual of Limington Congregational Church,** (Portland, Southworth Brothers, 1893), p. 22.
8. **Christian Mirror,** (Portland), Sept. 10, 1887.
9. **Ibid.**
10. **Probate Records,** (Alfred), Vol. 16:224.
11. **Manual of Limington Congregational Church,** p. 10.
12. **Ibid.**
13. Notes copied from the Atkinson's Bible, owned by Mrs. Frederick Baker.
14. **Congregational Records of Limington,** Vol. I.
15. **Deaths Kept by Francis Meeds of South Limington,** Manuscript.
16. **Maine Recorder,** (Limington), October 9, 1835.
17. **Maine Democrat,** (Saco), Sept. 5, 1843.
18. Ethel Maxim, **History of Congregational Church of Limington,** (Typewritten, September, 1952.)
19. Charles O. Gates, **Stephen Gates of Hingham and Lancaster, Mass. and his Descendants,** (New York: Willis McDonald and Company, 1898), p. 221-222.
20. **Biddeford Weekly Standard,** (Biddeford), October 23, 1889.
21. **Morning Star,** (Dover, N.H.), April 3, 1844.
22. **Ibid.**

23. **Maine Democrat,** (Saco), August 26, 1846.
24. John Buzzell, **Life of Elder Benjamin Randall,** (Limerick, Maine, Hobbs, Woodman & Co., 1827), p. 213.
25. Rev. Isaac Steward, **The History of Freewill Baptist for Half a Century,** (Dover, N.H.: Freewill Baptist Printing Establishment, 1862), p. 133.
26. **Limington Town Clerk's Record,** Vol. I.
27. **Morning Star,** March 24, 1847.
28. **Ibid.,** August 7, 1844.
29. Churches of Saco Valley and Vicinity, **Yearbook and Church Directory,** 1932-33, p. 25.
30. **Morning Star,** Mar. 24, 1847.
31. **Ibid.**
32. **Ibid.**
33. **Ibid.,** Nov. 5, 1845.
34. John Stevens, **Memoir of Life and Character of Rev. John Stevens,** (Dover, N.H.: Morning Star Job Printing House, 1878), p. 22.
35. **Morning Star,** April 14, 1835.
36. Rev. G.A. Burgess, Rev. J.T. Ward, **Free Baptist Cyclopaedia,** (Boston: Free Baptist Cyclopaedia Co., 1889).
37. **Morning Star,** March 24, 1847.
38. **Ibid.**
39. **Ibid.**
40. **Clerk Records of Adoniram Lodge, A.F. & A.M.**
41. Stevens, **Memoir of Rev. John Stevens,** p. 38, 40.
42. **Morning Star,** March 24, 1847.
43. **Clerk Records of Second Free-Will Baptist Church,** North Limington.
44. W.W. Clayton, **History of York County Maine,** (Philadelphia: Everts and Pecks, 1880), p. 405.
45. **Ibid.,** p. 404.
46. **Morning Star,** December 5, 1833.
47. **Ibid.,** April 14, 1835.
48. **Ibid.**
49. **Ibid.**
50. **Ibid.,** August 21, 1836.
51. **Ibid.**
52. **Ibid.,** Mar. 24, 1847.
53. **Ibid.**
54. **Ibid.**
55. **Maine Free-Will Baptist Repository,** (Limerick), March 9, 1850.
56. **Ibid.**
57. **Morning Star,** March 24, 1847.
58. **Ibid.,** Dec. 22, 1880.
59. **Ibid.,** Apr. 1851.
60. **Clerk Records Book of First Free Baptist Church,** South Limington.
61. **Maine Free-Will Repository,** March 9, 1850.
62. **Ibid.**
63. **Morning Star,** December 26, 1849.
64. **Maine Free-Will Repository,** March 9, 1850.
65. **Diary of Dennis Marr,** North Limington.
66. **Maine Free-Will Repository,** March 9, 1850.
67. **Maine Democrat,** Jan. 8, 1850.
68. **Biddeford Union & Journal,** June 10, 1859.
69. **Gorham Scrapbook,** Maine Historical Society.
70. **Ibid.**
71. Interview of Ada (Weeman) Manson, Waterboro, 1967.
72. **Maine Democrat,** Feb. 7, 1854.
73. Interview of Ina Emery, Kezar Falls, 1970.
74. **Biddeford Journal,** May 2, 1884.
75. **Maine Democrat,** Feb. 7, 1854.
76. Interview with Joseph A. Swett, (Saco), 1967.
77. **Ibid.**
78. **Lewiston Journal,** July 18, 1908.
79. **Ibid.**
80. **Biddeford Journal,** May 2, 1884.
81. **Maine Democrat,** Jan. 8, 1850.
82. **Biddeford Union & Journal,** Apr. 12, 1878.
83. Rev. G.A. Burgess, and Rev. J.T. Ward, **Free Baptist Cyclopaedia,** (Boston: Free Baptist Cyclopaedia Co., 1889), p. 382.
84. **Ibid.,** p. 618.

85. Ibid., p. 49-50.
86. Rev. Joshua Millett, **A History of Baptist in Maine**, (Portland: Charles Day and Co., 1845), p. 51.
87. Ibid., p. 52.
88. Ibid.
89. **Minutes of Twentieth Anniversary of Saco River Baptist Association, held at Biddeford, Sept., 1861**, (Biddeford: Union & Journal Office, 1861), p. 14.
90. Ibid., p. 15.
91. Ibid.
92. Ibid., p. 16.
93. Ibid.
94. Ibid.
95. Ibid.
96. **Oxford Democrat**, (Paris), Jan. 18, 1867.
97. **Lewiston Journal**, June 8, 1871.
98. **Maine Democrat**, Sept. 25, 1873.
99. **Ossipee Valley News**, (Limerick), Jan. 27, 1883.
100. Clayton, **History of York County, Maine**, p. 405.
101. Ibid.

CHAPTER VII
EDUCATION

1. Rev. Urial W. Small, **Small Family Notes**, Manuscript, Maine Historical Society.
2. **Eastern Argus**, (Portland), Feb. 17, 1903.
3. **Limington Town Clerk's Records.**, Vol. I, p. 17.
4. **Limington Town Clerk's Record**, Vol. I, Apr. 1800.
5. **National Republican**, (Biddeford), Aug. 14, 1833.
6. **Hamblen School**, by Mary Susan Hill, Newspaper Clipping, 1898.
7. Ibid.
8. **Lewiston Journal**, Jan. 25, 1912.
9. **Biddeford Journal**, (Biddeford), Feb. 8, 1884.
10. **Biddeford Journal**, June 15, 1883, Apr. 27, 1883.
11. Abstract Returns of Common Schools in Maine, 1840.
12. **Limington Town Clerk's Records**, Apr. 1847.
13. **Lewiston Journal**, Sept. 1, 1923.
14. **Cornish Maxima**, (Cornish), Feb. 21, 1880.
15. **Annual Report of the Town of Limington for the Fiscal Year, 1894**, (Portland: Southworth Bros.), p. 24.
16. **Eastern Argus**, Aug., 1910.
17. Arthur McArthur, Secretary, Original Record of the first meeting.
18. **Limington Academy Trustee Records**, Vol. I, p. 34.
19. Original Report made by the "Building Committee".
20. **Limington Academy Trustee Records**, p. 17.
21. **Limington Academy Catalogue**, (Portland: Thurston Printing Company, 1851), p. 14.
22. **Limington Academy Catalogue 1890-1900**, (Portland: Thurston Printing Company, 1901).
23. **Biddeford Union & Journal**, Oct. 25, 1861.
24. Ibid.
25. Ibid.
26. **Morning Star**, (Dover, N.H.), Aug. 30, 1854.
27. Ibid., Feb. 13, 1856.

CHAPTER VIII
MILLS

1. Austin J. Coolidge, J.B. Mansfield, **A History and Description of New England, General and Local**, (Boston: Austin J. Coolidge, 1859), p. 192.
2. W.W.Clayton, **History of York County, Maine**
3. Ibid.
4. **Water Wells, The Water Power of Maine**, (Augusta: Sprague, Owen, and Nash, 1869), p. 337-338.
5. **Maine Recorder**, (Limington), Deptember 27, 1833.
6. Ibid.
7. **Suffolk County Court Files**, Deposition of Amos Chase, No. 138378
8. **Eastern Argus**, (Portland), April 30, 1816
9. **Register of Deeds**, (Alfred), Vol. 184:61
10. **Register of Deeds**, (Alfred), Vol. 306:215
11. **Agreement Paper**, Document owned by George Chase
12. **Register of Deeds**, (Alfred), Vol. 240:231-32, 305:312, 305:372, 306:219

13. **Register of Deeds,** (Alfred), Vol. 379:261
14. **Register of Deeds,** (Alfred), Vol. 358:10
15. **Register of Deeds,** (Alfred), Vol. 82:160
16. **Register of Deeds,** (Alfred), Vol 82:181
17. **Register of Deeds,** (Alfred), Vol. 93:6
18. **Register of Deeds,** (Alfred), Vol. 61:31
19. **Register of Deeds,** (Alfred), Vol. 62:184
20. **Eastern Argus,** (Portland), October 2, 1806
21. **Register of Deeds,** (Alfred), Vol. 82:99
22. **Weekly Visitor,** (Kennebunk), March 11, 1815
23. **Register of Deeds,** (Alfred), Vol. 79:43
24. **Ibid.**
25. **Eastern Argus,** (Portland), Aug. 14, 1806
26. **Register of Deeds,** (Alfred), Vol. 100:108
27. **Register of Deeds,** (Alfred), Vol. 128:251,252
28. **Register of Deeds,** (Alfred), Vol. 139:265
29. **Register of Deeds,** (Alfred), Vol. 70:151
30. **Register of Deeds,** (Alfred), Vol. 82:100
31. **Register of Deeds,** (Alfred), Vol. 100:108
32. **Register of Deeds,** (Alfred), Vol. 118:70
33. **Portland Evening Express,** (Portland), Sept. 12, 1910
34. **Biddeford Journal,** (Biddeford), May 13, 1892
35. **Register of Deeds,** (Alfred), Vol. 56:122,222
36. **Register of Deeds,** (Alfred), Vol 62:213
37. **Register of Deeds,** (Alfred), Vol. 80:148,149,150
38. **Register of Deeds,** (Alfred), Vol. 107:117
39. Register of Deeds, (Alfred), Vol. 117:227
40. **Register of Deeds,** (Alfred), Vol. 117:226
41. **Register of Deeds,** (Alfred), Vol. 117:226
42. **Register of Deeds,** (Alfred), Vol. 117:206
43. **Register of Deeds,** (Alfred), Vol. 121:260
44. **Register of Deeds,** (Alfred), Vol. 236:286
45. **Register of Deeds,** (Alfred), Vol. 117:227
46. **Register of Deeds,** (Alfred), Vol. 128:113
47. **Register of Deeds,** (Alfred), Vol. 121:70
48. **Register of Deeds,** (Alfred), Vol. 282:404
49. **Limington Evaluation Book,** 1840
50. **Register of Deeds,** (Alfred), Vol. 282:412, 290:487
51. **Register of Deeds,** (Alfred), Vol. 372:18
52. **Register of Deeds,** (Alfred), Vol. 61:153
53. **Register of Deeds,** (Alfred), Vol. 63:102
54. **Register of Deeds,** (Alfred), Vol. 98:112
55. **Register of Deeds,** (Alfred), Vol. 84:230
56. **Register of Deeds,** (Alfred), Vol. 156:276, 158:155
57. **Register of Deeds,** (Alfred), Vol. 229:263
58. **Register of Deeds,** (Alfred), Vol. 159:207
59. **Probate Record,** (Alfred), No. 17195
60. **Register of Deeds,** (Alfred), Vol. 318:568
61. **Register of Deeds,** (Alfred), Vol. 206:341
62. **Register of Deeds,** (Alfred), Vol. 271:218
63. **Register of Deeds,** (Alfred), Vol. 275:504
64. **Register of Deeds,** (Alfred), Vol. 291:184
65. **Register of Deeds,** (Alfred), Vol. 332:403
66. **Register of Deeds,** (Alfred), Vol. 353:451
67. **Register of Deeds,** (Alfred), Vol. 353:452
68. **Register of Deeds,** (Alfred), Vol. 353:450
69. **Biddeford Journal,** (Biddeford), Sept. 22, 1882
70. **Biddeford Journal,** (Biddeford), Feb. 2, 1884
71. **Biddeford Journal,** (Biddeford), April 10, 1885
72. **Union and Journal,** (Biddeford), May 21, 1869
73. **Biddeford Journal,** (Biddeford), May 19, 1892
74. Interview with Miss Annie Stone, 1968
75. Ridlon, **Saco Valley Settlements and Families** p. 860
76. **Ibid,** p. 480
77. **Register of Deeds,** (Alfred), Vol. 134:71
78. **Maine Recorder,** (Limington), Dec. 13, 1833
79. **Register of Deeds,** (Alfred), Vol. 165:198
80. **Lewiston Evening Journal,** (Lewiston), Aug. 19, 1876

81. **Register of Deeds**, (Alfred), Vol. 197:553
82. **Men of Progress: Biographical Sketches & Portraits of Leaders in Business & Prof. Life in State of Maine**, New England Magazine, 1897
83. **Biddeford Daily Standard**, (Biddeford), Feb. 16, 1894
84. Alden Bradford, **Biographical Notices of Distinguished Men of New England**, (Boston J.G. Torrey 1842) p. 454
85. **Register of Deeds**, (Alfred), Vol. 51:79
86. **Register of Deeds**, (Alfred), Vol. 65:101
87. **Register of Deeds**, (Alfred), Vol. 195:241
88. **Register of Deeds**, (Alfred), Vol. 99:27
89. **Register of Deeds**, (Alfred), Vol. 143:12
90. **Register of Deeds**, (Alfred), Vol. 143:12, 147:160
91. **Register of Deeds**, (Alfred), Vol. 147:160
92. **Register of Deeds**, (Alfred), Vol. 158:101
93. **Register of Deeds**, (Alfred), Vol. 197:44
94. **Register of Deeds**, (Alfred), Vol. 197:46
95. **Register of Deeds**, (Alfred), Vol. 260:319
96. **Register of Deeds**, (Alfred), Vol. 279:186, 261:325
97. **Register of Deeds**, (Alfred), Vol. 283:134
98. **Register of Deeds**, (Alfred), Vol. 305:512
99. **Lewiston Journal**, (Lewiston), March 2, 1871
100. Blanche Clough, **Grandma Spins Down-East-Yarns**, (Portland:Fred L. Tower Co., 19537) p. 155-56.
101. **Register of Deeds**, (Alfred) Vol. 224:437
102. **U.S. Census Report**, 1870
103. Interview with Mrs. Ethel Boothby Colby, 1970
104. **Limington Evaluation Book**, 1808
105. **Register of Deeds**, (Alfred), Vol. 144:25
106. **Maine Standard**, (Biddeford), Nov. 8, 1866
107. **Register of Deeds**, (Alfred), Vol. 144:25
108. **Register of Deeds**, (Alfred), Vol. 144:299
109. **Register of Deeds**, (Alfred), Vol. 237:318
110. **Register of Deeds**, (Alfred), Vol. 167:63
111. **Maine Free-Will Baptist Repository**, (Limerick), Feb. 20, 1847
112. **Register of Deeds**, (Alfred), Vol. 167:63
113. **Register of Deeds**, (Alfred), Vol. 222:34
114. **Register of Deeds**, (Alfred), Vol. 222:281
115. **Register of Deeds**, (Alfred), Vol. 242:291
116. **Register of Deeds**, (Alfred), Vol. 237:320
117. **Register of Deeds**, (Alfred), Vol. 237:497
118. **Register of Deeds**, (Alfred), Vol. 242:291
119. **Register of Deeds**, (Alfred), Vol. 340:35
120. **Register of Deeds**, (Alfred), Vol. 340:38
121. **Register of Deeds**, (Alfred), Vol. 352:109
122. Notes of Emma Bailey, 1935.
123. **Lewiston Journal**, (Lewiston), Oct. 24, 1878
124. Interview with William Meserve, 1969
125. Notes of Arthur McArthur, Davis Library Limington
126. **Suffolk County Court Files**, Deposition of Amos Chase No. 138379
127. **Hollis Evaluation Poll and estates**, Oct. 1792
128. **Direct Tax of Mass.** Oct. 1798
129. **Register of Deeds**, (Alfred), Vol. 84:106
130. **Register of Deeds**, (Alfred), Vol. 150:15
131. **Maine Recorder**, (Limington), Aug. 16, 1833
132. **Register of Deeds**, (Alfred), Vol. 173:234
133. **Register of Deeds**, (Alfred), Vol. 190:70
134. **Register of Deeds**, (Alfred), Vol. 240:373
135. **Register of Deeds**, (Alfred), Vol. 252:180
136. **Register of Deeds**, (Alfred), Vol. 290:190
137. **Register of Deeds**, (Alfred), Vol. 215:343
138. **Register of Deeds**, (Alfred), Vol. 289:48, 298:219
139. **Register of Deeds**, (Alfred), Vol. 305:177
140. **Register of Deeds**, (Alfred), Vol. 341:370
141. Letter from Jesse Bradeen, Feb. 1967
142. **Register of Deeds**, (Alfred), Vol. 398:516
143. **Register of Deeds**, (Alfred), Vol. 74:177
144. **Register of Deeds**, (Alfred), Vol. 186:32
145. **Register of Deeds**, (Alfred), Vol. 220:185

146. **Register of Deeds,** (Alfred), Vol. 213:126
147. **Register of Deeds,** (Alfred), Vol. 242:449
148. **Register of Deeds,** (Alfred), Vol. 261:295
149. **Register of Deeds,** (Alfred), Vol. 332:310
150. **Register of Deeds,** (Alfred), Vol. 109:229
151. **Register of Deeds,** (Alfred), Vol. 121:187
152. **Register of Deeds,** (Alfred), Vol. 162:255, 170:223
153. **Register of Deeds,** (Alfred), Vol. 294:150
154. **Register of Deeds,** (Alfred), Vol. 351:182
155. **Register of Deeds,** (Alfred), Vol. 266:248
156. **Collection and Proceedings of Maine Historical Society** (Portland: Brown Thurston Company, 1893), Vol. IV., p. 379-81.
157. **Register of Deeds,** (Alfred), Vol. 63:163
158. **Register of Deeds,** (Alfred), Vol. 150:272
159. **Register of Deeds,** (Alfred), Vol. 99:197
160. **Register of Deeds,** (Alfred), Vol. 178:742
161. **Register of Deeds,** (Alfred), Vol. 96:68
162. **Clerk Records of Adoniram Lodge, A.F. & A.M.**
163. **Register of Deeds,** (Alfred), Vol. 62:96
164. **Register of Deeds,** (Alfred), Vol. 65:207
165. **Register of Deeds,** (Alfred), Vol. 251:107
166. **Register of Deeds,** (Alfred), Vol. 251:107, 279:263
167. Interview with Harland Richardson, (1969)
168. **Register of Deeds,** (Alfred), Vol. 125:94
169. **Maine Recorder,** (Limington), Oct. 18, 1833
170. **U.S. Census Report,** 1860
171. **U.S. Census Report,** 1870.
172. **York County Independent,** Apr. 12, 1870
173. **Register of Deeds,** (Alfred), Vol. 77:179
174. **Register of Deeds,** (Alfred), Vol. 68:95, 73:133
175. **Register of Deeds,** (Alfred), Vol. 78:60
176. **Register of Deeds,** (Alfred), Vol. 200:367
177. **Register of Deeds,** (Alfred), Vol. 259:475
178. **Register of Deeds,** (Alfred), Vol. 351:293
179. **Register of Deeds,** (Alfred), Vol. 390:45
180. **Portland Evening Express and Advertiser,** (Portland), Feb. 2-20, 1912
181. **Register of Deeds,** (Alfred), Vol. 48:95
182. **Register of Deeds,** (Alfred), Vol. 77:182
183. **Register of Deeds,** (Alfred), Vol. 73:30
184. **Diary of Catherine McArthur,** May 28, 1851
185. **Portland Evening Express and Advertiser,** (Portland), Feb. 20, 1912
186. **Biddeford Journal,** (Biddeford), June 2, 1882
187. **Oxford County Record,** (Kezar Falls), Nov. 20, 1886
188. **Oxford County Record,** (Kezar Falls), Nov. 13, 1886

CHAPTER IX
PROMINENT CITIZENS

1. **Portland Transcript,** (Portland), Jan. 24, 1900.
2. George T. Little. **Genealogical and Family History of State of Maine,** (New York Publishing Co., 1909), Vol. p. 308.
3. **Portland Sunday Telegram,** (Portland), Sept. 29, 1929.
4. W.W. Clayton, **History of York County,** p. 403.
5. **York County Independent,** (Biddeford), May 30, 1871.
6. **Morning Star,** (Dover, N.H.), Dec. 26, 1855
7. **Ibid.**
8. **Oak Hill Cemetery,** Auburn: Stone Inscription.
9. **Weekly Standard,** (Biddeford), April, 1892.
10. **Lewiston Journal,** (Lewiston), Jan. 10, 1912.
11. **Ibid.**
12. W.W. Clayton, **History of York County,** p. 403.
13. **Portland Press Herald,** (Portland), July 28, 1953.
14. **Boston Herald,** (Boston), Jan. 30, 1917.
15. **Portland Press Herald,** (Portland), Sept. 2, 1921.
16. George F. Plummer, **History of Town of Wentworth, N.H.,** (Concord, N.H.: Rumford Press, 1930), p. 210.
17. Harry H. Cochrane, **History of Monmouth and Wales,** (East Winthrop: Banner Co. 1894), p. 40.

18. **Harper Monthly Magazine,** — March 1888.
19. Rev. James Fetts, **History of Newfields, N.H.,** (Concord, N.H.: Rumford Press, 1912) p. 662.
20. **Register of Deeds,** (Alfred), Vol. 85:181.
21. Andrew N. Adams, **Genealogical History** of Robert Adams of Newbury, (Rutland, Vt.: The Tuttle Co., printers, 1900), p. 82.
22. **Christian Mirror,** (Portland), Dec. 3, 1824.
23. **Maine Recorder,** (Limington), June 20, 1834.
24. **Union and Journal,** (Biddeford), April 5, 1861.
25. Frederick C. Pierce, **The Descendants** of John Whitney, (Chicago, W.B. Conkey Company, 1895), p. 321.
26. **Maine Recorder,** (Limington), Oct. 10, 1834
27. Tristram F. Jordan, **Family Records of Rev. Robert Jordan, and his Descendants in America,** (Boston: Press of David Clapp and son, 1882), p. 357.
28. **Biddeford Journal,** (Biddeford) Sept. 23, 1888.
29. **Biddeford Journal,** (Biddeford) June 5, 1885.
30. George T. Little, **Genealogical and Family** History of State of Maine, (New York: Lewis Publishing Co., 1909), Vol. III, p. 1147.
31. **Biddeford Journal,** (Biddeford), Jan. 8, 1892.
32. **Biddeford Journal,** (Biddeford), Aug. 29, 1885.
33. **Biddeford Journal,** (Biddeford), Mar. 20, 1889.
34. **Biddeford Journal,** (Biddeford), Sept. 30, 1885.
35. **Bowdoin College Medical File,** Class of 1853.
36. C.C. Lord, **A History of Descendants of** Nathan Lord of Ancient Kittery, Maine, Concord, N.H., Rumford Press, 1912), p. 198-199.
37. **Ibid.**
38. **Portland Express and Advertiser,** (Portland), Apr. 21, 1911, **Biddeford Journal,** (Biddeford), Sept. 7, 1885.
39. **Oxford County Record,** (Kezar Falls), June 6, 1885.
40. **Maine Democrat,** (Saco), Sept. 30, 1829.
41. **Ibid.**
42. **Portland Advertiser,** (Portland), July 7, 1829.
43. **Ibid.**
44. **Lewiston Journal,** (Lewiston), June 8, 1871.
45. **Lewiston Journal,** (Lewiston), Oct. 1875.
46. **Biddeford Journal,** (Biddeford), Sept. 14, 1883.
47. **Maine Democrat,** (Saco), Feb. 2, 1889, **Weekly Standard,** (Biddeford), Feb. 5, 1890
48. **Portland Evening Express,** (Portland), Mar. 1, 1882.
49. **Ibid.**
50. **Portland Evening Express,** (Portland), Dec. 1, 1883.
51. **Francis Meeds' Daybooks,** (1816-1845), Maine Historical Society.
52. **Union and Journal,** (Saco), April 21, 1882.

CHAPTER X
MILITARY

1. **Maine Recorder,** (Limington), July 26, 1833.
2. George T. Little, **Genealogical and Family History of the State of Maine,** (New York; Lewis Historical Publishing Company, 1909), p. 85.
3. **Maine Recorder,** (Limington), Sept. 27, 1833.
4. **Oxford County Record,** (Kezar Falls), Nov. 24, 1883.
5. **Records of Massachusetts Volunteer Militia,** (Boston: Wright and Potter Printing Co. 1913), p. 155.
6. **Ibid.,** p. 270.
7. **Ibid.,** p. 312.
8. **Lewiston Journal,** (Lewiston), Dec. 6, 1925.
9. **Narragansett Sun,** (Gorham), Feb. 13, 1908.
10. **Oxford County Record,** (Kezar Falls), Oct. 11, 1884.
11. **Ibid.**
12. **Eastern Argus,** (Portland), Apr. 24, 1901
13. **Francis Meeds' Daybooks,** manuscript.
14. **Historical Sketch of Limington,** by Emma Marr Grace, 1936.
15. **Union and Journal,** (Biddeford), Nov. 12, 1880
16. **Ibid.**

LIMINGTON: THEN AND NOW

If a Limington Rip Van Winkle fell asleep at the "Corner" (Limington Village) in 1900, and awakened at the same spot today, he would still feel at home in familiar surroundings.

If he faced east down Waldron's Hill way, there at his right elbow he would see the same Town Hall he knew (built in 1871). A little further on would be the Congregational Church (1835). If he faced south, there to the left would be the same one-room schoolhouse (1835), and to the right the Limington Academy (1852). Turning westward, on the right he would notice the Masonic Building (1835), and a little beyond, the same McArthur Farm with its row of granite hitching posts.

These are village landmarks which haven't changed much in ninety years. But if our legendary Rip looked more closely, he could see some of the radical differences that have developed since he began his nap.

First, he might notice that the beautiful elm trees which lined the main entrances into the village are gone, and that the road he is standing on is hard and black instead of soft and brown. He has never seen those signs with numbers 11-117 before. And where are the horses, the wagons, the buggies, and the carryalls? He soon finds out as a speeding rubber-tired vehicle without any apparent means of locomotion, then another and another, scares away any of his lingering drowsiness.

These must be the "automobiles" he had heard rumors about as the new century began. And those big multi-wheeled vehicles which roar past him must be the new workhorses of farm and factory.

They certainly are, Rip. No other single thing has changed Limington so drastically, so completely; not only in its appearance, but in the way its people live and make a living. There are not many farms left, Rip; with their new-found mobility, not only fathers and sons but mothers and daughters go out of town to work in offices, stores, and shops for a daily or weekly paycheck. Even Grandma has left her kitchen to follow the crowd.

The constant heavy work that you remember--the digging, lifting, pulling, pushing, and sweating--has been simplified by the same fuel that propels the automobiles and trucks. The shovel, crowbar, crosscut saw, and hoe have been made obsolete by the backhoe, the chain saw, and the tractor. Trucks take away sand, gravel and lumber and bring in fuel, food, building materials, and every household necessity. Horses and oxen are now merely hobbies for show and recreation.

The second most important life-influencing change to occur in Limington during your nap was the coming of electricity: replacing the icebox with the refrigerator, the woodstove with the electric range; lighting up the buildings at night; and revolutionizing cooking, heating, and every household chore. When you went to sleep, Rip, there was hardly any leisure; now, with every home electrified, there is hardly any drudgery in everyday life.

The third most important change in twentieth-century Limington has been in the field of education. In 1900 there were several schools in town serving various neighborhoods, plus the Academy, which had recently assumed its role as Limington's high school. Today, there is only one school in town, and that is for the first six grades. It is named for Harold B. Emery, Jr., the only Limington soldier lost in World War II.

After the sixth grade, every girl and boy rides a school bus to a consolidated junior and senior high school in Standish known as Bonny Eagle. The scholars there are not only from Limington but from Buxton, Hollis, and Standish as well. The Portland Metropolitan Area has become their home town.

* * *

This, in a nutshell, is the story of Limington in the twentieth century: its evolution from an isolated farm community to an increasingly urbanized place. It has survived economic depressions; two world wars, as well as those in Korea and Vietnam; floods, fires, and many other hardships. But perhaps its greatest challenge yet, as it enters its third century, is to protect its environment; and to preserve, as much as possible, its country flavor.

Edward S. Lord, President
Limington Historical Society
1990

LIMINGTON IN PROFILE, 1900-1992

Population (U.S. decennial census)
Chronological List of Town Clerks
Alphabetical List of Selectmen, with Dates Served
Chronological List of Principals of Limington Academy
Some Noteworthy Events in Limington

LIMINGTON POPULATION, 1900-1990
(U.S. Census)

Year	Population
1900	1,001
1910	980
1920	803
1930	747
1940	864
1950	851
1960	839
1970	1,066
1980	2,203
1990	2,943e

LIMINGTON TOWN CLERKS
1900-1992

George Brackett	1901-04, 1906
Samuel N. Small	1905
Harry Maxim	1907-08
Guy Brackett	1909-11
William H. McKenney	1912-15, 1918-19
John H. Plaisted	1916
George D. Randall	1917
Harold B. Emery	1920
George A. Foss	1921-22
W. Freeman Smith	1923-24
Lawrence Clark	1925, 1927
Frost Pillsbury	1926
Edith Peters	1928-61
Phyllis Smith	1962-69
Elinor Edgecomb	1970-83
Marilyn Webb	1983--

LIMINGTON SELECTMEN
1900-1992

Anderson, Jerry H.	1906-07, 1909-10
Berry, G. Melville	1906-07
Blake, Leon	1940-41
Blake, Stanley	1964-66
Boothby, Bors	1983-
Boothby, Percy	1918
Boothby, Ray	1956-64
Brackett, Frank	1923-24
Brackett, George	1916-17
Brackett, Guy	1925-26
Chase, Charles N.	1904, 1915-17
Chase, George	1928-29
Chick, Edwin	1963-65
Chick, Edward L.	1901-05, 1919
Chick, Malcolm	1937-40
Cole, Guy	1913-14
Cole, James	1903-05
Cotton, Harry	1925-26
Durgin, Fred	
Durgin, Lindley	1941, 1965-67
Edgecomb, Howard	1942-49
Edgecomb, Kenneth	1955-63
Emery, Edwin	1953-55
Emery, Harold	1918
Estes, Ivory	1968-73
Foss, Frank	1981-82
French, Jerry	1911-12
Haley, George	1916-17
Haley, Stanley	1966-68
Hobson, Howard	1919, 1922-26
Holmes, Howard L.	1905
Holmes, Russell	1930-31, 1935-54

Selectmen (cont'd)

Hubbard, John	1977-80
Hubbard, Leroy S.	1913-14
Jones, Cecil	1973-78
Larrabee, James W.	1906-08
Lewis, Calvin	1974-76
Libby, Arthur	1935-36
Linnekin, Carroll	1952-53
Maxim, Harry	1907-08
McLucas, Ernest	1944-47
McKenney, A. Faulker	1915
McKenney, Fred	1932-36
McKinnon, William	1954-56
Meserve, William	1911-14
Pattee, Everett	1901
Pillsbury, Carleton	1979--
Pillsbury, Wingate	1928-31, 1949-51
Pulsifer, Reginald	1969--
Ramsdell, Herbert	1967-72
Randall, Fred	1918, 1920-21
Richardson, Wiley	1909-10
Robinson, Ansel C.	1903
Sawyer, Edmund	1932-33
Sawyer, Ralph	1942
Small, Charles	1908-09
Small, Joshua	1901-02
Small, Melville	1930-34
Smith, Harold	1934
Strout, Frank L.	1908
Thorne, Harry	1927
Webb, Raymond	1960-62
Weeman, Alvah	1920-22
Wentworth, Edgar	1915, 1920-27
Wood, Stephen	1902
Yennie, Richard	1950-52

PRINCIPALS OF LIMINGTON ACADEMY
1900-1990

Charles L. Orton	1899-1900
S. Everett Marks	1900-1901
Burton M. Clough	1901-1903
Walter H. Rusell	1903-1906
Willis F. Avery	1906-1916
Ralph G. Reed	1916-1918
Morton A. Campbell	1918-1919
William B. Smith	1919
Robert E. Brackett	1919-1920
John W. Hill	1920-1921
Lincoln J. Aikins	1921-1925
Ralph G. Reed	1925-1926
Clifton Hamm	1926-1928
Brainard C. Paul	1928-1944
Justin Johnson	1944
Earl W. Dolphin	1944-1946
Verner J. Wormlight	1946-1950
Arthur M. Griffiths	1950-1951
Roland M. Mayberry	1952-1954
Thomas L. Fairchild	1954-1956
F. Virgil Wood	1956-1958
John R. McCann	1958

SOME NOTEWORTHY EVENTS IN LIMINGTON
1900-1990

1907	Camp Moy-mo-day-o established on Randall place at South Limington
1910	Chapter of Eastern Star established at Limington
1911	Twenty-first Annual Small Family Reunion at "Dundee." Present about 125
1912	Schools named for New England authors
1912	Davis Memorial Library opens
1915	Old Quaker Meetinghouse on Quaker Lane was taken down
1917-18	World War I
1918	North Limington post office closed
1923	Academy "town" well drilled
1929	Covered bridge at East Limington replaced
1932	Naval observatory constructed for total solar eclipse
1938	East Limington post office closed
1938	First twentieth-century New England hurricane
1941-45	World War II
1943	Last Saco River log drive
1947	Destructive forest fires; Limington spared
1948	Sesquicentennial celebration
1950	Korean War
1951	Limington battlefield dedicated
1953	H.B. Emery Jr. Memorial School dedicated
1954	Academy dormitory destroyed by fire
1954	Hurricanes Carol and Edna
1955	Planning board organized
1958	Center Memorial Clinic opens
1959	South Limington Church destroyed by fire
1961-74	Bonny Eagle Jr-Sr high school complex developed
1964-69	Vietnam War
1967	Edgecomb Bridge on Little Ossipee River replaced
1972	Coventry North opens
1973	Limington Harmon Airport opens
1975	Historical Society organized
1978	Saco River new bridge/ Limington Rapids rest area opens
1983	First land use/building code/zoning ordinance adopted
1985	Last railroad freight service, Steep Falls; last passenger, 1958
1985	Camp Moy-mo-day-o property on Horne Pond purchased by the state
1988	Limington Plaza shopping center opens
1989	Locust Farm closes; cows discontinued 1963

1989   Locust Farm closes; cows discontinued 1963
1989   Congregational Church celebrates 200th anniversary
1989   First traffic light, at "Slab Street" - Routes 11/25

Errata

pge 5, line 19: covers
page 9, picture: built in 1896
page 18, line 15: between
page 30, line 37: Weeman
page 37, line 5: Small
page 44, line 4: omit "before"
page 45, line 29: Holmes
page 56, line 13: all
page 70, line 34: Ebenezer
page 97, line 18: Ezekiel
page 128, line 25: Meserve
page 129, 1820: 20 adults
page 129, 1825: 29 children

---- Watson 45
ABBOTT, Leonard 50 96
ADAMS, Clement J 117 Clement Jackson 121 Dr 122 Edward 117 John 52 Joshua 77 Mr 53 118 Mrs 122 Rev 53
ALLEN, Edwin 74 Fred J 56 Jedediah 74 Oliver 74 111 Oliver P 100 111
ANDERSON, Charles A 6 Jerry H 49 William 77 132
ANDREWS, John 77 131
ATKINSON, 81 John L 101 Jonathan 53 57 132 Rev 54
AVERY, John Jr 20 Willis F 154
BABB, John 128
BAKER, Arthur M 112
BANGS, Ebenezer B 125 Sylvanus 132
BANKS, Samuel 102
BASSETT, Ward 121
BEAN, 78 Charles 61 70 Daniel R 100 Elder 62 Mrs Cotton 125 Mrs Theophilus W 128 William 100
BENSON, 79
BERRY, Erastus 104 H O 11 Horace 9 Jake 9 James 77 G Melville 152 Richard 18 77 Samuel 18 23 31 33 34 77
BICKFORD, Lydia 121 Samuel T 108
BLACK, 81 Aaron 132 Edmund 95 Frank S 119 120 Frank Swett 119 Jacob 110 Jim 133 Joab 48 John 131 Josiah 77 128 131 Sewall S 95
BLAKE, 81 Benjamin 131 132 Howard M 96 Jennie 85 Leon 152 Sarah 85 Seth 131 132 Stanley 152

BOLDEN, John 93 131
BOODY, 81 133 Azariah 77 Harriet 110 Margery 58 Robert 20 58 74 77 131
BOOTHBY, 81 Alexander 125 Alice 86 Arthur 121 132 Asa 89 132 Bors 152 C Y 31 97 100 David 77 I 11 Harry 82 Israel 50 John 20 86 John D 89 97 John Moore 125 Jonathan 20 30 52 77 Maude 86 Mrs Thomas 31 Percy 152 Ray 152 Samuel 67 Samuel M 105 Thomas 31 97 Willard 26
BOYD, David 4 116
BOYNTON, Nathaniel 133
BRACKET, Blanche 85
BRACKETT, 81 108 Abraham 45 77 131 Elizabeth 123 Frank 152 Guy 151 152 James F 119 Joseph 131 132 Joshua 45 77 131 Manly 45 Mary 86 128 Reuben 77 Robert 84 Roy 86 Samuel 74 77 128 131 Susan 123
BRADBURY, 9 Dr 104 123 Elizabeth 123 Frank M 49 Samuel M 83 84 103 122 Samuel Moulton 122 Susan 123 Theophilas 99 Theophilus 18
BRADEEN, Henry 127 Jemima 127 M C 11 Melville 102
BRAGDON, 8 Arthur 131 132 Edmund 97 Elisha 77 Fred Augustus 125 H H 11 Hiram H 50 William 77 131
BRAGG, Samuel Jr 121
BRAINARD, C Paul 154
BRAY, Hazel 86
BROOKS, Avery 85

BRUNK, William 109
BUCK, James 60
BUCKNELL, Andrew R 47
BULLOCK, 81 Almira 65 66
 Christoper 59 Christopher 128
 Elder 61-63 65 66 Hannah 128
 Jeremiah 59-61 64-66 68 Mrs
 Jeremiah 60 Wescott 67 70
BURBANK, Samuel 62 101
BURNHAM, Joel 94 John 94 Levi
 72 Nicholas S 94 Perley 94
BUZZELL, 65 John 59
BYRNE, M 72
CASSIN, John 85
CASWELL, Clara 86 Ethel 86
CHADBORN, Humphrey 13
CHADBOURNE, Elder 71 John 70
 Mr 71
CHANEY, Reuben 99
CHAPLIN, Sidney 86
CHAPMAN, Edward 15
CHASE, 28 79 81 Abner 56 89 103
 Amos 18 20 27 30 31 33 43 44
 52 77 89-91 103 Amos H 90
 Amos Howard 89 Benjamin T
 93 Bessie 86 Charles 39
 Charles N 152 Daniel 90 91
 Deborah 90 George 91 152
 Hattie 86 Hooper 97 J C 11
 James 132 James M 89 James
 Madison 91 John 11 89 90 91
 John Elden 91 John F 49 89 90
 Josiah 90 91 Josiah E 6 89 95
 Josiah Jr 90 Lou 85 Moses 91
 132 Mrs Abner 44 Rufus 90
 Sumner Burnham 125 Uriah 64
CHICK, 92 Augustus S 49 Edward
 L 49 152 Edwin 152 Eliza 109
 James S 132 John 89 93 Lydia
 91 Malcolm 152 Nathan 15 16
 77 110 111 Nathan Jr 110 Peter
 79 89-91 Sarah 110 William 55
CHRISTIE, Isabel 85 Oliver 85
CLARK, 110 David Small 125
 Ebenezer 77 130 131 Ephraim
 77 109 128 130 131 Jacob 74
 131 Lawrence 151 Lewis 108
 109 Mary 117 118 Nathaniel
 117 132
CLIFFORD, George F 12

CLOUGH, Burton M 86 154 Levi
 47 Little Levi 47 48
COBB, Andrew 3 26 58 66 78
 David 20 Edenezer 70 Elisha
 103 J G 100 Joshua 74 Joshua
 G 100 Joshua R 50 Nathan 3 78
 Nicholas 74 Peter 15 16
COCHRAN, James 120 Jane 120
COFFIN, Edmund 15
COLBY, 65
COLE, Blanche 86 Christopher 99
 100 128 Christopher Jr 99 Guy
 152 Hannah 128 Isaac 93 94
 Ivory 99 James 152 Jim 99
 William 99
COLLOMY, Polly 128
COOK, Gideon 72
COOLEY, John F 67
COTTON, Carrie M 49 Harry 152
 William H 67
COUSINS, Abraham 131 132
 Lewis 85 Stephen H 102
CUMMING, Thomas 131
CUTLER, Charles Henry 96 Henry
 96 Mial 96 William 96
DAVID, William Goodwin 117
DAVIS, 81 Ezra 6 27-31 34 39 44
 49 77 100 104 Ezra 3rd 132
 Ezra Jr 28 James 103 Jeremi-
 ah 104 John 29 103 128 John L
 11 Joseph 104 105 Joseph Jr
 44 50 104 Mary 15 16 128 Mr
 118 Mrs Nicholas 29 Nicholas
 29 31 77 131 Robert 29 104 128
 Sarah 128 Walter G 29 Walter
 Sr 117 William G 117
DAY, 23
DEARBORN, Jacob 102
DELANO, Amaziah 131
DESHON, Noah 128
DIMMOCK, Charles E 49
DIMOCK, Charles 111 Helen 124
 Henry 120 Maria 112 Susan 120
 William 49 111
DIXON, Ed 82
DOLE, Loren 4
DOLPHIN, Earl W 154
DOUGLASS, Elisha 132 John 2 77
 131 132 John Jr 131 Leonard 3
DOW, Moses A 112 Oliver 103

DOW (continued) 104
DREW, Ira T 99
DROST, Jamie 86
DUNHAM, Ransom 72
DUNLAP, Henry 87
DUNNELLS, Martha 86
DURGIN, Fred 152 Lindley 152 Will 82
DURRELL, David 131
DYER, 47 Daniel 52 77 131 Isaac 45 77 131 Mr 48 Watson 128
EDGECOMB, 81 Elinor 151 Howard 152 Isaac E 104 John 132 Joseph 70 Kenneth 152 Nicholas 18 20 34 44 65 77 104 131 Nicholas Jr 103 Robert 110 William 77
EDGERLY, 5 Abigail 128 Richard 4 121 128 141
EDMONDS, Asa 20
EDMUNDS, Asa 52
ELLIOT, Zenus 97
ELLIS, John 77
ELWELL, Benjamin 103
EMERY, 62 81 Charles 135 Charles E 48 49 111 Edwin 152 Elder 61 Grover 86 Harold 86 152 Harold B 151 Harold B Jr 148 James 3 59 70 131
ESTES, Charles 40 S 11 Ivory 152
EVANS, Ben 44
EVELETH, John M 83
FAIRBANKS, Jonathan 36
FAIRCHILD, Thomas L 154
FELLOWS, John Albert 125
FERNALD, Pelatiah 36
FITCH, Fannie 85
FLANDERS, Abner 72
FOGG, Charles 77 131 Daniel 77 131 Frank 152 George 77 George A 151 Ivory 110 Joseph 77
FOSS, 74 81 Allen W 46 Alvin W 64 70 Anna 128 Elias 77 128 131 George 77 131 Isaiah 46 Jeremiah L 46 Job 77 John 26 45 46 77 131 Joseph 46 Joseph M 70 Mrs 26 Nahum 68 Randall 24 94 Susannah 46

FOSTER, Isaiah 27 Rosilla C 50 Thomas 120
FREEMAN, Frederic 57
FRENCH, Jerry 152
FROST, 81 Isaac 77 James 16 44 49 Joshua Wingate 14 Miss 111 Moses 77 Wingate 14 45 49 74 75 77 91 111
GARMAN, Charles Edward 55 John 83 John H 84 John Harper 55 57
GATES, C H 56 Charles H 56 Charles Henry 58
GILKEY, Betsey 128 Dennis 128 James 77 131 John 103 Reuben 39
GOODWIN, Amaziah 94 George K 57 George Kittredge 58 Martha 126 Samuel 126
GORGES, Ferdinando 12
GOULD, Ben 47
GOVE, John 131 Roland 85 Roland Sumner 125
GRAFFAM, Theodore 18
GRANT, Benjamin 132
GRAY, James A 22
GREENLAW, John 3 78 99 131 Leslie 37 Lizzie 85 Samuel 115 128
GREGG, William 53
GRIFFITHS, Arthur M 154
HAGEN, 81
HAGENS, Aaron 115 132 Fergus 114 Uncle Walter 114 115 Walter 77 114 115 131
HALEY, Benjamin 102 George 152 Stanley 152
HAMBLEN, 79 Gershom 5 35
HAMM, Clifton 154
HAMMOND, Christoper 15
HANCOCK, John 20
HANSCOM, Daniel 5 77
HARDY, Abel 103
HARMON, James 16
HASKELL, Hiram Brackett 125 Mr 79 William F 89
HASTY, Benjamin 132 David 77 131 Dominicus 132 Oliver S 64 68 Ralph 33 Robert 77 128 131
HAYDEN, Jeremiah 64

HAYES, Pearle 86
HEARD, John 132
HEATH, Daniel 101
HENRY, Patrick 79
HIBBARD, David S 56 David Sutherland 58
HIGGINS, Aaron 115 John 97 Walter 83 94 115
HIGGINSON, T W 121
HILL, James C 91
HOBSON, Andrew 63 Frank A 48 50 105 Howard 86 152 Jabez 101 102
HOGLE, Hollis 31
HOLMES, Howard L 152 Russell 152
HOPKINSON, Caleb 128 131 James M 87 118 James Monroe 118 John 99 132 Samuel 94 132
HOWE, Eben 47 Geo Wilson 68
HUBBARD, Allen 85 Augustus 72 Heard 131 John 95 153 John A 50 Leroy S 153 Silas 95 96
HURD, 42 Isaac 77 Isaac P 125
HURLIN, Charles 64
ILSLEY, Frank 85 135 Gilman L 134
INDIAN, Captain Sandy 12-14 21 27 36 Fluellen 21 Nick Sumbe 13 Squando 8 21 22 Wesumbe 13
INGALLS, Benjamin 127 Ruth 127
IRISH, Eben 46 47 Ebenezer 77 93 Obediah 77 William 131
JACKSON, Bartholomew 35 131 Eli 131 Robert 77
JACOBS, John 131
JENSON, Harold 44
JEWELL, Aunt Ruth 128 Enoch 127 Ruth 127
JOHNSON, 29 A H 56 Albion H 56 Albion Henry 57 Justin 154 William 77 131
JONES, Cecil 153 John Paul 109 Lemuel A 68 Paul 130
JORDAN, Cyrus 122 Larkin L 72
JOSSELYN, 22
JOY, James W 117 James Warren 117

KENNARD, Edward 16 77 131
KENNISON, John 76 Mrs 76
KIMBALL, 102 Ivory 54 57
LANE, 94 Isaac 94 John W 95
LARRABEE, Anna 82 Eben I 110 Ebenezer I 108 110 Isaac 77 James W 153 Joseph 104 Samuel 77 97 131 132 Samuel Jr 131
LEWIS, Calvin 153
LIBBY, 34 81 Aaron 35 77 128 Abner 2 19 47 77 109 112 115 Abner Jr 108 132 Arthur 153 Charles 111 Charles A 125 Cora 85 Daniel 132 Edward Norton 125 Elias 109 132 Gideon 131 Harvey 77 131 132 Isaac H 109 James 108 132 James Jr 132 Jesse 20 35 77 John 132 John Billy 2 Joseph 18 19 33 34 77 104 131 Levi Stone 91 Lewis 99 Lydia 91 Mrs Philemon 35 108 Parmenio 109 132 Philemon 27 35 77 108 Robert 77 131 Stella 125 Stephen 132 Stephen Meserve 125 William 132
LINNEKIN, Carroll 153
LINCOLN, Abe 134 Cotton 99 President 135
LITTLE, Edward 97
LITTLEFIELD, Edward 3
LOCKE, Jesse Frederic 122
LOMBARD, Calvin 131 Paul 3 78
LONGFELLOW, 97
LORD, 81 Benjamin Meads 15 16 Edward S 148 Fred Drake 125 George W 103 Helen 124 Inez 85 John 124 John F 70 John T 49 111 Mr 85 Thomas N 56 58 Tobias 101 William G 83-85 118 William Godding 118 Wm G 56
LUCAS, Hazel 54 57
LUMBARD, Luther 77
LYONS, Peggy 58
MADDOX, Daniel A 68
MANN, Edmond 102
MANNING, William 100
MANSON, 81 Albert G 87 B S 60

MANSON (continued)
63 Benjamin 42 45 60 Benjamin Small 69 George 33 Joseph 132 Mark 51 77 Melville Harrison 125 Miss 69 Mrs Benjamin Small 69 Samuel 128 William 45 51 77 131
MARCH, Benjamin 15 Elizabeth 15 Samuel 15 16 30 36 37
MARKS, S Everett 154
MARR, 81 Isaac 77 132 Issac 128 James 77 131 Mark 38 Mrs 128 Peletiah 77 William P 132
MARSHALL, Henry 99
MARSTON, Josiah 74 75 105 124 128 Sarah B 123
MATHER, Cotton 21
MAXIM, Belle 86 Harry 151 153 Truman 105 Truman F 50 68
MAYALL, Robert 91
MAYBERRY, Roland M 154
MAYO, Leroy S 94 Phillip 100
MCARTHUR, 35 Arthur 32 47 83 84 115 Charles S 87 James 32 44 50 87 108 112 122 John 31 44 77 104 Margaret 31 Mary 31 Mr 116 Mrs John 34 Peter 131 William 119 135 William Miltmore 118
MCCANN, John R 154
MCDONALD, John 110
MCKENNEY, 81 A Faulker 153 Dominicus 77 Emery 86 Eunice 128 Falker 82 86 Franklin 70 Fred 153 Hardy H 49 Humphrey 128 131 132 Humphrey Jr 131 132 Humphrey 77 James 77 131 John F 42 Joshua 40 128 Mary 128 Simon 131 Soloman 132 William H 151
MCKINNON, William 153
MCLELLAN, 79 Ebenezer 65
MCLUCAS, Ernest 153
MCPERKINS, John 87
MEADS, Asa 60
MEEDS, Artemas 132 Francis 128 Mary 128
MELICAB, 76
MERRIFIELD, Anna 128 Levi 5 44 45 82 Levi Jr 128

MERRIFIELD (continued)
Levi Sr 128
MERRILL, Bradbury B 102 Henry Ambrose 55 57 Isaac 94 William 61
MESERVE, 81 Abigail 128 Ava 86 Benjamin 38 C W 11 Charles W 100 David 132 Dr 124 Edwin W 100 Fred 85 George 2 77 Isaac G 100 Joseph 42 77 131 132 Nathaniel 77 131 Richard 84 Richard Hunnewell 123 Rufus 132 Sarah B 124 Silas 132 William 86 128 153
MILES, Ezra 49 Mae 86
MILLER, John 131 Mary 31 Thomas 77
MILLIKEN, Josiah 131 Nathaniel 15 16 Phineas 77 Susannah 46
MITCHELL, Daniel 77 Isaac 110 128 Isaac L 49 Kate 49 Martha 128 Mrs Isaac 110
MOODY, Benjamin S 68 Cyrus H 111 Daniel 125 132 Elizabeth 128 George 131 John H 42 Joseph 109 Leander 2 Moses 128 Simon 109 132 133
MOORE, Ada Small 14 David 104 Henry C 104 105 Jane 120
MORRILL, Thomas 18
MORRISON, Isaiah 131 Samuel 2
MORSE, Josiah 90 Mrs Josiah 90
MORTON, Ebenezer 77 128 Joseph 77 Sarah 128
MOULTON, A C 105 Alvin C 105 Arthur 85 Dr 112 Frank 85 George 11 105 John 86 John F 110 John Fairfield 124 Martha 124 Silas 64 67 87
MOUNTJOY, George 12
MULLOY, 26 Dennis 2 18 34 77 104 131 Edward 34 104 131 132 Ethel 86 Mrs Dennis 25 34 Thomas 131 132
NABOR, 76
NASON, Benjamin E 103 David 77 Edward 103 Isaac 15 16 James 96 Jemima 127 John 18 77 103 127 134 John Sr 77 Jonathan 77 Moses 103 Mrs 103 Nicholas 103 Samuel V 70 Simon 132

NASONS, John Jr 103
NORRIS, Jonathan 93
NORTON, Benjamin 18 131 Edward 128 Elston 77 Nathaniel 131
NOYES, Robert 57 Robert H 54
O'RION, John 131
OLD PHILIPS, 121
ORCUT, Molly 121
ORDWAY, Jonathan B 77
ORTON, Charles L 85 154 Mr 86
OSBORNE, Charles Frost 69
OSGOOD, Reuben D 56 Reuben Dodge 58
OTIS, David 49 111 131 132
PAGE, Caleb F 54 Caleb Fessenden 57
PAINE, Mr 54
PALMER, Fred A 68
PARKER, 8 Abraham 77 93 Kendall 132
PARKHURST, John F 95
PARSONS, John 56 57 Martha 124
PATTEE, Everett 153 Everett J 50
PEARSON, Samuel W 56 Samuel Wiggin 57
PERRY, T S 56
PETERS, Edith 151
PHILLIPS, Samuel 20
PILLSBURY, Alice 86 Carleton 153 Frost 86 151 William 74 Wingate 153
PITTS, Edgar Thomas 56 58 Lyman S 50
PLAISTED, Carrie Luella 125 John H 151 John Newton 125
PLUMMER, David 16 17
POLAND, Benjamin 93
PRATT, Henry B 112 Maria 112
PULSIFER, Reginald 153
PURINGTON, John 75 Stephen 74 131
QUINCY, Jacob 49 109 111
QUINN, Blanche 86
RACKLIFFE, Mr 53 Mrs 53 Sarah 77
RAMSDELL, Herbert 153
RAMSEY, Alexander 121
RAND, Isaac 103 James 61
RANDALL, 65 155 Benjamin 58

RANDALL (continued) Charles Lincoln 125 Edward B 42 Elder 58 Fred 153 George D 151 James 77 131 Jesse Andrew 125 Mrs Shadrack 58 Peggy 58 Shadrack 58
RANDELL, William 132
RANKINS, Andrew 131
REED, Ralph G 154
RICE, Frank 67
RICHARDSON, 81 109 David 32 77 128 Elisha 74 77 Isaac 132 James 132 James C 85 Marshall Lewis 41 Mrs Marshall Lewis 41 Ruhamah S 104 Susannah 128 Thaddeus 77 108 Thomas 132 Wiley 153
RIDLON, Carrie 85 Daniel 77 Elmer 86 John F 50 Thomas 103
ROBINSON, 102 Ansel C 153 George 128 132 Isaac 52 103 John 131 Thomas 132
ROSE, Joseph 77 131
ROUNDS, Charlotte 128 Daniel 128 Edith 86
ROWE, Ammi 128 Lazarus 125 126 131 Martha 126 Molly 125 Mrs Lazarus 126
RUMERY, Jonathan 103 Mrs Thomas 34 Thomas 34 77
RUSELL, Walter 154
RUSSELL, Martha 52
SABATTUS, 121
SANBORN, A F 102 Abner 99 100 Andrew F 102 Levi 102 Morrill 5 Rhoda 5
SAWYER, 79 Autien 2 Daniel 18 David 103 104 Ebenezer 77 131 Edmund 153 Isaac 11 94 James 70 John 93 John C 72 John Chadbourne 70 Joshua 18 30 31 35 36 77 Mary 52 Michael 132 Nathan 18 Nathaniel 31 35 36 77 93 128 131 Nathaniel Jr 110 Peter 36 Ralph 153 Samuel 20 77 94 131 Samuel Guy 125 Shuah 128 Stephen 70 William 2 18
SCHERMERHORN, Elizabeth G 94

SCRAMMAN, Col 130
SCRIBNER, 23
SEAVEY, Atkinson 102 Brother 72
  Elder 72 John 50 71 95 97 98
  99 Jno 11
SEWALL, 134
SHAPLEIGH, 15 18 Daniel 14
  Nicholas 14
SHEPARD, Thomas 58
SMALL, 81 A K P 56 Abbie 86
  Anna 15 Asa 97 Asahel 94
  Barzillai 94 Benjamin 15 16 19
  20 33 49 77 125 131 132 Carleton 104 Carrie Luella 125
  Charles 46 117 153 Charles
  Henry 111 Col 92 Cyrus 133
  134 Daniel 16 19 35 36 37 77
  131 David 122 132 Deacon
  Samuel 14 15 Ebenezer 132
  Edward 110 117 132 Elisha 36
  Elizabeth 15 Ephraim 132
  Erving 109 Evelyn 85 Ezekial
  97 Ezekiel 50 94 95 Fitz
  Elmer 125 Frances 13 Francis
  12 13 14 15 19 21 27 32 33 35
  36 37 52 127 132 Gen 117
  George 84 91 111 George M 49
  H 11 Hannah 76 Harold 86
  Henry 9 40 49 77 91 92 126 127
  131 132 133 Henry Audubon
  125 Henry C 79 Humphrey 127
  132 Irving 104 Isaac 44 77 94
  106 131 132 Isaac Jr 131 Israel
  94 97 Jacob 37 77 James 5 15
  30 36 37 76 77 94 97 131
  James M 94 Janet 86 Jeremiah
  36 John 77 110 128 John Jr 132
  John Megquire 125 John N 131
  Joseph 15 16 Joshua 14 15 16
  18 19 20 27 30 32 33 34 77 89
  105 106 131 132 153 Joshua Jr
  77 Kate 85 Lauriston Ward 14
  127 Lillian 85 Lillian H 92
  Marion 86 Mary 30 117 126 128
  Mary A 122 Mary G 122 Mary
  Susan 79 Melville 92 153
  Nathan 33 Nathaniel 32 Nathaniel C 89 132 Reuben 37 77
  Rufus 97 Samuel 14 15 16 18
  27 30 33 34 35 36 108 132
  Samuel Jr 15 16 32

SMALL (continued)
  Samuel N 50 96 151 Samuel Sr
  33 Scott 106 Timothy 36 37
  Uncle Isaac 106 107 William
  33 77 86 131 132
SMALLE, Francis 13
SMITH, 107 Charles Cogswell 86
  Daniel 37 Gamaliel E 112
  Greenlief 106 Harold 153 Ithiel
  36 John 47 John 2nd 132 Mary
  36 Mr 106 Phyllis 151 Thomas
  4 W Freeman 151
SNYDER, Brother 72
SPARROW, Jonathan 77
SPENCER, Thomas 18 93 131
  William 131
SPILLER, Alpheus 38 Charles 86
STANLEY, Dow 92 Lorenzo 92
  Moses 92
STAPLE, Enoch 77
STAPLES, Andrew 105 Anna 128
  Enoch 131 Enoch Jr 132
  George Dennett 125 James 131
  132 James Jr 105 John 131
  John M 128 Loring 67 Loring T
  70 Mrs 105 Nathaniel 128
  Robert 77 William 131 132
STEELE, James 122 Mrs James
  122
STEVENS, Almira 52 Elder 61 62
  James 70 John 59 60 61 62 69
  Theodore 60 61 63 70
STOCKIN, 79 James 91 Mrs
  Thomas 91 Thomas 91
  Thomas B 91
STONE, Fannie 85 Frank 41
  George 77 131 Hannah 128
  John 77 131 Marjorie 85
  Soloman 128 131
STORER, Joseph 67
STOVER, Eben C 74
STROUT, 81 Ada 86 Albion P 103
  Alvah 70 Annie 85 David 97
  Elisha 58 77 131 132 Enoch 77
  103 Frank L 153 George 132
  Gilbert 77 Isaac 77 131 James
  70 John 77 John Jr 77 Joseph
  132 Leonard J 48 Nathaniel 70
  Peter 108 Prince 131 Richard
  77 Sally 103 Samuel 77 132
  Simeon 38 74 77 Soloman 132

STROUT (continued)
William 77
STUART, Isambert Burnell 68
SULLIVAN, James 15 16
SUTTON, George 132 John 26 77 97 97 131
SWEAT, Jesse P 124 Moses 123 Moses E 84 123 124 Moses Erastus 123 Mrs Moses 123
SWETT, Thomas J 72
TARBOX, 35 Eliakim 18 34
TAYLOR, Evelyn 86 Walter 85
THAYER, H Otis 56 58 Henry Otis 58 Leila 85
THOMAS, Charles 33
THOMPSON, 127 Leonard P 18 Mary 126 Mrs 126 Wm 126 132
THORNE, Harry 153
THURSTON, David 56 57 58
TIBBETS, Chester 86
TOPLIFF, Calvin 123 Ruth 123
TRIPP, Leander S 72
TUCKER, Gideon 102 Gideon M 102 Mr 46
TUFTS, Esther 85 Gertrude 85 Helen 85 Henry 120 121 Lillian 85 Lydia 121 Simeon 121
TYLER, Abraham 77 Daniel 49 Joseph 77 Joseph S 126 131
USHER, Alherton 104
WALDRON, A C 109 Aaron C 105 109 111 Henry 109 134 Henry P 105 Leonard 109 Louise 85 Percy 85
WALKER, Addie 85 David 50 105
WALPER, 100
WARD, Cyrus K 67 Elijah 5 30
WARREN, Abner Chase 101 James 18 101
WATERHOUSE, Charles 100
WATSON, A H 11 Alfred 104 Alfred H 104 George 104 Roscoe 104
WEBB, Marilyn 151 Raymond 153
WEBBER, Molly 125 Stephen 71
WEBSTER, 96 Ben 82 J D S 11 James 95 James D S 95 96 Joseph 95 R Scott 95 Royal Scott 104

WEDGEWOOD, John Thatcher 123 Miss 123 Ruth 123
WEEKS, George Walter 124 Stella 125
WEEMAN, 37 Alvah 77 153 John 18 36 77 93 Winfield 9
WEEMEN, Alvah 30
WELLS, Howard 33
WENTWORTH, Benjamin 85 101 Benjamin Franklin 125 Edgar 153 Emery 101 Emily J 50 Henry 67 70 87 101 105 Ivory 101 John 77 John C 105 Stephen E 125 William 77
WESCOTT, Almira 68
WESTON, Belle 85 D 4 J W 87
WHEELWRIGHT, 79 Elizabeth G 94 George 94 97
WHITE, Joseph 62
WHITMAN, Herbert L 86
WHITMORE, Benjamin 57 Nancy 120 William 77
WHITNEY, Lewis 39 122 Luther 94 Mary A 122 William 78
WHITTEMORE, Nathaniel 72 74
WILDER, Charles S 57 Charles Samuel 58
WILSON, Woodrow 135
WING, Nathan 77
WINSLOW, Abram 74 111 Mrs Abram 111 Nathan 19 35 36 Thomas 86
WOOD, Enoch 11 F Virgil 154 Sarah A 94 Stephen 101 102 153 Stephen W 102
WOODBURY, Jerusha 36 Peter 19 35
WOODMAN, Joseph 94
WOODSUM, 94 Abiather 93 Abijiah 93 Abner 93 William 93
WORMLIGHT, Verner J 154
WRIGHT, John 15
YATES, Charles 49
YEATON, Franklin 55 57
YENNIE, Richard 153
YOUNG, David 77 103 David Jr 33 Thomas 33 103

www.ingramcontent.com/pod-product-compliance
Lightning Source LLC
Chambersburg PA
CBHW051103160426
43193CB00010B/1291